DOES THIS

MAKE

MY

ASSETS

LOOK FAT?

DOES THIS

MAKE

MY

ASSETS

LOOK FAT?

A WOMAN'S GUIDE
TO FINDING
FINANCIAL EMPOWERMENT
AND SUCCESS

SUSAN L. HIRSHMAN

ST. MARTIN'S GRIFFIN
NEW YORK

www.stmartins.com

The Library of Congress has cataloged the hardcover edition as follows:

Hirshman, Susan L.
    Does this make my assets look fat? : a woman's guide to finding financial empowerment and success / Susan L. Hirshman.—1st ed.
        p. cm.
    ISBN 978-0-312-38553-8
        1. Women—Finance, Personal. 2. Finance, Personal. 3. Investments. I. Title.
HG179.H543 2010
332.0240082—dc22

2010021668

ISBN 978-0-312-62048-6 (trade paperback)

10   9   8   7   6   5   4   3   2

A big thank-you to my family,
friends, and colleagues
who encouraged me to write this book.

To my mom, who instilled in my sisters and me
the importance of financial independence and financial literacy.

And a special shout-out to Big Ray,
who was my biggest fan, whose spirit will always be with me,
and who I know is getting the biggest kick out of this.

CONTENTS

· · · · · · · · · · · · · · ·

INTRODUCTION

· · · · · · · · · · · · · ·

In my work as an investment professional I notice three very interesting trends taking shape in the world of personal finance:

- Investment markets and products are becoming increasingly more complex.
- An increasing number of women are controlling more and more of the wealth in America (it is estimated that in the very near future women will control at least 60 percent of the wealth).
- The level of financial literacy in women is *not* increasing.

This last point is very disconcerting. On the surface, it doesn't seem to make sense. With women dominating men at every level of higher education (from associate degrees to Ph.D.s), why are these otherwise intelligent, effective, assertive women shying away from such a critical topic?

What I have learned over the last twenty-plus years in my conversations with clients and with audience members of lectures I have given across the globe is that there are four typical answers to this question of why too many of us shy away from such a critical topic. The four most common responses are as follows:

- They have neither the time nor the inclination.
- It's too overwhelming—and they will never know every-thing, so why bother.
- They're embarrassed to let anyone see their lack of knowl-edge.
- They assume their husband (or father or partner) will take care of it for them.

These reasons may seem valid, but in reality they are all nontruths that hinder your financial success and independence. The truth is, to have "fat assets" you do not have to spend hours upon hours on your investment portfolio—you need to know the basics and have realistic expectations. We don't learn this in school, so most people (both men and women) have very limited experience and knowledge, but when it comes to personal finances, the only person who is responsible for you is, well, you.

The last point is so important that it must be repeated: **The only person who is responsible for you is, well, you.** I say this with a heavy heart. I have seen too many bad things happen to too many good women because they did not take an active role in their own financial lives.

Now, taking an active role does not mean that investment termi-nology rolls off your tongue as if you had all my experience and knowl-edge, or that you are always aware of the value of the Dow or that you have to watch business news shows instead of your favorite reality show. What it does mean is that you have a broad awareness of the con-cepts and can apply them to who you are, what you want, and what you are willing to do to get there.

Taking control and gaining a basic knowledge of investment management is very possible. I say this with all the confidence in the world because I have seen this seemingly impossible task become a reality firsthand.

What I have found through my years of counseling a wide variety of investors (of all wealth ranges) on their personal finances, lecturing to hundreds of conference attendees, writing numerous articles, interviewing with financial reporters (on television and in print), as well as coaching other financial advisers, is that if you break investing down to its most basic elements and relate it to something that is familiar to that person or people whom you are advising, their comprehension of the subject matter as well as their confidence increases dramatically.

With that in mind and my deep passion for increasing the financial literacy of women, I decided to write this book. So, as I began to put pen to paper I had to answer a very important question: Is there a common experience (something that is very familiar) among most women that can be used to make the unfamiliar (investing) familiar?

I was able to answer that question with a resounding yes—dieting. I don't know about you, but just about every woman I know has been on a diet at least once.

As we know, the key to healthy dieting is a time-tested set of commonsense principles including balance, variety, and moderation. And anyone who's ever tried to lose weight knows these principles inside and out (even if she occasionally refuses to accept them or occasionally gets tempted by "quick fix" shortcuts). As luck would have it, the time-tested set of commonsense principles is the core to successful investment management. So most people already know how to approach it—they just may not realize that they do.

If you can learn to approach wealth management through the prism of healthy dieting, you can make great strides in your financial literacy and find financial empowerment and success by gaining a greater understanding of the ongoing, lifelong process of making sound financial decisions.

In thinking about diets, it's true to say that they often fail, but that's because we allow our emotions to get the better of us. The same is true in investing. As Warren Buffett said in the preface of Benjamin Graham's *The Intelligent Investor*, "To invest successfully over a lifetime does not require a stratospheric IQ, unusual business insight, or inside information. What's needed is a sound intellectual framework for decisions and the ability to keep emotions from corroding that framework." And that's what this book provides—a sound intellectual framework through which you can approach your own finances.

This is critical because your key to success is having and utilizing a framework that gives you the capability to be more intentional about your decisions and conscious of how the choices you make today will impact the life you'll have tomorrow. This book will give you the information you need to have a handle on your finances, the confidence you need to take control of them, and the mind-set to make it happen. Therefore, no matter your age, wealth, or market conditions, you will be able to make smart decisions about your money.

Being fabulous is never an accident. It's done by design. After you read this book, you will feel as comfortable deciding between investment vehicles as you do deciding between dinner entrées. Together, we will enhance your awareness and knowledge in a way that is simple, easy to identify with, and, perhaps, a bit of fun.

I know many of you may be somewhat gun-shy about investing because of the credit crisis back in 2008. I can't blame you—it was one of the worst financial crises in history. Simply, too many things went wrong at the same time (excess borrowing by corporations and by individuals, a bust of the housing bubble, regulatory lapses and mistakes), causing the whole market to basically collapse.

Recovering from such a crisis takes not only economic strength but also emotional strength on your part. The emotional strength comes from the knowledge that these types of events do not happen often or regularly (the Great Depression was more than seventy years ago) and that over time markets normalize.

But as you will see by reading this book, the markets are only 25 percent of the equation to your financial health and happiness. The other 75 percent of your success is gaining an understanding of who you are, what you want, and what you are willing to do to get there.

Therefore, the words that you will read and the work that you will do in this book will give you the encouragement and the confidence to answer the question "Does this make my assets look fat?" with an emphatic yes.

DOES THIS

MAKE

MY

ASSETS

LOOK FAT?

THE CHOICE IS YOURS

Dieting.

The word conjures up different emotions. One is dread. We know dieting isn't fun. A piece of chocolate is so comforting, the smell of a steak on the grill so enticing, a scoop of ice cream so satisfying. There's no way around it, it's difficult to give up the short-term gratifications of eating.

But the other emotion the word can bring to mind is satisfaction. That's how we feel when we see the results of a diet. Drop a couple of dress sizes and you feel better about everything—the way you look, the way you feel, the way others look at you. Life is better.

I know what you're thinking: If this is a book about investing, why am I reading about dieting?

You may not realize it yet, but there are many dieting principles that are applicable to investing. Both require discipline, both take time, and, if we're successful, both provide us with substantial rewards. The parallels are uncanny. I promise that you will find the concepts of investing and personal finance a lot more familiar than you think.

As you read this book, try to approach it with the same level of interest and focus you would use exploring an exciting new diet. Here's the truth: You don't need an MBA in finance to understand and take control of your financial life any more than you need a Ph.D. in nutrition to work toward your health and fitness goals. Understanding the basic concepts and tools of investing is attainable—anyone can do it.

The world is changing and a big part of that change is financial. In the past, a financially secure retirement was based on personal savings supplemented by Social Security and your employer's pension. As an individual, you had little risk and even less responsibility for planning your financial future; we didn't need to do much or make many decisions. But those days are gone forever. Today companies are reducing or eliminating guaranteed pension plans and politicians are talking about reductions in future Social Security benefits. Increasingly, we are being forced, whether we like it or not, to assume the burdens of planning and acting to ensure our future self-sufficiency. The risk and the responsibility are becoming ours. No longer is it enough to work hard; today we have to make conscious decisions to save, invest, and manage our assets.

Why have these changes occurred? In short, over the past twenty years or so corporate America has come face-to-face with new economic, demographic, and regulatory challenges. Business has become much more competitive. Severe cost pressures have forced companies to operate more efficiently by cutting costs and reducing overhead. At the same time the average American is living longer and using more resources in his or her retirement years. When traditional retirement plans that put the risk and responsibility on a company began, the average person spent somewhere between two and five years drawing retirement benefits before passing away. Today the time spent in retirement can be more than thirty years. Do you think companies want to keep paying you money for more than thirty years after you worked for them for maybe twenty years?

Of course not.

Some of you may think I'm being a little overoptimistic when I talk about retirement lasting more than thirty years. Our perceptions and expectations play a big part in financial planning and the sad fact is, *we're usually wrong!* Here's a fact: According to the U.S. Census Bureau, centenarians, people one hundred years old or older, are the fastest-growing segment of our population. The second fastest is the age group eighty-five or older. Currently, there are about 40,000 people at least one hundred years old in the United States. That's more than one centenarian for every 10,000 Americans. Of those, 85 percent are women. More important, it's estimated that 40 percent of women who reach the age of fifty this year will live to be one hundred years old. (If you want to get an idea of your own life expectancy, go to www.livingto100.com.) Now, remember the results of these kinds of exercises are based on averages and are not an exact science. So if the Web site tells you that based on your lifestyle you will live only to sixty-five, *don't bet on it!* You still need to save as if you had a longer life expectancy. I know too many people who maintained an unhealthy lifestyle—smoking, drinking, and carousing—until they drew their last breath in their nineties. Hey, Alfred Hofmann, the father of LSD, lived to be 102.

No matter how long you think you may live, you're going to have to apply the same three principles to your own finances that you apply to your diet: self-awareness, discipline, and commitment. What it all boils down to is who you are, what you want, and what you're willing to do to get there. Both dieting and financial success come down to one word: choice. Both disciplines require you to make the same kinds of decisions about instant gratification or delayed gratification on a regular basis. When you're dieting, you're constantly making a basic choice between indulging now or looking and feeling better later. That choice is forced on us by unchanging physical laws: The only way to lose weight is to reduce our calorie intake below our calorie expenditure over a reasonably long period of time. The calories that we take in go one of two places: Either they're burned as you go about the daily tasks of living, including exercise, or they're stored as fat. A pound of body fat is equivalent to about 3,500 calories. All else being equal, if we cut back our calorie intake by a thousand calories a day, we can expect to lose about two pounds each week. With that in mind, we can choose to have a bowl of ice cream now, but only at the expense of having to shed that extra five hundred or so calories sometime in the future if we want to lose twenty pounds. In the end, successful dieting boils down to that ancient maxim "You can't have it all." That's true of financial planning, too. There are only two things you can do with money: spend it or save it. If you want to build a solid financial future, you're going to have to make the constant choice between spending and saving. If you spend now, you won't have that money later. Worse, if you spend more than you make, you not only won't have that money later, you'll owe others more money. But if you save instead of spend, you'll discover the great secret of compounding (making interest on interest): Over time, the money you save will go to work for you making more money. It takes time for compounding to work its magic, but it can provide you with more money than you ever thought possible.

The following chart should give you a sense of the power of compounding. It shows the value of $10,000 compounded annually in five years and ten years at various interest rates.

INTEREST RATE	VALUE IN 5 YEARS	VALUE IN 10 YEARS
4%	$12,167	$14,802
6%	$13,382	$17,908
8%	$14,693	$21,589
10%	$16,105	$25,937
12%	$17,623	$31,384

We all know how easy and tempting it is to put off the start of a diet. *I'll start Monday. I'll start next month.* And, of course, every day that you delay adds more pounds that you're going to have to get rid of later. That same kind of procrastination in getting your finances in order is costing you money every day. Worse, just like dieting, the longer you wait, the harder it's going to be to start. Think about metabolism: It's always easier to lose weight when you're younger and your metabolism is nice and fast. Maybe you thought you could always stay thin without having to exercise. Then, as you get older, your metabolism starts to slow down, parts start to sag (and sag some more), and suddenly you're faced with the unpleasant reality of having to diet and go to the gym. The same is true in wealth planning, except the longer you wait to take control, the harder it may be to get what you want because you are not taking advantage of the miraculous power of compound interest.

Similarly with money, when we're young it's easy not to think much about our long-term future. We're too busy building careers, enjoying friends, and experiencing new things. But eventually the future arrives and we're forced to think about it. Sometimes that intrusion comes late in life when there is little time to do much about it. If we're lucky, something spurs us to think about the future earlier. Maybe it's the idea of retiring early and traveling, or figuring out how to finance a couple of college educations while our kids are still in diapers. The earlier we realize what we will need or want and what financial assets will be required to realize our long-term goals, the longer we have to build an effective financial program that gets us where we want to go. But no matter where you are in your life, remember this: *It's never too early to begin a financial plan, and it's also never too late.*

As a financial adviser, I find that one of the most puzzling aspects of helping people set up financial plans is the reluctance so many have to talk about money. I know when I'm out having drinks with friends we'll share the most amazing and intimate secrets about ourselves, except how much we earn and how much we have. I can't tell you how many stories I have heard about married couples where it turns out the wife hasn't a clue about how much money her husband earns or what kinds of investments they have. There are also some women who handle the day-to-day finances but don't make investment decisions. Their husbands take care of the long-term decisions—and as a result they have a very narrow view of their finances.

In either case, my advice is to open up! If you are single, seek out people with whom you can discuss your investment needs (if it's your father or boyfriend, "discussing" does *not* mean "do it for me"). If you're married, become a full partner or at least an educated one in your family's financial life. If your husband has more expertise in financial matters than you do, that's okay. I'm not saying you have to be a financial whiz. What you do have to be is aware and engaged in the process. At the very least you must have the confidence of knowing what the plan is and the comfort of knowing that should something happen to him, you won't be at the mercy of financial predators, and that you can safely keep the financial plan on track.

A cautionary note: If you think having your husband educate you about investing may be as torturous as when your father taught you how to drive (I can't remember how many times I walked home!), it may be a good sign that you need to work with a financial adviser, someone to help take some of the emotion out and be able to answer your questions over and over again. Don't be embarrassed; that's what they're paid to do. The only stupid question is the question not asked. To me, that is the biggest risk in investing because in that case what you don't know can hurt you. The risk I worry about the most is your failure to educate (and protect) yourself.

Whether you are single or married, an important aspect of working with an adviser is honesty, and not just partial honesty. Just as you wouldn't go to your doctor and tell her only a few of the symptoms that are troubling you, you shouldn't withhold critical financial information from your adviser. Without a full financial picture, the adviser won't be able to prescribe the best solutions to reach your financial goals. We'll talk more in Chapter 9 about choosing and using a financial adviser.

SETTING YOUR GOALS

Most people setting out to devise a financial plan think the first step is to take an inventory of income, spending, and assets so that they know where they stand. It doesn't work that way. Certainly it's important on any journey to know where you're starting from, but when talking finance, it's a lot more important to know where you want to go, otherwise you wind up wandering aimlessly and arriving somewhere you might not want to be. So the first step in taking control of your financial life is to understand what you want from it. The way to do this is to set goals, both short term and long term, and rank them in order of importance.

Goals are critical because they dictate the shape of your financial plan. They also provide discipline. Without goals it's too easy to become susceptible to whatever is happening at the moment. Distractions are endless and expensive. Keeping your eye on your goals will do a lot to prevent you from getting sidetracked and falling short of what you want to achieve.

I cannot emphasize enough the importance of prioritizing goals. Too often I see people make lifestyle changes without really comprehending what, if any, future needs or wants they are sacrificing. Unfortunately, we can't escape it: For every action there is an equal and opposite reaction. Every dollar spent today cannot be spent for something else tomorrow. No matter what your choices, they have consequences, both now and later. As you go through this exercise, keep one of my favorite expressions in mind: "My wants always outweighed my needs until my needs became critical." Knowing what is truly important to you now and in the long run will bring you a great sense of fulfillment in your life.

To further explain the importance of goals, let's look at how goals work in dieting. If you think about it, dieting is a four-step process. The first thing you do when starting a diet is to decide what your target weight is. That sets you up to take the second step, which is determining which foods will be part of the diet and which ones will be excluded, as well as how much and what kind of exercise you have the time, motivation, and skills to undertake. The third step is to plan each of your meals to be sure you're getting balanced nutrition and avoiding the high-calorie foods with little nutritional content. Finally, you periodically weigh yourself to see how well your plan is working and what adjustments, if any, should be made.

Believe it or not, that's exactly the way you set up a financial plan. The goals come first: What do you want to do and what will each goal require in financial assets? The second step is to use those goals to determine how to save and invest your money. In financial terms it's called "asset allocation," and all it means is balancing your investments among the "big three" asset classes: cash, stocks, and bonds. Cash is used to meet short-term goals, and stocks and bonds are typically for your longer-term goals. (There are other investments, too, that can be used to fatten up your assets and we'll talk about them later, but the core of any portfolio is built on the big three.) The third step is to decide what specific investments you should have to implement your asset-allocation strategy. This involves decisions about where to put your cash so that it is making at least a little money for you but is easily available when you need it, and which stocks and bonds to include in your long-term portfolio (don't worry, I won't be asking you to pick your own stocks and bonds; there are plenty of ways to invest in them without having to be a stock picker). Finally, just as you weigh yourself to measure how well your diet is working and to make adjustments if necessary, you will also periodically review your finances to be sure your plan is producing the results you want. If it is, fine, keep it up. If it isn't, make whatever changes are needed to get it on track.

THE PROCESS OF INVESTING

Step 1: Set goals.
Step 2: Develop asset-allocation strategy.
Step 3: Select investments.
Step 4: Continue to review.
Repeat process as needed.

So let's get back to setting goals. First we need to figure out your short-term, mid-term, and long-term goals. Short-term goals are those things that you want to achieve within the next three to five years (say, paying off debt or setting up an emergency account), mid-term goals are those six to ten years away (like saving for a larger expenditure, say, a car or a house), and long-term goals are those that you want to achieve in ten or more years (focusing on retirement and aspirational purchases, for instance).

In order to identify your goals, you need to think seriously about what makes you happy, what you want your life to look like, and what you want to get out of it. This requires honest, thoughtful, and truthful reflection. There's no point here in trying to fool yourself, because you are the only one to whom this is vitally important. And be prepared to encounter a little emotional upheaval. You may not have ever thought carefully about where you're going and how you plan to get there, and, as with any long journey, getting started can be a little scary.

As I said before, you can't have it all. But at this early stage of setting up your financial plan I want you to ignore that truism and think not so much about goals as about dreams. It doesn't matter, at least for the moment, how practical your dreams are. We'll come back to reality fairly soon. Right now I want you to list, either on a piece of paper or on your computer, your wildest dreams, the things you most want to do, the places you most want to go, the things—clothes, cars, homes—that you most want to own.

For many of you this may be an easy exercise. For others, perhaps not. Take me, for example. When I first sat down to determine my goals, I freaked out and had to go straight to the cookie bag. My "freak-out" was on two levels. First, it was a commitment thing. Just having to think about what exactly I wanted to do five, ten, and even twenty years out was overwhelming. I remember screaming at the paper, "I can't commit to what I'm having for dinner tonight, much less what I'm going to be doing in twenty years!" Once I got through that little crisis, I realized that the second issue was the fact that I didn't know what I wanted. "Oh, no," I thought, "I'm goalless!" If you're like me, don't despair. There are ways to overcome your commitment issues.

Fortunately, I was able to put on my professional hat and realize that the point of the exercise was not to commit to a life sentence, but to give myself *goals to work toward*. My goals may change over the years, but at least I'll have the ability to choose twenty years from now which job I take or whether to retire early. Keep in mind that what you articulate now may change over time, but the goals you set now act as a road map for your life's financial journey. We all know, too, that working toward something helps tremendously to keep us focused, disciplined, and engaged.

WHAT'S IN MY BUCKET?

I was still left with the problem of not knowing what I wanted. But again, with the help of my professional hat, I realized that I knew what I wanted my life to feel like, but I was too overwhelmed to articulate that feeling in terms of specific goals. With the help of my alter ego, it occurred to me that money can only be used to the benefit of four categories: you, your family, charity, and the government. I call these the "money buckets of life" and they're illustrated in this diagram:

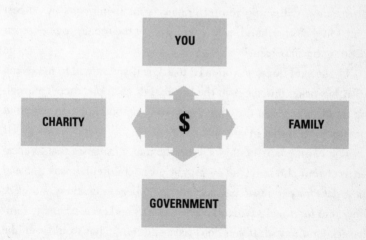

Note: The box labeled "Government" represents the taxes you pay on your income and investments.

The best way to attack the You box is to focus on your lifestyle now and what you want it to be in the future, including in retirement. You should be able to answer two questions.

First, do you envision your lifestyle changing significantly over the years as you approach retirement? Consider three answers to this question: I want my lifestyle to be about the same; I want to live it up more, which means spending more on things like travel, dining out, and nicer cars; or I want to tone it down some, live a simpler life that requires less spending.

If you chose to "stay the same," no problem. When you do the exercises in Chapter 2, you'll be able to estimate your lifestyle costs fairly accurately. But if you picked "tone it down" or "live it up," you need to think about how much less or more you'll need to pursue that particular lifestyle. A good rule of thumb is to go up or down no more than 20 percent. That doesn't sound like much, but believe me, a 20 percent reduction or increase in your current spending, spread over years, is a very big deal! You need to ask yourself what that really means. What, for instance, will you give up to reduce your living costs by 20 percent? On the other hand, where will you get the money to boost your spending by 20 percent?

The second question you need to ask is if you intend to make any really big-ticket purchases in the future. For example, there's a growing trend throughout the country to have a second home to retreat to for vacations. Is that in your plan?

The Family box should focus on the major expenses that loom in terms of your children (and eventually grandchildren). It isn't unusual these days for parents to pay not only for college educations and weddings, but for down payments on new homes and even expensive family vacations abroad. If you don't have children, what would you like to provide for other family members? You may want to help with a partner's further education or a niece's trip to Europe.

Finally, the Charity box is all about the basic question of contributing now and after you've passed away to various charitable undertakings. Do you want to spread out your contributions among many charities or focus all your financial efforts on a particular cause? Should you wait until you have your financial ducks in a row to make contributions or can you make them part of your daily financial life?

We know the future is coming, we just don't know what it holds. There are bound to be surprises, both good and bad, along the way. Having a plan and working toward your goals helps prepare you for whatever lies ahead. You may have to change certain behaviors to reach your goals, but the earlier you do so, the less drastic the change may be.

A word of warning to people in two very different situations: those who are already retired and those who have not yet married. People who are already retired often think they don't have any goals. Wrong! You need to think about ensuring that you don't outlive your current resources, which may be needed down the line for possible large health-related expenses, such as nursing homes or prolonged in-home care, and how also you will leave money for loved ones. And for you young single ladies reading this, who are in your twenties and thirties, don't make the mistake of *assuming* you're going to get married and therefore you don't need a financial plan. Whether you marry or not, you still need a plan. Plan based on your situation today and try to always remember what one of my favorite bumper stickers says: "A man is not a financial plan."

JULIE'S GOALS

While you're thinking about your own goals (there's a worksheet at the end of the chapter to help you), let's take a moment to look over the shoulder of someone else going through the same process. Her approach and her thinking may illuminate this process of goal setting for you. Julie is a thirty-five-year-old advertising executive. She's married with two kids under the age of five.

To determine her goals, Julie approached this exercise using the "money buckets" system. She first focused on what she wanted for herself and her husband, starting with **short-term goals:**

- Become a stay-at-home mom.
- Keep my lifestyle intact.
- Create a savings cushion of two months of salary.
- Pay off credit cards.
- Get a new car.

All those should be targets for the next few years. Next we identify **mid- and long-term goals.** In Julie's case they were:

- Finish paying off student loans.
- Remodel the kitchen.
- Buy a beach house on Lake Michigan.
- Take a family trip to Europe when the oldest child turns fifteen.
- Get her husband to retire at age sixty.

Okay, that takes care of the You box. Now what about the Family box? Since her children are so young, Julie mostly thought about long-term goals for them:

- Pay for college and grad school for the kids.
- Contribute to a down payment for their first homes.
- Pay for her daughter's wedding (and help the young couples out financially if the need arises).

Finally Julie turned her attention to the Charity box:

- Continue limited annual contributions to favorite charities.
- Don't worry now about leaving a bequest to a charity.

It goes without saying that Julie's objective for the Government box was to pay as little in taxes as is legally permissible.

Julie's list of goals seems pretty typical. But now comes the big question: Which ones matter most? She needs to rank her goals as "must-have," which means that goal is essential to her basic happiness; "like to have," which suggests the goal is important, but not critical to happiness; and "dream to have," which is a goal that would really be nice, but won't wreck her life if she can't have it.

Now, applying the rule that "you can't have it all," Julie needs to think about both the rational and the emotional value of each of her goals. This is an important step because Julie is going to have to make trade-offs, an essential part of every financial plan. For example, let's say based on her financial situation today Julie realizes that in order to fund her children's educations she has to adjust her current lifestyle. Will she or won't she? You may think the "right" answer is obvious, but, in fact, it is not. There is no right answer. It all depends on who Julie is and what her values are. She's the only one who can decide whether an ultraluxury car is more important to her in terms of defining her success and happiness than expensive college educations for her two children, who, after all, can get scholarships or loans.

As Julie pondered her goals and their rational and emotional significance, here's how she ranked them:

SHORT TERM
- Must-have: Become a stay-at-home mom and establish a cushion of two months of living expenses.

- Like to have: Pay off credit cards and buy a new car.
- Dream to have: None

MID TERM

- Must-have: Pay off student loans and redo kitchen.
- Like to have: Lake Michigan beach house
- Dream to have: European vacation for the family

LONG TERM

- Must-have: College for both children and pay for daughter's wedding
- Like to have: Her husband retire at sixty and make down payments for each child's first home
- Dream to have: Leave an inheritance for the children.

Do you notice anything a little bit worrisome about Julie's prioritization? What pops out to me is her lack of a deep commitment to paying off her credit card debt under her short-term goals. We all run up credit card bills every once in a while, but it should always be a top "must-have" priority to pay off your balances as quickly as possible. The reason is simple math: In some circumstances (especially if you pay just the minimum balance due) you are in a compounding nightmare. Just as the concept of compounding works to increase the value of your investments, it works to increase the amount you owe when you're in debt. (Look to the appendix's debt-to-income ratio to see an example of this issue.)

So what are your goals and how did you prioritize them? If you need a bigger home to be happy, then be honest with yourself about that. By the same token, if you *don't* need that, don't say that you do. This exercise is not about validating or justifying your goals. It's simply about identifying them. So be honest with yourself. The purpose of doing this is to help you understand your trade-offs. It's difficult to muster the enthusiasm, discipline, and courage to reach a goal that you don't really feel is vital to your happiness. And please understand that by "happiness" I don't mean the short-term high that comes from buying a designer bag or a great pair of shoes. Rather, I mean the true inner satisfaction that comes from having financial freedom and the ability to choose a lifestyle.

If you are married, make sure that you and your spouse or partner do this exercise together. I suggest you each do it independently and see where you agree and where the gaps are. If you are having a hard time coming to an agreement, don't worry. It's a common problem. A research study by Fidelity Investments indicates that many boomer and preretirement couples are not "in sync" with regard to retirement-planning issues. Among the findings:

- 41 percent of couples disagreed when asked whether one or both spouses would work during retirement.
- Wives generally had an accurate picture of when their husbands expected to retire, but husbands tended to underestimate the retirement age of their wives.
- 37 percent of couples could not agree whether their overall lifestyle would be better, worse, or the same as it is currently, with husbands indicating a more optimistic outlook than wives.
- When asked about their top three sources of retirement income, most respondents answered workplace savings plans, pensions, and Social Security; however, 61 percent

disagreed on which of the three would be the primary
source of retirement income.

I suggest that you schedule wealth-planning date nights. Have a
glass of wine (it's only 120 calories, so take a walk after dinner), relax,
and let your minds go away from everyday problems to what you really want. Too many times I see husbands and wives who have completely different goals, especially when it comes to prioritization. The
boat may be a "must-have" for the husband, while giving the children
a down payment for a house is the wife's. In order to plan, you have to
have consensus. In the long run this may save you both a lot of heart-
ache (and money).

CALCULATING THE COSTS OF GOALS

Unfortunately, there's a price for everything. Now that you have your
various goals, it's time to assign a dollar cost to each of them. This
doesn't call for precision, but it does require you to become somewhat
more specific with your goals. Getting back to our example, Julie
states that one of her goals is to fund her kids' college educations.
What exactly does that mean? Home or away? Public or private school?
Tuition only or all costs? Each of those decisions results in a different
goal. If you are not sure what you want, then go for the gold. I would
rather see you set a higher goal now and have some extra if it turns
out something less expensive is the later choice than come up short
and not be able to achieve what you really wanted. And as her children grow, Julie will have a greater sense of what is right for them
and can adjust accordingly.

Like I said, don't kill yourself trying to figure out exact values. Just
make some reasonable estimates. Take a look at Julie's cost calculations:

GOAL	COST
Short Term	
Become a stay-at-home mom	$100,000 each year (Julie's salary)
Establish a two-month expense cushion	$40,000
Maintain current lifestyle	$150,000
Pay off credit cards	$5,000
Buy a new car	$55,000
Mid Term	
Pay off student loans	$18,900
Remodel kitchen	$65,000
Lake Michigan beach house	$140,000
Long Term	
College for both kids	$200,000
Daughter's wedding	$30,000
Down payments on kids' first homes	$50,000
Husband retire at 60	$125,000 per year

If you think this exercise has been a lot of work, you're right. It has been. But in the words of Vidal Sassoon, "The only place success comes before work is in the dictionary." So don't give up! Because like Julie you will now know what you want (overall goals), when you want it (short to long term), how important it is to have it ("must-have" to "dream to have"), and how much it will cost. The next step is to see how your current financial picture matches up with your goals and determine what you have to do to be able to achieve the present and the future that you desire.

AT THE VERY LEAST

Choose one or two goals for each category, and determine how much each will cost and its priority:

TIME	COST	PRIORITY
Short Term		
1. _____	$ _____	_____
2. _____	$ _____	_____
Mid Term		
1. _____	$ _____	_____
2. _____	$ _____	_____
Long Term		
1. _____	$ _____	_____
2. _____	$ _____	_____

CHAPTER SUMMARY

1. To achieve any level of success, we must know what we want.
2. No matter our age, we all have goals.
3. A good framework to help you identify your goals is to think in terms of what you want for yourself, then your family, and then charity.
4. Goals should be broken down by time frame, priority, and cost.
5. Prioritizing your goals allows you to achieve your "must-have" goals.
6. What you've learned:

NAKED IN FRONT
OF THE MIRROR

I'm the queen of excuses. If my pants are feeling a little too tight, the dry cleaner must have shrunk them. If my chin is hanging over my turtleneck, it's because of the cut of the sweater. And we all know how inaccurate bathroom scales are—strange, isn't it, that they always seem to err on the high side?

I can tell myself these little white lies for days on end. But they don't help me get closer to what I want.

Eventually I give up on the excuses. That's when I take the cure, learn the facts, and see the truth. That's when I stand in front of the full-length mirror. Naked. All is revealed and I can see without any excuses where I stand. Only then am I able to really appreciate the magnitude of the task that lies ahead. I know where I am, I know where I want to go, and I can now develop both the motivation and the fortitude to stick to my weight-loss plan.

Believe me, it is not always pretty and not necessarily a bundle of fun. But I know from years of experience that I can't execute my weight-loss plan without that painful review of my naked body. We all have a dream body in our mind. Often it's an idealized version of ourselves that we'll never totally attain. Face it, our bodies are the sum of what we've been given, much of which is beyond our control: bone structure, genetics, and age, for example. Some of us will never be supermodels and we need to recognize that. But how close we come to achieving what is realistic depends on things we *can* control: our lifestyle, our attitudes, and how much effort we are willing to invest in reaching our goals. If we start out trying to deceive ourselves about who and where we are in life and what we are willing to do, chances are that we'll never attain what we want.

A successful weight-loss program isn't just about *perceptions* of how we look now and how we want to look. It's also about *measurements*— the numbers that help us keep score on how well we're doing in the weight-loss game. We determine our baseline by weighing ourselves, putting the tape measure to our hips, waist, and bust, and, if we're really serious, by measuring our percentage of body fat. Then we create a food and exercise diary that tells us daily how many calories we're taking in and how many calories we're burning up. If we find that we're taking in more calories than we're burning, we know something has to change—fewer calories in or more burned up—if we're going to be moving in the right direction.

In this chapter we're going to see how and why you must stand naked in front of the financial mirror. Chapter 1 was all about dreaming, thinking about a wide range of things that you want to achieve for yourself, your family, and your charities. Those goals are important, make no mistake about it. But understanding what you need to do to achieve them is equally important. We're going to start by doing a personal financial inventory so you'll know exactly where you stand now. We'll call it a net worth statement, and it will be the financial equivalent of getting on the scale to see how much you weigh. Then we'll set up the financial equivalent of your food and exercise diary to measure how much money you have coming in and how much is going out. That will tell us what changes in your current lifestyle (if any) you need to make to be sure you're moving toward your objectives. It may also tell us that there simply isn't enough coming in to ensure that you'll meet all your goals. If that's the case, then we'll start thinking about making some trade-offs to be sure you reach those goals that are most important.

Here's the deal. Just like we can hide our weight excesses by wearing some sort of body-shaping hosiery, eventually it comes off and you've got what you've got. We can only pretend for so long. The same is true for your finances. You can keep your head in the sand, hide behind your credit cards or your significant other, but sooner or later you have to come to terms with what you have (or don't have!). So now is the time to expose yourself. Let's look at your assets, your liabilities, and your monthly cash flow. What we want to determine is what you have saved so far toward your goals and what you can expect to save now and in the future.

STEPPING ON THE FINANCIAL SCALES: YOUR NET WORTH STATEMENT

A net worth statement measures the net difference between your assets (what you own) and your liabilities (what you owe). That difference, **Assets − Liabilities = Net Worth**, amounts to a snapshot of your financial position on a given date. Unlike your morning ritual of stepping on the bathroom scale, you'll update your net worth statement much less frequently, perhaps quarterly, and at least annually. But like the bathroom scale, your net worth is the single most important measure of how much progress you're making toward reaching your goals. Just as you know you're doing something wrong if the bathroom scale is steadily creeping higher, you'll know your financial program is off-track if your net worth is steadily creeping lower.

The easiest way to calculate your net worth is to begin by separating your assets—the things you own—into four categories:

- **Liquid assets**—those that can easily be converted into cash, usually within a day or two (for example, checking accounts and money market accounts)
- **Investment assets**—those that are more longer-term assets (such as brokerage accounts)
- **Retirement assets**—IRA or 401(k) accounts
- **Real estate**—personal residence, as well as any vacation homes, vacant lots, or office property

The four categories we have set up are in descending order of liquidity. It's easy to write a check, not quite so easy to sell stocks or bonds, quite a bit more difficult to cash out of a 401(k) plan, and most difficult to sell real estate.

You might be thinking to yourself, "What about my car, our Jet Skis, and all that nice furniture in our house?" We aren't counting them for several reasons. First, we're assuming you own a car because you have to use it to get to work, to the store, and to the gym. If you sell the one you own now, you'll just have to buy another one. I know your furniture is nice, but unless you have some particularly fine antiques, you love your furniture much more than anyone else ever will. Should you try to raise cash by selling your furniture, you'll be shocked and disappointed by how little it will bring. Most jewelry and virtually all clothing, while initially expensive to buy, will bring only a small fraction of what it cost when put up for sale. As for the Jet Skis, sure, they're worth something, but in the overall scheme of things they're not really worth much more than a few evenings out on the town.

Once you have your assets in the proper categories, it's time to assign a value to them. That's easy for your liquid assets. Take the balance of your checking account, your savings accounts, and your money market account (see Chapter 3 for more information on money markets), and add them up. Valuing stocks and bonds may require a little more effort, but not much. Stock price quotes are carried every day in most newspapers and they're also easy to obtain on the Internet. Many financial Internet sites provide stock-tracking screens on which you can enter your holdings and get constant updates on the price. All you have to do is multiply the number of shares you own by the price of one share to get the value of your stock holdings. To value your bonds, just use the face value (there's more to the price of bonds, but for projection sake, it is good enough). That's the amount you'll receive when the bond matures. Valuing your mutual funds (an investment vehicle that is a pool of funds; see Chapter 5 for more information) is pretty easy as well. All you have to know is the symbol of the fund and the number of shares you own. The business section of a newspaper or a variety of financial Internet sites will provide you with something called the "net asset value," or NAV, which is the price for one share of a mutual fund. Multiply that price by the number of shares you own and you have the total value of your holdings in that fund.

If you have more esoteric investments—say, a hedge fund, for example—you'll have to rely on your fund manager to keep you up-to-date on the value of your holdings at the end of each quarter. Now, if this sounds too confusing, don't worry. Just get out your latest statements (you do keep them, don't you? It's advisable to keep year-end statements for three years and monthly and quarterly statements for one), and use the account values you see under market value.

Valuing your home is a little tougher. Basically, you're making an educated guess. Look at some recent home sales in your neighborhood and make an effort to identify sales of houses that are about the same size as yours (real-estate appraisers tend to assign values to houses based on earlier sales of houses with approximately the same square footage).

This exercise may be the first time you've ever seen all your assets and investments together in one place. Most people get episodic glimpses of parts and pieces of their investments, for instance when they get a statement from their bank or financial adviser. A continual fragmented view of the parts and pieces often results in a portfolio of investments that is not in sync with who you are, what you want, and what you like. Once you have your entire portfolio in front of you, it will be easier to make decisions about how to consolidate various accounts to streamline your investments and focus them more precisely on the goals you're trying to achieve.

Now, let's look at the other side of the ledger, your liabilities. For most people, adding up liabilities is pretty easy. Start with how much you owe on your home mortgage, which, if you have one, is probably the single biggest debt you have. Add to that the balance owed on any other loans, including student loans, investment loans, car loans, or home equity loans. Finally, take a look at your credit card bills for the past few months. Are you paying off the balance in full each month? In that case, your credit card bill is not a liability. But if you're carrying a balance of $5,000 or so from one month to the next, that amount is a liability.

The final step: Add it all up. Take the total of your assets, subtract the total of your liabilities, and what emerges is your net worth. In a sense that's your financial weight on the date you do this exercise.

For those of you who have a neatness streak and have kept your financial records in good order, preparing a net worth statement shouldn't be very difficult. Also, if you've applied for credit lately, either for a home mortgage or for a credit card, you probably had to fill out an application that would give you a head start now on preparing your net worth statement. And if you haven't done any of those things, that's okay, too, because once you've done this exercise the first time, it becomes much easier to do it again as you track the ups and downs of your net worth in coming years.

Technology can be a big help in the area of financial records. I have had clients over the years with fairly complex financial lives— stock and bond investments, retirement accounts, and more than one real-estate investment—who use a spreadsheet on Microsoft Excel to keep track of all their assets and liabilities. As an alternative, you might want to invest in a software program like Quicken or Microsoft Money that prompts you on how to organize your finances and then automatically tracks and updates most of your holdings with just a few mouse clicks. If you use a financial adviser, he or she can provide plenty of help in setting up a net worth statement, or they just might wind up doing it for you. (In Chapter 9, we will discuss selecting and monitoring a financial adviser.)

Here's a form that will help you sort out the various components of your net worth statement:

LIQUID ASSETS

Cash in bank or credit union	$_____
Money market accounts	$_____
Total liquid assets	$_____

TAXABLE INVESTMENTS

Stocks	$_____
Bonds	$_____
Mutual funds	$_____
Other investments	$_____
Total taxable investments	$_____

RETIREMENT ASSETS

Cash value life insurance	$_____
Current value of 401(k) plan or similar retirement account	$_____
Individual Retirement Account (IRA, Roth IRA)	$_____
Total tax-deferred	$_____

REAL ESTATE

Home $_____
Vacation home $_____
Other $_____
Total real estate $_____

OTHER

Collectibles $_____
Other $_____
Total other $_____
TOTAL ASSETS $_____

LIABILITIES

Personal mortgage $_____
Home equity loan or line of credit $_____
Credit card balances $_____
Investment loans $_____
Student loan balance $_____
Other $_____
TOTAL LIABILITIES $_____

NET WORTH $_____
(Assets – Liabilities)

Calculating your net worth is the fundamental starting point for determining your financial health and figuring out how to get from your starting point to achieving your various goals. Your net worth statement will become increasingly useful over time as you plot your progress over months and years. It will show you the impact both of things you can control—how much you spend or save—as well as things over which you have no control, like the performance of the stock market in any given period. For example, you may have been doing a great job of saving money each month to add to your assets, but the recent market conditions resulted in a current lower net worth despite those savings. Not to worry, though. It's just a matter of recovery and perhaps goal adjustments.

For those of you in your early working years, your net worth may not mean much because you simply haven't accumulated a lot of assets. At this stage of your life it's a lot easier to accumulate liabilities, and too often I see this mostly in the form of credit card debt. That's something to be both aware of and wary of. Credit makes it easy to live beyond our means, but the bill always comes due and paying off big credit card debts can keep us from accomplishing more desirable or more important goals.

The trend line in your net worth is what is important. If you're like most of us, you'll find your income rising over time. But you may also find your lifestyle demanding heavier spending, whether for larger families, elegant restaurants, fancy toys like boats, or for expensive travel. By looking at your net worth statement from year to year, you will be able to see whether you are overdoing the spending. And when you finally reach retirement age, your net worth becomes a critical component in determining how well you'll live in retirement. Those who do the best planning will have sufficient investments to fund their entire retirement period, while those who fail to plan will find themselves worrying constantly about how to make ends meet. Think of your net worth statement as the fuel gauge in your car. You feel like you can go anywhere with a full tank of gas, but you really get worried if you're out there on the highway and the needle is sitting close to Empty.

GOOD OR BAD

How do you know if your own net worth is good or bad? Well, if you're twenty-five years old and have a negative net worth, it isn't something that should keep you awake at night. But if you're fifty-five and have a negative net worth, it's concerning and deserves some examination. Look at the past ten years. Has your net worth been growing or shrinking? Why is it acting that way? If it continues on the trend line it has been following, will you be able to realize all your goals? Some of your goals? Few? None? It's important to keep in mind that it isn't whether your current net worth is really good or bad, it's the direction where your net worth is taking you.

Now I need to add a note of caution: You can't always take your net worth at face value. Here is what I mean: Say you are in your late forties or older and your house has appreciated significantly since you bought it. Too often (especially prior to the recent real-estate bust), people confuse the equity in their homes with retirement savings. To get the equity out of your home and available for use in retirement, you must sell your home and, presumably, move somewhere else. Will your new home be cheaper than the home you are selling? If you are downsizing significantly or you are moving to a less-expensive city or state, the answer may be "Yes, my new house will cost substantially less." That means you'll have money left over from the sale of your old house to fund some retirement spending. But I see many retirees who plan to downsize but don't. They wind up buying a new house that costs just as much as the old one. In that case, your equity in your old house is contributing nothing to funding your retirement. Even worse off are retirees whose homes did not appreciate as they expected.

We've all seen the height-and-weight charts that doctors and insurance companies put out to help us determine if we're overweight, underweight, or just about right. If you're five feet three and weigh two hundred pounds, you're in a lot different situation than someone six feet six who weights two hundred pounds. The chart below is the financial equivalent of a height and weight chart. The median is the midpoint, the figure at which half of those in the age bracket have more wealth and half have less. The negative figure shows the percentage of those in the age bracket who have a negative net worth. These kinds of statistics are interesting, but take the chart below with a grain of salt. Just because you are above the median for your age group doesn't necessarily mean that you're well on your way to living the way you want to live and achieving the goals you have set for yourself.

AGE	MEDIAN	TOP 25%	TOP 10%	NEGATIVE
20–29	$7,900	$36,000	$119,300	24.7%
30–39	$44,200	$128,100	$317,800	11.1%
40–49	$117,800	$338,100	$719,800	7.5%
50–59	$182,300	$563,800	$1,187,600	5%
60–69	$209,200	$647,200	$1,429,500	5.8%

SOURCE: Federal Reserve Board's 2004 Survey of Consumer Finances.

For an additional check, see the appendix for some benchmark calculations you can do.

CASH FLOW: YOUR FINANCIAL CALORIE COUNTER

The net worth statement that you just set up is the starting point for getting control of your finances. But whether your net worth grows or shrinks depends in large measure on what we call your cash flow. The term is simple enough. Money, or cash, flows into your life, mostly in the form of income from salary, but also from various other sources such as interest and dividend payments. It flows out again in the form of payments, whether small—that latte to get you cranked up each morning—or large—monthly health insurance premiums. Mortgage payments are often the biggest source of cash outflow, but credit card bills can give your mortgage a run for the money if you aren't careful. Think of your cash flow statement as if you're counting calories. You know that if you take in more calories than you burn up over a given period, you gain weight. With cash flow, it's just the opposite: If you burn up more money than you take in over a given period, you lose financial weight. Believe me, this is one circumstance in our lives where it is joyous to feel fat rather than thin. Embrace it!

Determining whether your cash flow is good or bad is a simple exercise in arithmetic. If more cash flows into your life in a given period of time than flows out, you have a positive cash flow. That means your net worth probably is growing (a decline in the value of your investments, which don't count as cash flow, can more than offset positive cash flow in some periods). If you find that more cash is flowing out of your life than is flowing in, then you have a negative cash flow. All other things being equal, a negative cash flow means your net worth is shrinking. The only time in life that this is an acceptable situation is when you are well into your retirement and in your spend-down phase.

If you've ever kept a really serious food diary, you know how surprising it is to discover how many calories you actually consume without even thinking about it. That bag of M&Ms ("But it's snack size!") as an afternoon pick-me-up, the extra bowl of pasta ("But it's whole wheat"), or the second glass of wine at dinner ("It was a tough day")— those are the calories that only get counted when we are conscientiously trying to lose weight and paying very close attention to what we eat. But whether we count them in our diary or not, they still count when it comes to gaining or losing weight.

I'm pretty sure you're going to be surprised when you start keeping track of your cash flow, and for some of you, it won't necessarily be a pleasant surprise.

If you recall, as we discussed in Chapter 1, there's a double whammy attached to every dollar you spend that is the "opportunity cost." It's the trade-off between using money to do one thing rather than another. A dollar you spend is a dollar you can't invest. And since an invested dollar often earns more money, the dollar you spend is really more than a dollar. Opportunity cost is just a way to measure the impact of making trade-offs when you can't have it all. And with a few exceptions like Bill Gates, we *can't* have it all. It's important to understand and accept the concept of opportunity cost because it's going to play a big role in helping us determine which goals we want to achieve and how we achieve them. As you'll see in all the chapters ahead, we will be faced over and over again with the choice of short-term gratification versus long-term goals. I'm no different than you. I don't like to deprive myself, and constraints make me crazy. But when I think about it, the idea of not being prepared for retirement and having to live hand-to-mouth makes me even crazier. Cash flow is the key to your financial life. Everything else—your lifestyle, investments, retirement plans—flows from it. So once again, I am going to ask you for a little self-awareness here. Are you ready and open to accepting your trade-offs? Because just like dieting, you will not find success until you are.

Here's a form that will help you prepare your cash flow statement:

MONTHLY CASH FLOW STATEMENT	$
SOURCES OF CASH	
Take-home pay*	
Dividends/interest	
Rental income	
Other	
Total sources of cash (A)	
USES OF CASH	
Fixed expenses	
Mortgage	

Loan payments	
Utilities	
Insurance	
Property taxes	
Other	
Total fixed expenses (B)	
Variable expenses	
Charitable Contributions	
Clothing	
Travel and entertainment	
Gifts	
Other	
Total variable expenses (C)	
TOTAL EXPENSES (B + C)	
Positive/negative monthly cash flow available for investing A − (B + C)	

*Make note of employer saving plans' monthly contributions.

We can start constructing our cash flow statement by looking at our last paycheck, which tells us our gross pay for the period and how much is deducted for income taxes, Social Security taxes, and medical and dental insurance. If you're making contributions to a 401(k), that's shown, too. The number we're really interested in is the "net pay," or what we typically call "take-home pay." That's the main source of your cash flow. If you have other substantial regular income from some other sources (alimony or rent payments from tenants, for example), those, too, will become part of your cash flow under income. In most cases, our income remains about the same from month to month and thus is fairly predictable.

Now we can turn our attention to the expense side of the ledger to see where all that money we have coming in is going. Fixed expenses are pretty much just that. You're obligated to make them, usually monthly, and the amounts don't vary much from month to month. Your mortgage payment or rent is probably the most important fixed expense you have, followed by a car payment, property taxes, and insurance. Some mortgage lenders include your property taxes and home owner's insurance in your mortgage payment. If that's the case, don't worry about breaking them out separately. We'll include utility bills in fixed expenses, too, even though the amount varies from month to month and season to season. The fact is, you aren't going to do without utilities, so you know you have to pay those bills.

Variable expenses are those that are optional. You can decide whether and when to incur those expenses and you have some degree of control over how much you're going to spend on them. Clothes (not only yours, but your kids' as well), accessories, restaurant meals, and vacations are all variable expenses.

Now, with your income and your spending written down on paper, it's time to add and subtract to see if your cash flow was positive or negative for the past month or the past quarter. If it's positive, congratulations. You're building up your net worth and making more goals attainable. If your cash flow is negative, you're losing ground and perhaps jeopardizing some of those future goals. In either case, it's time for you to ask yourself, "Are my balance sheet and income statement aligned with my long-term goals?" If the answer is no, the next question is, "Do I want to commit to my future? Do I want to make this better?" If the answer to that one is yes, then you have to figure out how.

Can you see where this is heading? We're coming back to

opportunity costs. Current lifestyle versus future needs and wants. As I have said, everything you buy not only costs you whatever the purchase price is, it also costs you some future amount that you could have by saving and investing rather than making that purchase. Believe me, I'm not saying that you have to live in a cave and wear animal skins rather than having nice clothes, or never go out for dinner or on vacation. I'm just saying that the ancient adage "All things in moderation" is very good advice whether applied to diets or finances.

Now that you have all your financial information nicely organized and documented, it's time to see how aligned your goals are with your financial condition. The best way to do this is to use goal-based financial-planning tools. If you invest in mutual funds or if you have a bank account, they usually have some online tools that can be helpful. Alternatively, you may want to try some consumer programs such as the advanced versions of Quicken or Microsoft Money. I suggest those of you who have multiple goals and more complex situations to seek professional help in the form of an experienced financial adviser. Keep in mind that planning is not a onetime event. Your plan is based on a number of assumptions, and as time goes by your assumptions may have to be refined. So use these numbers not as a bible but as a guide. Our objective here is projection, not perfection—we want to make the best decision today based on the information we have in order to give us the best possible chance we can to meet our goals tomorrow.

Some of these goal-based financial-planning tools will give you a specific dollar amount and others will give you a probability amount (for example, you have a 75 percent chance of meeting your goals). For your longer-term goals I prefer using tools that show probabilities because they more accurately reflect the wide variety of market conditions—some good, some bad—we may face years from now. What you are looking for in terms of an acceptable probability is around 75 percent to 80 percent. These probabilities are determined by using tools that utilize a "Monte Carlo" system. An oversimplified definition of this type of system is that it simulates a variety of scenarios and the probability of occurrence. It's important to remember that no matter what tool you use, or what you call it, these are only projections and not precise predictions. There is no perfect tool, but without any tools you are diving into the pool blindfolded and are almost guaranteed failure. This is why you need to continue to monitor your finances over time. These projections should be updated at a minimum every five years and as you move into retirement every three years.

FACING FACTS

If, once you have prepared your projections, you see that you can meet all your goals (including your "dream to have" goals) with plenty of room to spare, you may want to loosen up a bit. Perhaps you want to add some new goals or, instead, live it up a little today. I know we talked a lot about debt up to now, but there are many of you out there who are in fantastic financial shape yet are so in tune with the hand-to-mouth syndrome that you are compromising your life today. Don't live like a miser unless you have to or you truly enjoy it.

If you can't meet all your goals, now the hard work really begins, especially if you can't meet all your "must-haves." This is a serious issue and needs serious thought. The decision is yours; no one else can make it for you. The choice is simple: What, if anything, are you willing to give up today for the future or give up in the future for today? Let the trade-offs begin!

Let's go back to the goals you developed in Chapter 1 and their respective priorities—"must-have," "nice to have," and "dream to have"—and their costs. Remember, this is about needs and wants. Your "must-haves" should include all your "needs," and the "nice" and "dream to have" can only be your "wants." Obviously, it's no good having a second home if you have no money to pay your health-care costs when you are in retirement.

First, make sure your needs truly are needs and not wants. Ask yourself this question to help you really determine your needs versus wants: "Would it be life-altering if I did not achieve that specific goal?" In our example in Chapter 1 Julie said a "must-have" is to redo her kitchen for $65,000. Based on our calculations, doing that would put paying for her kids' college education at risk. If she does nothing different from what she is doing today, she is making a choice, even if she doesn't realize it.

What we have to recognize is that all choices involve trade-offs, and that some have short-term and others have long-term effects. Obviously, it's easier to decide what the best course of action is if our decisions have short-term consequences. It's those that have long-term ramifications where we must step back and truly focus on the balance between today and tomorrow.

We must constantly determine which trade-offs we can best live with. Be honest with yourself about your personal values and priorities. These drive the choices you make. We can be so much better satisfied with our lives when we take full responsibility for the fact that we are not "victims," but are always living our lives by choice.

To further help along your thought process, understand what your choices are. You basically have four different choices: give up something today for tomorrow, increase the expected rate of return on your portfolio, extend the time frame for your goals, and redefine or modify your goals. Let's look at Julie for an example:

- She can give up something today for tomorrow. In her case that might mean continuing to work rather than becoming a stay-at-home mom.
- She might be able to increase the potential growth rate

(expected rate of return) on her investments. That is an option, but as we will soon see, higher returns are almost always accompanied by higher risks.

- She can extend the time frame for her goals, perhaps by delaying that kitchen redo for five years.
- Finally, she can redefine her goals. If the kitchen really is a "must-have" goal, then she can consciously choose to allocate less money to the kids' college educations. After all, there are loans and scholarships available.

Remember that there is no single right answer here, only the right answer for you. And you know what? Your decisions may not always be the soundest financially, but as long as you are aware of and ac-knowledge the consequences of your choice both from a short- and long-term perspective, you are in control.

For example, let's say that you discover you have $1,000 available for investing each month, but to reach your "must-have" goals, you need $1,200 available monthly. You review your situation and discover that you don't want to give up anything today, you can't increase your rate of return, and you don't want to change the time lines of your goals. Your only choice, then, is to change your goals to match your available cash flow. You take a good, hard look at your list of goals and you decide you're not willing to give up the dream family vacation, but you are willing to give up the three-month emergency savings account.

So you're trading off security for family memories. Is this the "perfect" financial decision? No! But is it right for you? Maybe. It's fine as long as you understand the trade-off: Should you suddenly need cash (and do stop to consider the likelihood of this, because it does happen and more times than you think), you'll have to get it out of the equity in your home, or your life insurance policies, or you'll have to ask someone for a loan. Those alternatives will incur additional costs, which may very well have an effect on your other goals down the road. Furthermore, in this day and age of tightened credit markets, you may not be able to get the credit you need at the exact moment you need it. Are you willing to accept this risk? Does this decision feel comfortable and guilt-free? If not, try a happy medium. You could adjust both goals: Trim the emergency savings to one month and scale down the trip. Whatever you want is okay as long as you make these decisions consciously and with a full and clear understanding of the risks and the consequences. Only then will you have the peace of mind and the motivation to stick to your plan—when you find the best answer for you individually. And that is what this is all about: you.

It all boils down to making sure that your short-term and long-term goals are compatible. We are constantly choosing between the two, even when we don't realize it. Unless you unify your goals, there will be a conflict, which fosters turmoil in your life. This in turn causes many of us to feel out of control. But by doing the work and analysis we've discussed, you will gain a sense of control over money, rather than letting money have control over you.

These exercises are not easy. They force you to make tough decisions. The best advice I ever heard when making these types of decisions is this: Do not focus on what you are "giving up"; instead focus on what you will be "getting" from the path you take. You aren't giving up designer purses, you're preparing for a fulfilling and desirable retirement!

THE FIVE PHASES OF YOUR FINANCIAL LIFE

To help you with your trade-off decision making, I suggest you focus on different issues at different stages of your financial life. You can break your financial life into five phases:

1. Wealth creation
2. Wealth growth
3. Wealth accumulation
4. Wealth preservation
5. Wealth transfer

PHASE ONE: WEALTH CREATION

The wealth creation phase is generally at the beginning of your working career. Typically you are in your twenties and unless you are an investment banker or an associate at a top-tier law firm you're just making ends meet. You may think you have no assets and you may even have a negative net worth thanks to all those student loans. Don't despair! You have one of the greatest assets of all—time. Your basic financial goals at this stage in your life should be cash flow planning, debt reduction, and retirement planning. I know it's hard to have your newfound freedom limited by concerns about retirement, but by using your best asset—time—effectively you can achieve financial independence decades earlier.

The key to cash flow planning is to avoid frivolous spending. For many twenty-somethings, one of the biggest areas of excess spending is entertainment. One trick I highly recommend is to leave your credit card at home. It's too easy for the tab to get out of control. If you can, only use credit cards for emergencies. If you can eat it, wear it, hear it, or drink it, is it really an emergency? And if you withdraw cash regularly from the ATM, leave a chunk of that at home, too. I find that if I have money in my wallet it tends to want to escape into the hands of some merchant. I have to fight to be disciplined.

When you're at this stage of life, student loans may be a big part of your debt. In fact, according to a report by the Project on Student Loan Debt, the average student loan debt for graduating seniors in

2008 was approximately $23,200. But in addition to the student loans you also have credit card debt and auto loans. The Federal Reserve reports that nearly twenty-five cents of every dollar a twenty-five-to-thirty-four-year-old earns is spent on such debts. So look at all your debt and be strategic in paying it down. Look to the higher-interest-rate loans and the nondeductible debt first. Have payments deducted automatically from your bank account to avoid any late payments and applicable charges.

Not only is minimizing debt good for your financial health, it's also good for your mental health. A survey conducted by Myvesta Foundation, a nonprofit consumer education organization, found that nearly half of the people who have problems with debt experience symptoms of depression, and credit card debt is the generally at the root of it. Given our credit card culture, you can build credit card balances easily. But don't kid yourself, the day of reckoning will come and come sooner than you think. The longer you wait to get your financial life in balance, the more the cure is going to hurt.

Believe me here. I am truly talking from personal experience. Yes, as my family and friends know all too well, I am a reformed credit card junkie. My attitude was live for today and if you want it, charge it. But alas, just like with any bingeing, my day of reckoning came. To my great chagrin I was forced, at age thirty, to move in with my parents in order to pay down my ridiculous debt. (Oh, did I forget to tell you that it was their credit card but they didn't remember I had it until they ran a credit report? Oops.) Now, my parents are great, but having to move back in after being on my own for so long was extremely traumatic for me (and I am sure for them as well), and what I learned is that all the short-term gratification I received each time I swiped my credit card was not enough to compensate for all that it cost me later. Furthermore, although I have reformed, I still feel somewhat behind the eight ball because I misused my most powerful asset—time.

MINIMUM PAYMENTS ON CREDIT CARDS

According to www.bankrate.com, if you only make the minimum payment on a $8,400 credit card balance at 15 percent interest, it will take more than twenty years and nearly $16,700 to pay off the balance plus interest. You may want to consider visiting www.bankrate.com or another financial Web site for access to calculators that will help you determine the amount of time and money it will take to pay off your credit card balances using alternative monthly payments.

Today I'm finding people in their twenties who are very anti-debt. That's good, to a point. But it can be overdone. Believe it or not, if you don't have any history of carrying debt and paying it off consistently over time, you may not be considered an A+ credit risk, because the people loaning you the money want to see evidence of your ability to manage your debt. I know it sounds counterintuitive, but it's true. As you get ready to purchase a new home you should check your credit rating. The appendix has more detail on credit ratings and scores. The average age of first-time home buyers is approximately thirty-two. And being totally anti-debt may lead some people to decide they would rather pay off their student loans than contribute to their 401(k). Bad idea! If your company contributes to your 401(k), you will be walking away from free money if you don't pony up your share. Between the match and your aggressively invested portfolio, you most likely are earning more than the interest rate of your loans.

Although retirement seems an eternity away when you're in the wealth creation phase of your financial life, the power of compounding is huge, and even small amounts can mean great differences over long periods of time. As you will recall from Chapter 1, we now live in an age of self-sufficiency, and time is one of the most important components of your success and happiness. A Roper Center survey shows that people who save just 5 percent of their income are much happier overall than those who don't save at all. Unfortunately, according to the Washington-based Employee Benefit Research Institute (EBRI), in 2006 71 percent of full-time workers aged twenty-one to twenty-four were not enrolled in their employers' retirement savings plans. Furthermore, it's interesting to note that (according to Brightwork Partners LLC, a financial services consulting company), almost 60 percent of retirees say if they knew then what they know now, they would have set up a disciplined savings program much earlier in order to have accomplished their objectives. They probably never paid attention to this chart:

The Benefits of Investing Early*		
	TOTAL CONTRIBUTIONS	TOTAL SAVINGS
Early saver—starts today Contributes $150 month for 40 years and earns 8% annual return	$72,000	$527,142
Late saver—starts in 15 years Contributes $300 month for 25 years and earns 10% annual return	$90,000	$401,367

*Assumes monthly compounding and consistent returns.

PHASE TWO: WEALTH GROWTH

The wealth growth phase is an exciting time in life. It typically corresponds with your thirties and the birth of children, home purchases, and increasing responsibilities at work. Those increasing responsibilities often come with greater income, but with increasing expenses as well. If you were having financial problems in your twenties, chances are those problems are going to get worse now. Unfortunately, according to the Center for Consumer Financial Research, the average age of a person filing for bankruptcy is thirty-eight.

Keeping track of where your dollars are going, continuing to save for retirement, and laying the foundation for your children's college funds should all be "must-have" goals. It can be helpful to have a few rules of thumb for tracking expenses. One is that your basic expenses should take no more than 50 percent of your after-tax income. The rest of your income is to service your debt and your variable expenses. Cars are a common source of overspending. Credit counselors suggest that total car costs, including car payments, fuel, insurance, and maintenance, shouldn't exceed 20 percent of net (after-tax) income. Your income and expenses may be different, so use these as a guideline and adjust accordingly.

Continuing to save for retirement goes without saying. On average, we stay at our jobs for five years or so, so we may have a 401(k) left at our previous employer. If you are happy with the investment opportunities in your new employer's plan, you may want to consider rolling over the old into the new. That way everything is under one roof and you will be better able to keep track of it. You should be increasing your contribution rate as your salary increases until you hit the maximum limit.

Saving for children's college education causes angst for many parents. The question often comes down to "Us or them?" That is, you may have to choose between saving for retirement or saving for your children's college education. Which one do you do? When push comes to shove, the answer is simple. You can finance your kids' college education, but you can't finance your retirement. And don't forget, this is not an all-or-nothing deal. If you can't save to fund the entire amount of college, then focus on what you can do.

No matter what you save, you may want to consider using a 529 college savings plan to accumulate the funds. These types of plans are pretty easy to understand, especially if you get how a 401(k) plan works. Just like with a 401(k), your contributions are invested in a portfolio of mutual funds (generally managed by an investment manager or "program manager") and the earnings grow tax-deferred (that is, the earnings are not taxed until you actually use them). Simple? Yes! Just keep in mind that the purpose is to save for college and the tax rules require that the money be used for "qualified college expenses" (tuition, books, supplies, and room and board). A further benefit is that if you use your state's own plan your state may offer some income tax breaks as well (like an up-front deduction for your contributions or income exemption on withdrawals). There are other ways to save for education, but 529 plans are often the best bet.

PHASE THREE: WEALTH ACCUMULATION

One day, age fifty will loom startlingly close. That's when financial priorities become really simple: It's make-or-break time for retirement. Remember the four places toward which you could direct your money: yourself, your family, charity, and the government? At this stage it has to be all about you. These are your peak earning years and you have to make up for lost time and bad investment decisions. If not now, when?

Do you know how much you should be saving? Probably not.

EBRI states that fewer than 37 percent of us have ever tried to calculate how much money we will need in retirement. Most people's guesstimates are too low. If you do nothing else, at least develop a ballpark estimate. You can go to www.choosetosave.org and complete the "ballpark estimate" retirement planning tool. It takes no more than five minutes. Women especially need to do this. You may be thinking you have been saving well, but it's a sad fact that although women who have access to employer-sponsored savings plans put the same percentage of their income aside each month as men do, they end up with far less money at retirement than their male cohorts. This is partly because they earn less for the same work (don't get me started), and partly because their opportunities for career advancement are stunted from being out of the job market for blocks of time while rearing children. As a result, they earn less over their careers.

So please use a planning tool or work with your adviser to determine whether you're on the right path to accumulating wealth and preparing for retirement. Don't just put your head in the sand. And don't say, "Whatever, I'll just work until I die or I'll work until I can no longer walk or talk." Unfortunately, many current retirees said the same thing during their working years but were forced into retirement before they wanted because of health and/or opportunity issues. A Merrill Lynch survey shows that 65 percent of the nation's 76 million baby boomers will not have sufficient funds to retire at age sixty-five. They really will have to work until they die or more likely until poor health forces them into substandard retirement. It's interesting to note, though, that a study by the Pew Research Foundation found that more than three-quarters of today's workers (77 percent) expect to work for pay even after they retire. But these expectations are dramatically out of step with the experiences of people who are already retired, just 12 percent of whom are currently working for pay (either part- or full-time).

Additionally, the study found there is also a disparity between the age at which today's workers say they plan to retire and the age at which today's retirees actually did retire. The average worker expects to retire at age sixty-one, while the average retiree actually retired at 57.8. I don't know about you, but I know plenty of fifty-five-year-olds who wanted to keep working but their companies didn't cooperate. A 2006 study by McKinsey & Company confirms this. Their research found that 40 percent of current retirees were forced to retire earlier than they had planned. Of those retirees, 44 percent cited job loss or downsizing as the reason they were no longer working. Also cited was caring for aging parents. According to www.sandwichgeneration.com, the vast majority of caregivers for parents are women, and according to the National Center for Women and Aging, the average caregiver will lose over $600,000 in wages, pensions, and Social Security benefits over a lifetime.

So don't rely on the fact that you will work until you drop—often life happens to get in the way.

PHASE FOUR: WEALTH PRESERVATION

Congratulations on your retirement! You are now in your sixties and you have worked hard to accumulate your savings. Now that you earned it, you must make sure that you not only protect your wealth but that it keeps growing for you. For more than twenty years you have focused on accumulating a pot of money to fund your life after you stop working. Now, in order to have these funds last as long as you do, you need a strategic spend-down plan. Your spending plan will be dependent on inflation and your longevity genetics, health, and lifestyle.

This concept of a strategic distribution plan is somewhat new to the financial services industry and there are new tools and products coming out every day. The consensus seems to be that someone sixty-five years old may not want to withdraw more than 4 percent of retirement assets annually. A higher withdrawal rate can quickly deplete your savings, causing you to run out of money. And when you run out of money in your seventies, there's no "do over"!

Withdrawal Rates (too high a distribution rate can derail your plan)	
WITHDRAWAL RATES	YEARS PORTFOLIO MAY LAST
10%	10 years
9%	11 years
8%	12 years
7%	14 years
6%	17 years
5%	21 years
4%	27 years

SOURCE: Fidelity Investments.

PHASE FIVE: WEALTH TRANSFER

"The person who dies with the most toys wins" may not be your motto. You are in your mid-seventies and are confident at this stage that you will not outlive your assets and thus you are more focused on your legacy. Your goal is to ensure that your assets will be distributed to your heirs as you so desire. Careful planning is needed. To be blunt, the decision at this point comes down to this: Do you want to give money and assets away before you die, after, or both? Some people want to pass on wealth so they can watch their loved ones enjoy it. Others don't want to surrender control and prefer to make bequests after their own death. Obviously if you're in this latter group you need to make the plans before you're gone. Don't get legacy or estate planning confused with estate tax minimization. Your first goal should be about your assets going to the right people at the right time. Only then should you think about tax efficiency.

WEALTH PHASE WRAP-UP

No matter what stage of life you are at, I'd like you to think about this process. Many of us avoid getting on the scale if we think the number will be bad. But eventually the day comes when we finally stand in front of the mirror naked, confront our issues, and get honest with ourselves. The irony is that when we finally do get on the scale, we feel instantly better, no matter what the number is, because we are now taking control of our lives. The same is true with your finances. Going through these planning exercises may hurt a little up-front, but I promise you that the process will bring you a greater sense of contentment.

KEEPING IT REAL

Now that you are "in the know" about your situation, it's time for you to learn about behaviors that may set some barriers in the way of our financial success. These behaviors are driven purely on emotion with tried-and-true psychological underpinnings. In fact, there is a growing academic discipline called behavioral economics that's all about how we, as human beings, think about money. For a long time economists just assumed that we were all rational animals who made intelligent decisions about things like spending, saving, and earning money. Of course, the rest of us who aren't economists knew that was far from true.

Here's a classic example of how behavioral economists view the rest of us. They start by asking a simple question: What's a dollar worth?

Well, it could be worth one hundred pennies, ten dimes, twenty nickels, or four quarters. But it's still a dollar and one dollar is equal to any other dollar. Easy enough, so far. But if that's true, why do most of us treat some dollars as being worth more than other dollars? Let's say you're shopping for a new purse and you find one priced at $200 at a store near you. But then a friend tells you that you can get that exact same purse at another store for $150. Trouble is, that store is twenty miles away. Do you make the drive to save $50? Most of us would.

Now, instead of a purse, let's go shopping for a car. Let's look at a new economy car. The dealer in your town will sell you one for $19,000. But you find out by phoning around that a dealer twenty miles away will sell you the identical car for $18,950. Will you drive twenty miles to save $50? Probably not.

Isn't that weird? You're willing to drive twenty miles to save $50 on a purse, but you won't drive twenty miles to save $50 on a car. The savings is exactly the same and the distance is exactly the same. To drive that far for one $50 savings but not for another is irrational.

There are lots of other irrational behaviors that we engage in when dealing with money. For example, we tend to value income from our jobs more highly than the money we receive in the form of tax refunds or gifts. Why? A dollar in the form of salary is exactly the equal of a dollar from a tax refund or a gift.

This irrational thinking about the value of money becomes especially dangerous when we begin thinking about some dollars as being less valuable than others because of the way we spend them. Credit cards are perhaps the most dangerous example of this way of thinking. I don't mean to keep harping on credit cards, but with the average credit card debt somewhere between $8,000 and $9,000 (and because I'm a reformed chargeaholic), I just can't help myself. Many women don't even know their credit card balance because their husband or partner takes care of all the bills. These women assume all is well because nothing is said, only to find out one day that they're up to their ears in debt. Behavioral economists have found that most of us value a dollar of cash more than we do a dollar spent on a credit card purchase. In simple terms, we might not part with $400 in cash for a new purse, but we don't think twice about swiping away with our credit card and charging that $400 purse. Yet in either case we have spent $400 for a purse. It gets worse. We think of our dollars in our savings account as much more valuable than we think about the amount of dollars on our credit card balance. That's why so many of us aren't willing to take money out of a savings account where it earns, say, 3 percent interest to pay off a credit card balance that may be costing us as much as 18 percent interest.

In other chapters throughout this book, we will address additional behaviors that you should be in the know about that may be barriers as well to your financial success.

The importance of knowing what you have, what you can expect to save, and what it is that you want cannot be understated. Without this knowledge your future is nothing more than a hope and a prayer.

I think the best way to close this chapter is by quoting from the song that was on the B-side to the Rolling Stones' "Honky Tonk Women": "You can't always get what you want, but if you try sometimes, you just might find you get what you need."

AT THE VERY LEAST

Focus on your retirement goals. Log on to your 401(k) site and use the tools there or find one online to better understand where you stand today, what your options are, and what you'll need to change (if anything) to achieve your retirement goals. If you don't have access to a retirement planning tool, you may want to check out the article "National Savings Rate Guidelines for Individuals" by Roger Ibbotson et al. in the April 2007 *Journal of Financial Planning*. There you will find several charts showing what percentage of your income you should save for retirement given your age, income, desired retirement income, and the amount already saved.

CHAPTER SUMMARY

. . . .

1. You must identify your goal in terms of time, priority, and cost.
2. You must know what you own, what you owe, and what's available.
3. You must compare what you have with what you want and identify, if need be, what you are willing to do to achieve what is really important to you.
4. This analysis should be done at least every five years (every three if you are near or in retirement).
5. Do not focus on what you are "giving up"; instead focus on what you will be "getting" from the path you take.
6. What you've learned:

THE FOUR BASIC FOOD GROUPS

Any effective and well-balanced diet is built around a working knowledge of the basic food groups: fruits and vegetables, proteins, carbohydrates, dairy, and fats. Each supplies us with necessary nutrients to fuel our bodies. The trick, though, is to combine the various food groups in such a way as to get the optimum amount of nutrition with the minimum number of calories.

Investing is very similar. Instead of food groups, we have four asset classes: cash, stocks, bonds, and alternatives. Each provides us with an essential ingredient for a healthy portfolio, but each has very different characteristics. This chapter is all about the various asset classes, their characteristics, and the roles they play in our portfolios. We're laying the foundation here to plan our overall financial diet. The terms may sound unfamiliar at first, but as you'll see, the explanations for each of these asset classes are pretty simple.

Before we look at each asset class individually, we need to understand that our long-term financial plan will be a constant process of balancing the two essential factors of investing: risk and reward. The most important concept to remember is that generally speaking you can't have one without the other. To me, the relationship between risk and reward is just like the relationship between calories and taste. Think of calories as risk and taste as reward. Typically the greater the calories in something (the greater the risk of gaining weight), the better it tastes (and thus the better your reward). All throughout your dieting life you are constantly asking yourself if the reward—thirty seconds of heavenly taste—is worth the risk of another pound gained. For example, think of a rice cake and a chocolate chip cookie. A rice cake is thirty-five calories. That's great because the risk of gaining weight from eating one is minimal. But then there's taste. If you like eating cardboard, you'll *love* eating rice cakes. Now think about a big, fat chocolate chip cookie and the 450 calories packed into it. Eat a few of those and you'll have taken in a day's worth of calories. But, boy, do they taste good! So you see, dieting becomes a challenge of matching risk and reward.

When we think about various asset classes we're also balancing risk and reward. The risk comes in the form of what we call "volatility." The reward is called "expected return." The key thing to remember is that each asset class, as well as the specific investments in each class, has a risk-and-return profile, and the higher the risk, the higher the expected return.

Rewards at a Glance	
HISTORICAL RETURNS OF STOCKS, BONDS, T-BILLS, AND INFLATION FROM 1926 THROUGH 2008*	
Large-cap stocks	9.6%
Small-cap stocks	11.7%
Intermediate-term government bonds	5.4%
U.S. Treasury bills	3.7%
Inflation	3.0%

*This chart is for illustrative purposes only and does not represent the performance of any particular investment. Past performance does not guarantee future results.

SOURCE: Morningstar.

Just as no single food or food group can provide you with all the nutrients that you need, no single investment can supply all the risk and return that you need to achieve all your goals. That's why I recommend that you utilize a variety of different investments and different classes. As we go through each asset class, we will spend some time on the risk-and-reward profiles of the various instruments within each asset class as well as the profile of each class itself.

As I wrote earlier, there are four main asset classes that make up the foundation of a robust investment plan: cash, stocks, bonds, and alternatives. Briefly, we can say that cash is like your fruit and vegetables. If you have more than the recommended portion amount, you won't necessarily gain a lot of weight, but you won't make tremendous progress toward your goal either. Bonds remind me of dairy because they give portfolios a foundation. What's more, bonds are like milk in that the higher the fat content and respective calories (or expected return from a bond), the greater you like it. Unfortunately, that increase in pleasure (or reward) comes at an increased risk to our health and weight (and risk of financial losses from a bond). Stocks are like your carbs and proteins. They are your investment plan's main source of energy and are necessary if your portfolio is going to grow. Finally, alternative investments are like fats. A little can go a long way.

FRUITS AND VEGETABLES: CASH AND LIQUID INVESTMENTS

Many people dieting for the first time are surprised to learn that they cannot eat an unlimited amount of fruits and vegetables. Although they provide great nutrients and should be a part of your menu, too much of a good thing is, well, not a good thing. The same is true of cash. Cash provides us with great liquidity (remember, this means your money is readily available if you need it), but too much of it can prevent you from reaching your long-term goals.

The problem is that cash has a very low risk-and-reward profile. That means that on a day-to-day basis the value of cash doesn't go down—that is, there's no real risk of losing much cash—but it also doesn't go up very much. About the best you can expect is to earn a percentage point or two on the money in your bank account. Hence, you have an asset with little risk and little reward. To that you might say, "So what?" The "so what" is inflation. You can think of inflation simply as an increase in prices. The box of cereal that cost you $3.99 last year now costs $4.99. If the value of your cash stays the same while prices are going up, you have a problem: Your "purchasing power" has declined. Without making any less money you're slowly becoming poorer. Bummer, isn't it?

INFLATION

Here's how inflation can undermine a financial plan. Let's say that at the end of the year you had $1,200 under your mattress. But if, during the course of that year, inflation rose 4 percent, that $1,200 in cash can now buy you only $1,152 of goods and services compared to what it would have bought a year ago. You actually lost purchasing power! If, instead, you had parked that $1,200 in a money market mutual fund with a return of 4 percent annually, your $1,200 would have earned $48, exactly the amount by which inflation grew. So you are still able to buy the same things without eating deeper into your portfolio. In other words, you broke even. That doesn't sound good, I know, but breaking even is a lot better than losing money.

You may be thinking, "Why a section on cash? Cash is cash. How much is there really to know?"

Well, not so much as to be overwhelming, but enough that it deserves some attention. Yes, cash is cash, but different cash vehicles have different degrees of liquidity. The cash in your purse is very liquid. To get at it, all you need to do is reach in and grab a handful. The trade-off for that liquidity is that the cash in your purse isn't working for you, making more cash. It's just sitting there. That's where "liquid investments" enter the picture. They are simple investments that, while still providing you with liquidity, put your cash to work earning a return, albeit usually a very small return.

There are four major types of liquid investments that you can use to keep your money handy, but keep it working for you at the same time. Here's a brief overview, then I'll go over each one in more detail.

- *Certificates of deposit*: Offered by banks, CDs are federally insured by the Federal Deposit Insurance Corporation (FDIC) and usually are offered in various terms ranging from a few months to several years.
- *U.S. Treasury bills (T-bills)*: These are short-term loans that you make to the U.S. government for six months or less. They have a set maturity date and are backed by the full faith and credit of the U.S. government.
- *Bank money market accounts*: They usually pay higher interest rates than a bank savings account because they have higher minimum balance requirements and restrict the number of withdrawals to six per month with no more than three checks written per month. When offered by banks, money market accounts are covered under the FDIC up to the FDIC limits.

- *Mutual fund money markets*: You own a fractional interest (shares) of a pool of assets invested in different types of very short-term debt. They are *not* FDIC-insured and thus, because of that slight extra risk, tend to pay a higher interest rate than bank money market funds. Your interest is paid to you in the form of additional shares in the fund, all of which are priced at $1.

The best way to think about cash and liquid investments is that you will use them as a parking lot. Money sits in the parking lot until it is needed for something within the next few years. Remember that I told you earlier that stock prices are volatile, that is, move up and down a lot? While we want a big part of your portfolios invested in stocks for the long term, the risk that stock prices might decline for a while—a year or more, for example—suggests that if we know we're going to be spending a few thousand dollars for something in the next year or so, that money ought to be safely parked in a liquid investment, earning enough to prevent inflation from destroying value, but accessible enough that we can get to it easily when we need it.

Let's focus more closely now on each of the four types of liquid investments. Generally, the major differences between them are if they are FDIC-insured or not and if you have daily access without restriction or penalty.

Certificates of Deposit (CDs) These are "time deposits" that earn a specified rate of interest over a specified period of time. Basically you're lending money to a bank for a fixed period of time and, in return, the bank is paying you a stated rate of interest, paid in various installments over the term of your CD. The term can range from three months up to five years, with the longer terms typically paying higher returns. The risk with a longer-term CD is that during the period your money is locked up at a specified rate, interest rates can rise and you could have earned more money if you didn't have it tied up. You may be tempted at that point to withdraw your money prior to the maturity date. Remember that when you sign up for a CD, the expectation is that you won't withdraw your money before the term you agreed to is up. If you do, the bank typically charges you a penalty that can substantially reduce the return on that CD. Read the fine print to make sure you know the specific terms and conditions. You want to understand the rate of interest (APY, or annual percentage yield), the time frame, minimums, call provisions (the bank ends it early), and early withdrawal penalties (you take it out before the end of the term).

CDs are often used when you have a specific need for a specific amount of cash within a few years and not before. For example, you need $50,000 in two years to redo your kitchen. You "park" your cash in a CD. CDs are good for people who want to add an extra layer of discipline to their cash holdings. By that I mean if you're tempted to spend cash that's just sitting around in your bank account you can remove that temptation by locking the money away in a CD. The penalty on early withdrawal will help keep you honest.

U.S. Treasury Bills (T-bills) T-bills are very short-term loans that you make to the U.S. government. They are sold in denominations ranging from $1,000 up to a maximum of $5 million and commonly have maturities (expiration dates) of one month (four weeks), three months (thirteen weeks), or six months (twenty-six weeks). The unique aspect of T-bills is that you don't earn interest in the traditional sense of the word. Instead, your return on a T-bill comes from the fact that they are sold at a discount from their face value. For example, you might pay $970 for a $1,000 bill. When the bill matures, you get back the face value, $1,000. Your interest is the face value ($1,000) minus the purchase price ($970), or $30. You can buy T-bills directly from the government (www.treasurydirect .gov) or through a traditional brokerage account. Financial intermediaries, large companies, and governmental units buy most T-bills.

Bank Money Market Accounts Bank money market accounts earn a return in much the same way that mutual fund money market accounts do: They pool the money from lots of investors and use it to make short-term loans to government entities and corporations. The interest rate returns from money market accounts will vary over time and are somewhat unpredictable, unlike, for example, a five-year bank CD. The major difference between a bank money market account and a money market mutual fund is that the assets in the bank are insured by the Federal Deposit Insurance Corporation. That safety factor can result in slightly lower returns than what you might find available among mutual fund money market funds. You'll also find more stringent regulations covering such things as minimum amounts and the number of withdrawals in a given time span. The return paid by any money market fund is the result of competitive forces. Bank money market funds are handy places to keep your "emergency fund" because you will only need to get the money in rare circumstances.

Mutual Fund Money Market Accounts Money market funds offered by the mutual fund industry aren't insured by the FDIC and often don't have as many restrictions as bank money market accounts. When you own a mutual fund money market investment, you are issued "shares" in the fund at the rate of one share for each dollar invested. As your account earns interest, you are issued additional shares at the same rate of one share for each dollar. Money market funds are classified according to the kinds of debt securities they own. Some invest only in federal government (very) short-term debt securities, some municipal government (tax-free), and some corporate short-term debt securities. Money market funds offer the greatest flexibility and should be your first choice when flexibility is important.

The value of a money market share could drop below a dollar if your fund made a bunch of loans to companies that then defaulted or went bankrupt. In financial lingo this is called "breaking the buck." Every fund knows that if it "breaks the buck," it will suffer huge outflows as investors take their money to other, better-managed competitors. Prior to 2008 this was practically unfathomable; in fact, if we look back over the thirty years that retail money markets have existed, no fund ever "broke the buck." Sadly, the extreme events of the recent credit crisis caused unimaginable happenings and we did see the value of a share of a few funds go below a dollar (to ninety-seven cents).

Keep in mind that like all mutual funds, there is a cost to you for using a fund company's money market fund but you may not be aware of it (although during the credit crisis many waived their fees). If you compare two money market funds that invest in similar securities and one really outperforms the other, the problem may lie in the two funds' expense ratios, the amount they charge investors. Most money market fund expense ratios are in the range of 0.15 percent to 0.50 percent. The expense ratio can be found in the fund's prospectus. Alternatively, if you compare two money market funds that have similar expense ratios and one really outperforms the other, the difference most likely is in the underlying securities. Typically if it appears too good to be true—it is. The underlying securities may be of higher risk than you anticipate.

When looking to put your cash somewhere, it's actually good to shop. Look around to find the kind of investment that meets your needs for liquidity, safety, and return. Use the chart below as a guide, and you may also want to check out one of the financial rate aggregator Web sites like www.bankrate.com to compare rates of different cash products.

LIQUID INVESTMENTS	FEATURES
Certificate of deposits (CDs)	• CDs are good to park your cash in when you believe interest rates will be falling during the term of your CD. • CDs are good to use if you need an additional layer of discipline, because of the penalties for early termination. • FDIC-insured*
U.S. T-bills	• U.S. T-bills are the ultimate in safety since they are backed by the full faith and credit of the United States.
Bank money markets (BMMs)	• BMM accounts are good to use in a rising interest rate environment since the money market rates change as market conditions change. • BMMs are good to use if you do not need unlimited access to the funds. • FDIC-insured*
Money market mutual funds (MMMFs)	• MMMFs like BMMs are good to use in a rising interest rate environment. • MMMFs give you unlimited access and check-writing capabilities. • Not FDIC-insured

*Go to www.FDIC.gov for a more detailed look at the specific rules and restrictions and updates.

PROTEINS AND CARBS: STOCKS

Stocks are the meat and potatoes of any long-term investment plan. Why? Stocks pack the biggest punch—that is, the potential highest returns—of the big three asset classes. Over the long haul—I'm talking about many years—stocks have produced, on average, annual (nominal) returns of more than 10 percent. That doesn't happen every year, of course. The price of any single stock or of most of the stocks in what we think of as "the stock market" can go down, sometimes sharply, and stay down, sometimes for years. Therefore, while we want to get the long-term returns from stocks, we don't want all of our money tied up in stocks.

Stocks are also known as "equity securities" because they represent an ownership share in a company. If you own Microsoft stock, you own a little tiny chunk of Microsoft and you and Bill Gates have something in common. Never mind that he owns a few million shares and you own just a few shares. You both gain or lose depending on how well Microsoft performs in a very competitive world.

Deciding which stocks are going to be best for your portfolio is incredibly difficult. To do so effectively you must be able to understand and predict how something as complicated as a corporation will perform in the future. Think about it. To be able to analyze any company you have to know who is managing it and how good they are. You have to know all about the company's products, how they are produced and sold, and what competitors are doing to steal customers now and in the future either with better products or lower prices. You have to know if the company is deeply in debt or generating lots of spare cash. How much is it plowing into research and development? How does it treat its workforce? Does it pay enough to attract the best and brightest? What external factors can either boost or hurt the business?

The list goes on and on. There are lots of smart people working for financial firms on Wall Street who are paid large amounts of money to figure out all this stuff and they don't always get it right. Do you think you have the same or better skills than those professional stock pickers? Probably not. That's why I'm very adamant about this: Most individual investors should *not* be picking individual stocks; rather, they should be using an investment vehicle where a variety of stocks are packaged together such as a mutual fund (more about this in Chapter 5).

There are two ways to make money by owning stocks: capital appreciation and dividends. Capital appreciation is a fancy name for an increase in the price of the stock. Stocks that appreciate over time do so because the underlying company is innovative, well managed, and competitive. In other words, the company becomes more valuable over time.

The other way to make money on stocks—dividends—is about real money, not paper gains. A company, especially a big, successful company, often generates more in profits than it can wisely reinvest in its business. Rather than simply hold on to those excess profits, the company distributes them to its shareholders as dividend payments, usually on a quarterly basis. For those companies that pay dividends (many don't, because they need to reinvest profits in growing the business)—the rate is about 2 percent or 3 percent of the stock price. Keep in mind, though, that often a company that is reinvesting all its cash back into its business may have a greater chance of capital appreciation than one that doesn't.

STOCKS AND RISK

Stocks have provided the best returns of the big three asset classes over the years, but rewards don't come without risks, and stocks have their fair share of risks. The two main categories are market risk and

company-specific risk. Market risk and company-specific risk are best
explained by using an analogy to a tossed salad. Here's what I mean:
Think of the stock market as a mixed salad and salad dressing as the
economy. If you put bad dressing on your salad, no matter how fresh
the vegetables, that salad will taste bad. But if you have a good dressing and all your ingredients are fresh except a rotten cucumber, you
can pick out the cucumber slices and still enjoy your salad. Market
risk is like the bad salad dressing; it's the chance that the entire stock
market will decline. Company-specific risk is like the rotten cucumber; everything else is fine, only the cucumber (or company) is bad.

Market risk is also known as systematic risk or nondiversifiable
risk. At some point because of a weak economy or some other problem (as we saw in the last quarter of 2008 and into 2009), almost every
stock suffers. Not every stock will go down, but the majority usually
do. They won't fall in just one day. Rather, they decline in fits and
starts over a period of weeks, months, or years. The underlying health
of the companies whose stocks you own may be fine, but when the
market trends down, people get scared and tend not to want to own
stocks. That means there is more supply of stock than demand for it.
More supply than demand equals price drops. Market risk cannot be
"diversified" away, meaning buying a broad variety of stocks won't
prevent you from feeling some pain. If you invest in any stock, you
will be subject to market risk. It's just one of the things you have to
live with because risk is not to be avoided, it is to be managed.

Company-specific risk stems from all the possible mistakes an
individual company can make and is the reason why analyzing and
choosing individual stocks is so difficult. Management may make a
bad decision or not see a competitive threat emerging in time to coun-
ter it. As a result, profits fall or disappear and consequently stockholders want to get out before things get worse. In other words, more
supply of shares than the demand for shares. Thus, the stock price

falls, sometimes precipitously. Every individual stock has its own respective risk, some higher than others, some lower. Company-specific risk can be "diversified away" by investing in more than one company. That way you minimize the potential bad impact that one respective stock would have on your portfolio.

There are literally thousands of stocks in the market today. They come in many different shapes and sizes with different risk-and-return profiles. It is important to understand something about the various categories of stocks out there, because many of the investment vehicles you will use specialize in certain categories of stocks and that influences their risk-and-reward profile.

A SMORGASBORD OF STOCKS

There are three basic ways that stocks are categorized:

- Size
- Style
- Location

Each category performs somewhat differently than the other categories. Taken together the different categories provide the best possible diversification for long-term portfolios.

SIZE

The financial size of a company is measured by its market capitalization, or "market cap." In its simplest terms, market cap is equal to the share price of the stock times the number of shares outstanding of the corporation. If a company has fifty million shares outstanding and each share has a market value of $100, the company's market capitalization is $5 billion (50,000,000 × $100 per share). Obviously, a company's capitalization changes each time the stock price changes, but usually the changes aren't big enough to make a significant difference in how investors think about the company's size. The three basic categories by financial size are:

- Large cap—more than $10 billion
- Mid cap—between $2 and $10 billion
- Small cap—less than $2 billion

Size matters here, because there is a correlation between size and risk. Typically, the greater the size (capitalization of an organization), the lower the risk of a company going out of business in the near future. Think about it this way: Which company would you think would have a greater chance of going out of business, P&G or a small computer start-up company?

The following is a summary of how they are similar and how they differ.

Large-cap Stocks Large-cap stocks are stocks with a market capitalization of $10 billion or greater. Large-cap stocks tend to be household names because they tend to be large, well-established companies. Microsoft, IBM, ExxonMobil, Coca-Cola, Wal-Mart, and General Electric are all large-cap stocks. The very largest, like those we just named, are often referred to as "blue chips," a term derived from the game of poker in which the blue chips are the most valuable. Blue-chip stocks generally are considered to be safe, in excellent financial shape, and firmly entrenched as leaders in their fields. The exact criteria used to classify a company's stock as a blue chip is subjective, but they generally pay dividends, have a long history, and are favorably regarded by investors. Two of the ways most commonly used by investment professionals and the press to measure the health of the stock market are the Dow Jones Industrial Average and Standard & Poor's 500 index. Both consist almost entirely of blue-chip stocks. (See the appendix for a list of the different indexes.)

Because large-cap stocks are so large, it is generally assumed that they will have slower growth than smaller stocks, although there are always exceptions, such as Apple and Google, both of which have recently exhibited remarkable growth. But the slower growth is offset by the durability of most large-cap stocks. It's awfully hard to kill off a company with a $100 billion market cap (but not impossible, as we saw in 2008, when circumstances were beyond extreme). So we come back to our ever-present concept of risk and return. Large-cap stocks simply aren't as risky as small- or mid-cap stocks. As a result, large-cap stocks tend to offer less reward, too. Obviously we don't live in a perfect world and sometimes we are surprised when a big-cap stock grows—or falls—very fast.

Mid-cap Stocks Mid-cap stocks are sort of the Goldilocks of stocks, neither too big nor too small. The financial industry tends to define the mid-cap segment of the market as stocks with market capitalizations of between $2 billion and $10 billion. Mid-cap stocks tend to be a little more risky than large-cap stocks, but they also tend to have greater potential for growth than the large caps. A simplified way to think of mid caps is that they are either the small companies that made it past the dangerous start-up phase of their lives but haven't yet reached full potential or they are larger companies that are in decline for some reason or another. The companies on the way up may not be industry leaders, but they have the potential to rise to that position. The declining companies may once have been leaders and may, with the right management and under the right circumstances, still achieve leadership again. Recognizable mid caps are Under Armour, Vail Resorts, and Ross Stores. Mid-cap stocks don't always get the attention they deserve, but in recent years investors have begun to pay more attention to the category. Just as the S&P 500 index measures the health of the large-cap stocks, the S&P Mid-Cap 400 Index is the most widely used index for midsized companies. Generally, you can find the values and the risk-and-return measurements of the different indexes on a variety of financial Web sites.

Small-cap Stocks Finally we come to the small caps. Small-cap stocks are those that have a capitalization of less than $2 billion. These companies tend to be younger companies with a potential for great growth. Notice the word "potential." A great way to think of small caps is that they can behave like someone with bipolar syndrome. For a period of time the price of a small cap can rise at euphoric rates, only to hit a peak and then plunge with depressing, even shocking, speed. Some will simply disappear. That price volatility makes small-cap stocks one of the most exciting and dangerous segments of the market. Risks are high, but so are rewards when things go well. The Russell 2000 is the most widely used index for small-sized companies. The average market cap of a company in the Russell 2000 is $530 million. To give you some sense of proportion, the market capitalization of ExxonMobil (as of this writing) is $325 billion. You can find the market capitalization of many companies on the same financial Web sites that you find index information.

STYLE

Size isn't the only thing that counts when we're talking about stocks. All three sizes of stocks also come in two different styles:

- Growth
- Value

Growth stocks have typically been growing faster than the average stock in their size (and industry) category. For example, large-cap stocks tend to grow on average about 5 percent per year. A large-cap stock that is gaining faster than that is, by definition, a large-cap *growth* stock. The average small-cap stock, on the other hand, tends to grow at a rate of about 10 percent per year. Any small-cap stock growing faster than that warrants the small-cap growth stock label. Growth stocks tend to grow because they are high-quality, successful, and probably very innovative companies. Value stocks aren't growing as fast as the average stock in their size classification, and therefore act very different from growth stocks. Thus they tend to command somewhat lower prices, at least for a while. Investors often look to a stock's price-earnings ratio (P/E ratio) as an indicator of its style tilt. You can read more about the P/E ratio in the appendix.

While growth and value stocks can be found in any sector of the stock market, certain sectors have historically lent themselves to one style or the other. Growth stocks tend to be found in the technology and health care sectors. Value stocks tend to be from the financial, energy, and telecom sectors. Now, just because a stock is classified as value or growth doesn't always mean that it will forever remain in that category. Microsoft, for example, was classified as a growth stock in the 1980s and '90s. But as we entered the new century investment pros were increasingly thinking about Microsoft, besieged as it was by competitors like Google, as a value stock. Apple is the opposite. It was long seen as a value stock, but with its great product innovations over the past several years, including the iPod and iPhone, many investors now classify it as a growth stock.

There are investors who swear by either growth or value stocks, but they both have their pros or cons. Growth stocks are growing fast but at some point that growth is going to have to slow. When it does, disappointed investors are likely to sell the stock and knock the price down sharply. Value stocks, on the other hand, are considered to be those on the discount rack, like last season's fashions. You can get a really good deal and if enough other investors eventually realize what a good deal the stock is, they'll rush to buy it, too, resulting in a juicy price increase. Neither growth nor value stocks come with any guarantees. They both fluctuate with market conditions and they both reflect the good and bad things that can happen to individual companies. Growth and value also tend to run in cycles that can be difficult to correctly time. The bottom line? They both carry investment risk, but both are worth considering as potential investments in a well-diversified portfolio.

LOCATION

For the U.S. investor a company is either foreign (headquartered somewhere outside the United States) or domestic (headquartered in the United States). Why should that matter? The basic reason is opportunity. The U.S. stock market represents less than half of the total market capitalization in the world. When people question me on the benefits of international investing, often I will have them think about the following: How boring would life be if we only got to eat hot dogs and apple pie? We would be missing out on pizza, paella, and pumpernickel bread, to name just a few. Through exposure to different cultures we have developed more sophisticated palates and have been able to enjoy fantastic flavors that bring us great satisfaction. Clearly, we are more apt to try foods from the more developed countries than those of the more exotic countries, such as those in parts of the Far East, Africa, and South America. Usually we hesitate to try new foods because we are not familiar with the ingredients and are unsure about its safety. But sometimes if you are willing to take the risk you may be rewarded with sensational treats.

What I am trying to say is that investing in international stocks increases the diversification of our portfolios. Some international stocks are from regions or countries that are very developed and that we are familiar with like Western Europe or Japan, and some are from the less developed or "emerging market" countries. The economies of these emerging markets are not as stable as those of the more developed countries, so the risks of investing in their stocks can be much greater. But just like exotic foods, taking a little risk on stocks from emerging markets can produce fantastic results. Overall, foreign stocks give us exposure to more dynamic economies and companies, as well as other currencies, all of which provide valuable diversification benefits.

DAIRY: BONDS

When you own a stock you own a piece of the company. Bonds are very different. They are essentially loans to a company. A company wishing to raise money without selling more shares can issue bonds. If you buy one, you're loaning your money to the company. Furthermore, it isn't just companies that issue bonds. So does the federal government, as well as state, local, and foreign governments.

There are four basic terms to be aware of when discussing bonds: issuer, face value, coupon rate, maturity or term.

Issuer	Organization getting the "loan" from you
Face value	The amount of the "loan"
Coupon rate	The specified rate of interest on the bond
Maturity or term	Amount of time until you get the principal, or face value, of the bond back

Let's see those terms in action. Assume you bought a brand-new U.S. Treasury bond. It has a face value of $5,000, a 6 percent coupon rate, and a ten-year maturity.

Issuer	U.S. Treasury	If you buy the bond when it is first issued
Face value	$5,000	and hold it for ten years, each year you will get a *fixed* interest payment of $300 (6% of $5,000) from the U.S. Treasury and at the end of the *fixed* ten-year term you will get back the *pre-fixed* amount of $5,000 from the U.S. Treasury
Coupon rate	6%	
Maturity or term	10 years	

Thus, if you invested in this bond, you would get a fixed amount of interest for a fixed amount of time and get a fixed amount of principal back when the bond matures. These *fixed amounts* are why bonds are often referred to as fixed-income securities. But keep in mind that just because these amounts are fixed does not mean they are guaranteed.

Just like stocks, not all bonds are the same. The two key ways people look at bonds is by the issuer and by the length of time the bond has until it matures. The issuer is important because different organizations have different levels of health with different likelihoods of making the interest payments and paying the face value back. The length of time the bond has until it matures is also important because, in its simplest form, it is how long you will get paid that rate of interest.

This tells us that there are two major risks of bonds that you must be aware of:

- Credit risk
- Interest rate risk

RISK TYPE	DESCRIPTION
Credit risk or default risk	• The risk that the organization can default on the loans • Dependent on the organization that issues the bond
Interest rate risk	• The risk that the value of the bond will change due to changing interest rates • Dependent on the term of the bond

The coupon or interest rate (reward) that an organization would assign to a newly issued bond and the price of an existing bond will be a factor of both the creditworthiness of the organization and the term of the bond (risks).

THE FAT ON BOND ISSUERS

One reason I called this section about bonds the dairy section is that, as I said earlier, bonds remind me of milk. There are five general categories of milk: nonfat, low fat, reduced fat, whole milk, and heavy cream. They're all basically the same thing—milk—but as you move up the fat-content scale the flavor gets richer (greater reward) but the calorie count rises as well (greater risk).

There are five general categories of bonds:

- Treasury (U.S. government)
- Municipal (state, cities, and so on)
- Corporate
- Foreign governments
- Foreign corporate

They're all basically the same thing—bonds—but as you move down the credit quality scale (U.S. government to foreign corporate) the returns can get greater but the chance of default (risk) rises as well. So let's see which type of bonds are "nonfat" and which ones are the "heavy cream."

NONFAT: TREASURIES

U.S. government bonds are often called Treasuries. They're just like nonfat milk, not that exciting but they provide less risk to your portfolio's health than other types of bonds. They are essentially free of default risk and consequently provide the lowest returns in exchange for that safety.

There are three subclassifications of Treasuries. The difference lies in their maturities.

TYPES OF TREASURIES	MATURITY
Treasury bill	6 months or less
Treasury notes	Between 2 and 10 years
Treasury bonds	Greater than 10 years

Besides the three subclassifications of Treasuries, there are two other categories to be aware of: Treasury Inflation Protected Securities (TIPS) and Agencies.

TIPS	The maturity value of TIPS rise if inflation rises, thus protecting the spending power of the face value of the bond
Agencies	They are affiliated with the U.S. government and they have its "implied," but not actual, taxing power. Thus, they tend to offer somewhat higher returns than Treasuries with a somewhat higher risk, because they are not necessarily guaranteed

The three most common agency bonds are Ginnie Maes, issued by the Government National Mortgage Association (GNMA); Fannie Maes, issued by the Federal National Mortgage Association (FNMA); and Freddie Macs, issued by the Federal Home Loan Mortgage Corporation (FHLMC). These agencies may ring a bell with you because they were headline news in 2008. They suffered severe losses during the recent housing crisis and the federal government had to step in to protect their viability. In the fall of 2008 the concept of implicit guarantee by the federal government became explicit as evidenced by the billions of bailout dollars directed toward these organizations.

LOW-FAT: MUNIS

Next down the credit (default) risk scale are municipal bonds. Muni bonds are issued by states, cities, and counties. What's more, there are two types of munis:

- Government obligation bonds (GOBs)
- Revenue bonds

The difference between the two is the source of funds used to pay them off.

General obligation bonds (GOBs)	Use the full faith, credit, and taxing powers of the municipality that issued the bonds
Revenue bonds	Depend on a specific revenue stream, such as user fees or lease payments

So whoever issued the GOB will raise taxes on its citizens if necessary to make sure you get your interest and principal, whereas revenue bonds depend on the specific revenue of the project. As a result, typically revenue bonds have a higher credit risk than the respective municipalities' GOBs. But be warned: Not all municipalities are the same; some municipalities are on a better financial footing than others.

People like muni bonds because of their implied safety and because the interest they pay is usually tax-free income (as always there are some exceptions; some private activity bonds may be subject to the alternative minimum tax). Thus, you get to keep more of it.

Of course, the municipalities issuing bonds know that you're going to get a tax break if you buy their bonds. That's why muni bonds tend to offer lower interest rates than taxable bonds (there's no free lunch!).

REDUCED FAT: CORPORATE BONDS

Corporate bonds tend to be characterized by higher yields than Treasuries and (most) munis because there is a higher risk of a company defaulting than a government. But again, each company has a different credit quality and it is important to understand the amount of credit risk you are taking when you buy a specific corporate bond.

TAX EQUIVALENT YIELD

Often when people discuss muni bonds they will use the term "tax equivalent yield" (TEY). The formula to determine the TEY is as follows:

Tax-free yield ÷ (1 – your federal tax rate)

For example, if your tax rate was 30 percent and you had a $1,000 muni bond with a 5 percent coupon rate, you would end up with $50 in your pocket. To get that same amount ($50) after tax in your pocket a taxable bond would need to pay you approximately 7.15 percent interest, which is 5 percent divided by (1 – 30 percent). Therefore, the TEY for a 5 percent muni bond is 7.15 percent.

WHOLE MILK: FOREIGN BONDS

Foreign or international bonds are bonds issued by foreign governments, generally in their own currency. They are sometimes called "sovereign bonds." Like U.S. Treasuries, they are backed by the full faith and credit of the issuing government. Does that mean that they are as safe from default as U.S. Treasuries? Not necessarily. The full faith and credit of a foreign country may not be so secure, especially if the country is emerging, less industrialized, or is subject to political strife. We only have to look back ten years to the Russian default or the Asian financial crisis to see examples of this. Thus many foreign government bonds are rated well below investment grade.

HEAVY CREAM: FOREIGN CORPORATE BONDS

In addition to foreign government bonds, investors can buy bonds issued by foreign companies. Like any other corporate bond, owners of international corporate bonds must rely on the continuing ability of the issuing company to repay its debt. You can think of them as the "heavy cream" of bonds. They will have to pay a richer interest rate, but with a respective higher risk of default.

Bonds issued by the U.S. Treasury have no real risk of default and are said to be free of credit risk. After all, the Treasury can simply print money if it must to repay its debts. To determine the credit quality of the other type of bonds, one turns to a bond-rating agency, such as Standard & Poor's, Fitch Ratings, or Moody's. The rating companies use different symbols to describe how likely a company is to default, but they're not that different (see the table below). The higher the quality of the bond, the lower credit risk it is said to have; in fact, bonds with ratings from AAA (Aaa) to BBB (Baa) are referred to

MOODY'S	STANDARD & POOR'S	WHAT THE RATING MEANS
Aaa	AAA	Highest quality
Aa	AA	High quality
A	A	Upper-medium quality
Baa	BBB	Medium quality
Ba, B	BB, B	Below investment grade
Caa, Ca	CCC, CC	Highly speculative
C	C	Typically bonds that are paying no interest
—	D	In default, interest and/or principal

as investment-grade bonds and those BB and below are referred to as junk bonds. Since junk bonds' credit ratings are less than pristine, they pay high yields to compensate investors for the risk.

INTEREST RATE RISK

As we discussed earlier, besides the creditworthiness of the issuer of the bond, the term or the maturity of a bond also affects the "risk" of investing in it. Bonds have different maturities, generally ranging from one day to up to thirty years. They are often categorized as short term, intermediate, and long term.

TERM	MATURITY
Short term	Maturities of up to 5 years
Intermediate term	Maturities of 5 to 12 years
Long term	Maturities of 12 or more years

Let's look at this simplified example to demonstrate why the term matters:

	FACE VALUE	MATURITY (PAYBACK DATE)	INTEREST RATE (COUPON RATE)	LIKELIHOOD OF INTEREST RATES INCREASING DURING TERM OF BOND
Bond A	$10,000	1 year	5%	Low
Bond B	$10,000	13 years	5%	High

If interest rates are anticipated to increase in the future, which bond do you think you would rather have? The one that you will be able to reinvest your $10,000 at the new higher prevailing rate of interest in one year or the one where you have to wait thirty years to do it?

Obviously, you would want to earn the higher interest rate as soon as possible and thus if interest rates are rising you would not be willing to pay $10,000 for Bond B (if you could buy Bond A for the same amount) you would want to pay less for Bond B, since you will not be getting the higher interest rate for a longer period of time. Therefore, the price of the bond goes down. What this tells us is that interest rates and bond prices have an inverse relationship. That means that as interest rates increase, the price of an existing bond issued at a lower rate will decrease, and vice versa.

Thus the price you can get for a bond if you choose to sell it before it matures varies. Therefore, if you sell a bond before maturity, it is possible to have a capital gain or loss, or in other words, you can make money or lose money on the sale of a bond just as you do with stocks (but the range of possible outcomes is usually not as great for bonds as it is for stocks. See the appendix for additional discussion on selling a bond in the secondary market). Putting together a bond portfolio is no easy task. My advice? Don't try this at home. What I mean is that, as with stocks, most investors should not own random individual bonds. Instead you have a better chance of getting the best reward for the risk you take when a variety of bonds are packaged together. We will discuss the different packages in Chapter 5.

FATS: ALTERNATIVE INVESTMENTS

The last category of investments we need to examine are alternatives. What is an "alternative investment"? An alternative investment basically is an investment in a "nontraditional" or "noncorrelated" asset. How helpful was that? Not a bit.

The truth is, a discussion on alternatives can get complex. But not to worry, all you really have to know is there generally are two basic categories of alternative assets. The first we'll call "pure play," the second "mixed play." In simple terms, investments classified as alternatives that fall into the "pure play" category are out-of-the-ordinary assets like commodities, real estate, or private equity for example. Investments that can be classified as "mixed play" are not necessarily out-of-the-ordinary assets, but the way they are put together is—usually we are talking about some type of hedge fund or hedge fund–like product.

Both categories are used to give an investment portfolio a boost. Keep in mind that the definition of "boost" here is very broad. The goal with some alternatives is to really try and "knock the lights out," where others are about bringing down the risk of an overall portfolio without giving up any potential return.

The push you get from alternatives, especially the "knock the lights out" sort, isn't always in the right direction. It can be a very wild ride. That's why they remind me of fats: Not everyone can tolerate them or only in small portions. If you're the kind of person who would freak if you saw a portion of your portfolio fall 50 percent then you'd better stay clear. They don't call some alternatives "portfolio octane" for nothing.

The variety of alternative strategies can fill book after book. Thus we are not going to go into the various strategies. (Believe me, you will thank me.) This is another instance in which I'm compelled to say, "Do not try this at home." If alternatives are something that interest you, you'll be best served by utilizing the skills of a well-experienced adviser.

Congratulations ! We're finished with the chapter. I know we dealt with a lot of information in these pages, but with your newfound awareness you now have the foundation to begin developing a portfolio (an asset allocation) for your specific situation that is the perfect balance of risk and reward.

AT THE VERY LEAST

Be aware of the intricacies of the big three asset classes—cash, stocks, and bonds.

CHAPTER SUMMARY

. . . .

1. Under each of the four basic asset class categories are subcategories that all have different risk-and-return profiles.
2. Cash has the lowest risk-and-return profile out of the four. The major risk with cash is inflation risk.
3. Stocks are categorized by size, style, and nationality. Each has an effect on the risk-and-return profile of a stock. Due to the economy, interest rates, and other uncontrollable external factors the market as a whole is subject to systematic risk. Individual stocks are subject to their own unique risks known as unsystematic risk. The goal of diversification is to minimize unsystematic or company-specific risk.
4. Bonds are loans to organizations. Issuer and time to maturity are the key differentials. They are subject to credit risk and interest rate risk. Treasuries are said to have the lowest credit risk whereas international corporate bonds are said to have the highest. Generally speaking, the longer the term to maturity the greater the interest rate risk.
5. Alternatives are basically anything that does not fall into the "big three" asset classes. Their risk-and-return profiles vary greatly.
6. What you've learned:

4

PORTION CONTROL

In Chapter 3 you learned about the "food groups" of investing—the various asset classes. Now we're going to take a look at how to craft the best possible financial diet for you by combining those financial food groups—cash, stocks, bonds, and alternatives—into a healthy investing plan. To continue with our metaphor, we can explain the process of asset allocation by looking at the fundamentals of healthy dieting.

No doubt you agree that for optimum long-term weight loss (and, perhaps more important, to ensure that we are getting the proper nutrients that our bodies need to be working effectively), we should eat a robust variety of foods from each of the various food groups in specified portions. Thus, it's not only about the type of food, it's about the combination and the serving size of the food as well. In other words, it's about achieving variety, balance, and moderation. All three need to be in sync for maximum success.

For example, say you go on a diet and eat from a variety of the food groups but limit your choices within the groups to just one—chicken, apples, and yogurt, for example. Yes, you have some balance. But your variety and moderation are way out of whack. Or let's say you go on a fad diet and only eat from one food group, such as various forms of protein—chicken, beef, pork, and fish. You certainly have some variety, but, again, your balance and moderation are out of whack. If, like me, you've tried both of these diets, you know that the end result is far from what you wanted to achieve. We can all do it for a short period with some limited success, but sooner or later it backfires on us—and often we end up heavier than when we started. Thus, for optimal long-term results the foundation of our diets must be variety, balance, and moderation. Let me add one more "must" here: customization. What you need to do to lose weight is likely different from what your mom, sister, or friend has to do. It depends on your age, sex, body size, activity level, and personality, among other things. Simply put, you have to tailor your diet to who you are and what you want.

Asset allocation is the same. The basic fundamentals to success are variety, moderation, balance, and customization. Variety and moderation equal "diversification" and balance refers to "asset allocation" in investment-speak.

There is one underlying issue that makes the need for asset allocation so compelling—the market is fickle. If we look at the annual returns for key indexes over the last twenty years ranked in order of performance, what you will see is that there is no pattern to the returns. Rather, they occur pretty randomly—one year an asset class can be the best performer and the next year the worst. Additionally, one year an asset class can have a positive return and the next year it can have a negative return. To see this for yourself go to the Web site www.callan.com/research/institute/periodic/files/Pertbl.pdf and check out the periodic chart of investment returns.

Thus, since markets do not always behave as predicted or expected, it makes it practically impossible to know when or which asset class is going be the best performing in any given year. This makes it very difficult for anyone to time the market perfectly. So to increase your probability of investment success from a portfolio, your best bet is to keep in mind the old adage "Don't put all your eggs in one basket." In other words, be a student of multi-asset class investing (asset allocation).

DOES DIVERSIFICATION ALWAYS WORK?

Investors during 2008 would certainly answer this question with a resounding not necessarily. That is because the past credit crisis caused pain throughout the total market—it was universal or systemic. There was no place to hide, and the loss of portfolio value was basically impossible to avoid. Generally speaking, you only see this during times that are unprecedented and extreme. Success during these times is defined as *not being as down as you could have been*. For example, the results of investors whose portfolios were well diversified and allocated came through the market crash better than those investors who were heavily invested into, say, stocks of financial services companies and auto companies.

It's important to keep in mind that markets eventually do come back to a normalized state. It's just a matter of time, patience, and discipline.

It's important to note that the terms "diversification" and "asset allocation" are often used interchangeably but not necessarily correctly. Indeed, the principles are closely related; both are designed to reduce risk in your portfolio. But asset allocation takes this principle a step further by diversifying your portfolio not just among different investments, but also among different investment classes.

So before we get into the particulars of asset allocation, let's take a step back and make sure we are clear on the distinction between the two terms. To do that I would like you to think about the following two questions.

- If a portfolio is diversified, does that mean it is well allocated?
- If a portfolio is well allocated, does that mean it is well diversified?

The answer to both these questions is not necessarily. Here's why.

A portfolio that is diversified does not necessarily mean that it is well allocated, because you may have lots of different investments but the allocation or the balance between the asset classes is not optimum. For example, your portfolio is composed only with the stock from the forty largest U.S. companies where you are well diversified because you have many different investments, but you are not well allocated because they are all from the same assets class (U.S. large-cap stocks). On the other hand, a portfolio that has good balance between the various asset classes is not necessarily well diversified, because the investments in the respective asset classes may not have enough variety and moderation. For example, your portfolio has just a few individual securities in each asset class.

The bottom line is this: Simply owning many investments does not mean that you own asset classes in the proper and most efficient weightings or that you have good diversification within the asset class. Therefore you are not getting the best bang for your buck. As such, your risk versus your return is not being maximized. For that reason your overall objective is to have diversification within the asset class as well as among the asset classes.

When you don't have either you tend to have what is known as a concentrated position—think "too much of a good thing" or " all my eggs in one basket." With concentrated positions you can create wealth but you can destroy wealth as well. To learn more about the typical profiles of people who tend to have concentrated positions, misconceptions, and challenges surrounding them, see the appendix.

ASSET ALLOCATION: A BALANCE
BETWEEN RISK AND REWARD

How you decide which asset classes and what proportion to use for your diversified portfolio is based on mathematics and your personal preferences. The right way for you (just as with your dieting plan) is likely different than for your friends and neighbors. The appropriate asset allocation plan for you is contingent upon your goals, age, time frames, available resources, and your tolerance for volatility or risk. In other words, your investment plan must be customized to who you are and what you want.

Let's first focus on the mathematics. Wait, don't close the book! You don't have to memorize any formulas or get out financial calculators. An adviser, a software package, or even some investment products design portfolio allocations and therefore do the calculations for you. Although you don't have to "do the math," it's important for you to understand what goes into the calculations and what these calculations are trying to solve for.

The basic inputs into the calculations are the three R's: return, risk, and relationship.

- Return—expected
- Risk—range of potential outcomes or standard deviation
- Relationship—similarity (or lack thereof) of behavior among the asset classes or correlation

THE THREE R'S—RETURN, RISK, AND RELATIONSHIP

You don't have to an expert on these concepts but you do need to be aware of them, because not only are they frequently referred to in the press, in investment literature, and in investment proposals, your investment adviser (if you utilize one) may also use this terminology.

Return Return (growth of the portfolio) is stated as a percentage—for example, 5 percent, 10 percent, and so on. The most important thing for you to understand is that expected returns are "probable" not "guaranteed."

An expected return is the average growth over an investing cycle (seven to ten years). Hence, it does not necessarily mean that day to day, quarter to quarter, or even year to year you will achieve that specified return. During these shorter time frames (day to day, quarter to quarter, and so on) and depending on the investment, you may see wide swings or variations from the expected return.

Risk (Standard Deviation) These swings are referred to as volatility or risk and are often reported as standard deviation. Standard deviation is stated as a percentage (plus or minus) from the expected return. The larger the standard deviation, the wider the potential swings of an investment's returns, either positive or negative, and therefore the greater the risk.

Let's look at an example of two investments with the same expected return but with different standard deviations—and the respective potential range of returns:

INVESTMENT	EXPECTED RETURN	STANDARD DEVIATION	RANGE OF POTENTIAL OUTCOMES
A	10%	10%	0% to 20%
B	10%	5%	5% to 15%

THE SCALES OF STANDARD DEVIATION

Whenever I discuss standard deviation it always reminds me of stepping on the scale and the variability of my poundage. To get a sense of why I do, have a think about your own weigh-ins and weight history and write down your weight for each of the past fifteen years. Some of us may find that the number has been pretty consistent year to year give or take five pounds, while others may find that it fluctuates more dramatically.

Therefore, from one year to the next, those of us with a smaller volatility of weight should have an easier time than those with a greater volatility in predicting accurately what our weight will be from year to year; those with the higher standard deviation unfortunately run a greater risk of our pants not zipping.

Now look over your fifteen-year weight history again. You will probably notice that there were a few times over the course of the past fifteen years where your weight was outside of your usual range (either higher or lower). Typically, these outlier years were caused by some extenuating circumstances—such as a freshman year of college, pregnancy, a work project, or some other extremely stressful situation. Therefore we can say that a majority of the time your weight is within a consistent range, but there are times when atypical events cause a different and sometimes extreme result.

What this tells us is that for any given year, A's return could be plus or minus 10 percent from its expected return (that is, 20 percent to 0 percent) and B's could be plus or minus 5 percent (i.e., 15 percent to 5 percent.) Which investment would you choose? Are you willing to risk a 0 percent return to get a 20 percent return or would you feel more comfortable giving up some upside (20 percent down to 15 percent) for the protection of your downside (0 percent up to 5 percent). The answer depends on the balance between your risk and return.

Now, as we know, the only things that are guaranteed in life are death and taxes; standard deviation does not mean that your investment return will always fall within that range. It means that a bit more than two-thirds of the time the return should fall within the stated range—and a little less than a third of the time it won't. When the return is outside the most likely range usually something unusual and infrequent is going on—like a severe recession, a political con-

| Sample Expected Standard Deviations* ||
ASSET CLASS	STANDARD DEVIATION (%)
Cash	1.0
Intermediate bonds	6.0
High-yield bonds	10
U.S. large-cap stock	16.0
Small-cap stock	22.0
International stock	19.0
Emerging markets stock	28.0
Private equity/venture capital	35.0

*These do not represent any specific investment vehicle and should not be relied upon as a specific recommendation.

flict, or a technology boom. Sometimes these results are very positive (boom times) and regrettably sometimes they are not.

Relationship (Correlation) When you create a portfolio, to get the balance between risk and return you are looking for, it is not enough to look at just the expected risk and returns of the respective investments, you also have to look at the relationship between the investments as well. The relationship (that is, difference and similarity in behavior) between investments is known as correlation. Because it is practically impossible to time the market on a consistent basis, we need to spread our bets so that when one asset class is doing well, it can shelter the asset class that is doing poorly and vice versa.

OUTPUT—PORTFOLIO OPTIMIZATION

As we said earlier, it's good to know the inputs into the formulas, but what you must really understand is what they are trying to solve. Simply, you are trying to create the most efficient combination of asset classes. By efficient, I mean an asset allocation that provides the greatest overall return for a given level of risk—or in investment-speak, to make sure the "weighted average of volatility" for the whole portfolio is less than the volatility of each of the individual portfolio components.

This concept is known as "portfolio optimization" and is often referred to as modern portfolio theory (MPT). I have found that the best way to explain this concept is by comparing it to baking apple pies.

So, suppose you are going to bake some apple pies. Your objective is to create a series of apple pies that for a given level of calories (risk) have the best taste (reward) possible.

The pies are composed of a variety of ingredients—apples, flour, butter, raisins, sugar, lemon zest, and so on. Each ingredient has distinct characteristics (as in flavors, consistencies, calories, and chemical makeups). To create pies with the best taste for a given level of calories, not only do you have to understand the distinct flavors (returns) and the calorie counts (risk) of each respective ingredient but also the similarities and/or differences (correlations) among the various ingredients.

Take, for example, sugar and raisins. They behave similarly—they sweeten; keep adding one when you have enough of the other and the pie becomes not only too sweet, it becomes too fattening. For the extra calories, you are not getting the flavor you deserve. Your pie is not optimized—there is a better recipe. (In other words, for a higher level of risk you should have gotten a greater reward.)

Or conversely, take sugar and lemon zest. They work in opposition to each other—keep adding lemon zest without adding more sugar and you end up with a pie that is not sweet enough for the relative calorie count. For the same number of calories, you could have gotten a pie with a superior taste. (In other words, for the same amount of risk you could have gotten a greater reward.)

There are countless ways these ingredients can be combined together, but as we said earlier, the best combinations are those that produce pies that maximize flavor (reward) for a given level of calories (risk). So pies, just like portfolios, are a balance between risk and reward. But keep in mind, the pie or portfolio for you is the one that meets your personal needs and preferences.

PORTFOLIO (ASSET ALLOCATION) FLAVORS—
A BALANCE BETWEEN RISK AND RETURN

Asset-allocated portfolios generally come in three broad flavors, which are defined by their risk-and-return characteristics. The three broad categories are:

- Conservative
- Moderate
- Aggressive

Conservative portfolios have the lowest risk-return profile and usually value the safeguarding of capital over maximizing investment returns. They have relatively lower levels of allocations to equities.

Aggressive portfolios have the highest risk-return profile and usually are focused on growth over the long term. They have the highest levels of exposure to equities.

Moderate portfolios are between the two and are meant to provide an attractive level of growth and preserve an element of capital.

The following chart shows very basic and generic sample allocations across the broad categories. These are examples and should not be relied upon as a specific recommendation; rather, their purpose is to demonstrate the changes in asset class allocations (increases in equity and alternatives and a decrease in bonds and cash) as we go up the risk scale.

	CONSERVATIVE	MODERATE	AGGRESSIVE
Cash	10%	6%	2%
Bonds	43%	30%	19%
Stocks	42%	54%	64%
Alternatives	5%	10%	15%

Within these broad-based risk categories often you will find subcategories or risk gradations. The differences are subtle and many times reflect not so much the overall allocation as much as the further diversification within the asset classes. For example, a highly aggressive portfolio may have a larger allocation to emerging markets in their overall stock allocation than does a more temperate aggressive portfolio. No matter what your asset allocation is, always keep this in mind: Asset classes and thus portfolios all have some sort of risk attached to them, so the goal of portfolio optimization or asset allocation is not to eliminate risk (because that is virtually impossible), but to control and manage it.

PERSONAL RISK PROFILE

As discussed earlier, the portfolio or asset allocation that is right for you is the one that matches your personal needs and preferences. I refer to this as your personal risk profile (PRP). Your PRP depends on your balance between risk and return. The balance is determined by examining two key aspects of your PRP—your "financial risk capacity" and your "emotional risk capacity."

FINANCIAL RISK CAPACITY

When we talk about your financial risk capacity we are trying to learn if you are financially able to take on uncertain investment returns. Financial risk capacity is based on a variety of variables idiosyncratic to you—basically, time and money.

Let's look at an example. Mr. Smith wants to buy a house in three years. He decides to invest in an aggressive portfolio, because if it does really well, he will be able not only to buy the house but to furnish it as well. Unfortunately, though, the market crashed. Instead of getting a home and furniture, he now doesn't have enough to even make the down payment on the house.

What this example shows us is that the shorter your time horizon, the less able you are to take on uncertainty, the more you become concerned with the risk of losing money ("loss" adverse) and the less capacity for risk you have. Therefore, the longer your time frame, the greater your capacity for risk because you have the time to ride out the market cycles and the more volatility you can handle, and thus the greater your capacity for risk. That is why if you are between, say, twenty and forty-five it is often said that your asset allocation should resemble an aggressive target portfolio, if you're between forty-six and sixty-five a moderate target portfolio, and over sixty-five a conservative portfolio.

EMOTIONAL RISK CAPACITY

Your financial risk capacity tells you how you "should" invest (conservative, moderate, or aggressive), but you need to balance this somewhat against your emotional risk capacity for the up-and-down swings of the marketplace. In other words, what you feel comfortable investing in. For example, let's say you have more money than you could ever spend and want to leave a legacy. Financially you can take on a lot of risk without putting your goals in jeopardy. You should be using an aggressive target portfolio. But the volatility (the up-and-down movements) of an aggressive high-risk portfolio makes you so uncomfortable that you are convinced that any day now you will lose everything. So your financial capacity is high but your emotional capacity or your tolerance is low.

If you have a high financial capacity and a low emotional capacity and you invest in an aggressive portfolio, what do you think the chances are of you sticking with that investment plan is? Most likely slim to none.

I can't overemphasize the importance of being aware of your emotional capacity. Too often we focus on just the return and not the risk and then we react to risk (volatility). Remember, there is always a trade-off between risk and return, so the higher the potential return, the greater the potential for volatility.

Due to the abysmal experiences many investors had during the financial crisis of 2008, their emotional risk tolerance may be at an all-time low. I urge you to remember that (as we mentioned earlier) these types of crises happen very infrequently. Try and think about how you reacted to market volatility during more normal market conditions. During those times of average market stress did you abandon the basic principles of sound investing? If so, you have a low emotional risk capacity. If you are able to stick with your plan, your emotional capacity is high.

If you are a person who is hypersensitive to market movements, take a step back and think about if you are fearful of something irrational. Becoming a bag lady? Losing it all? If you are, you may want to delve somewhat into your past. Growing up, how was money handled in your family?

For example, in my family my father was a child of the Great Depression. I heard story after story about how one day they were living a very comfortable life and the next they were living behind a candy store with his mother working eighteen-hour days. So my father, although successful in his own right, always lived with the feeling that we were on the brink of disaster. The message was that there was never going to be enough money and that risk was to be avoided at all cost. So, along with his insatiable sweet tooth, this fear was passed on to me. Luckily for me I am able to get the irrational voice out of my head and instead replace it with the two things I really know to be true: that the market will always move up and down, but as long as I stay on my plan I will have the greatest probability of success, and I can do more harm to myself by being so overly conservative that my investments don't keep up with inflation. In other words, too safe is not too good. Therefore, by being anti-volatility one protects oneself from market risk but exposes oneself to possibly an even more dangerous hazard—a severe case of inflation risk.

So what is your emotional capacity? Don't judge it. There is no right answer. Again, it's about you. I know because of the happenings of 2008 and into 2009, for many of us, committing to who we are may be challenging. But try to keep in mind that financially speaking, those years were a time of unimaginable extremes. Hopefully, reading this book has given you the confidence, the competence, and the comfort to move forward with your investing life.

PUTTING TOGETHER YOUR PERSONAL RISK PROFILE

The three basic personal risk profiles (overall risk tolerance) are categorized very much like asset-allocation models are categorized:

- Conservative
- Moderate
- Aggressive

Coincidence? No! Because for optimum investment success the construction of your portfolio must be in line with who you are, how you think, and, most important, how you act (or react).

Conservative Investor As a conservative investor you generally can expect a calm, perhaps even a somewhat boring ride. You don't have a lot of room for error. The key disadvantage of being a conservative investor is that you have limited growth potential. Typical characteristics of a conservative investor are as follows:

- Has low financial and/or emotional risk capacity
- Requires more current income than investment growth
- Seeks to protect the investment value from the effects of inflation
- Has a relatively shorter investment horizon

- Seeks principal preservation
- Not necessarily adding assets to accounts over time
- Is in later wealth preservation phase and/or wealth transfer stage*

Moderate Investor As a moderate investor you can generally expect a nice ride with a few somewhat challenging times along the way. As a moderate investor you understand the concept of risk and understand that the market cycles over the long term. The key disadvantage here is that if you have a very long time frame, you may be limiting your potential. Typical characteristics of a moderate investor are as follows:

- Has moderate financial and/or emotional risk capacity
- Seeks a broad, diverse investment portfolio
- Prefers to limit volatility but can handle some ups and downs
- Invests for the medium to long term (doesn't need the funds for current living)
- Seeks acceptable growth
- May be adding assets to accounts over time
- Is in later wealth accumulation and/or earlier wealth preservation phases of financial life

Aggressive Investor As an aggressive investor you are up for the ride—and know it can vary from times of glee to times of despair. But you know you are in it for the long term. Typical characteristics of an aggressive investor are as follows:

- Has high financial and emotional risk capacity
- Is comfortable with taking risks with her investments
- Invests for the longer term

---

*If you are leaving a large legacy for future generations, the time frame becomes their time frame and not yours, so you can be more aggressive with this type of portfolio.

- Seeks growth
- Most likely will be adding assets to accounts over time
- Is in the wealth creation, growth, and early accumulation phases of financial life

Because we are people we can't always be pigeonholed into an exact profile, but try to choose the one that you most closely resemble. If you need additional help in determining the kind of investor you are, there are a variety of risk profile tools on the Web. As a starting point, check out the sites of your 401(k) plan, bank, or mutual fund company for these tools.

No matter what your asset allocation is and how you decide to implement it, the most important aspect to your investment success is keeping your expectations in check. Remember, diversification and its respective asset allocation do not guarantee a profit or guarantee against market loss. What it does do is to try to manage your risk and try to give you the biggest bang for your buck compared to other portfolios. In other words, the biggest return for a given level of risk.

Furthermore, as we said earlier, what is right for your neighbor is not necessarily right for you. The portfolio that is right for you is the one in which risk and return are controlled and managed in such a way that they are in sync with your personality, lifestyle, and attitudes. Bear in mind, like so many things, your personal risk profile, life situations, and markets may change over time, so you should reexamine your risk profile every so often.

CAUTION FOR COUPLES

There is one very important last thing about your risk profile: If you are married, you and your husband (or significant other) may very well likely have different risk profiles. If you have not discussed this or have been a passive participant in the investment process, I suggest you each think separately about your own respective risk tolerances before discussing them together. Really focus on why you feel the way you do. It is a good check to see if any of your reasons are irrational. Many times in risk tolerance decision making I see women fall victim to what is known as "the recency effect" and men to "overconfidence." Both of these are identified common psychological phenomena that are very prevalent in investment decision making.

The recency effect causes people to make decisions based on the most recent experience while ignoring the studied facts. For example, as markets begin to recover, some people will stay very frightened and get out of equities completely because they believe that the same unprecedented market collapse is going to happen over and over again (in the short term). We know the markets will always go up and down, but not to the extremes we just experienced; therefore, if you come to the table with irrational arguments too often, you will be dismissed as being overly emotional or silly and it will be difficult to win your argument.

Overconfidence is just what it sounds like—people overestimate their abilities. Typically they think their results are much greater than they are (in fact, according to a Northwestern University survey, 88 percent of investors overestimated their actual portfolio returns, and a quarter of those who thought they'd beaten the market were actually 15 percent behind it), and/or they blame past investment mistakes on random events (their adviser, you) rather than poor planning, and they consistently use the argument "this time is different." In other words, they overrate their opinions and tend to exaggerate their ability to control and manage their financial portfolio.

During bull markets the tendency for people to be overconfident and the likelihood of abandoning the principles of asset allocation become very great. I say this because asset allocation is just not sexy—if you properly diversify within and among asset classes, you will most likely not consistently "beat the market."

By now we know that over a single period there will always be a single asset class that gives the best return, most likely superior to that of a diversified portfolio. Of course, nobody knows in advance what the "hot" asset class of a given year will be, so this information can only be viewed in hindsight.

BEATING THE MARKET

When people say they "beat the market," I am always a bit concerned. Whenever someone says they "beat the market," three questions must be asked:

1. What market are they referring to?
2. Over what time frame are they referring to?
3. What were their risk parameters?

Without this information, too many people end up feeling bad about their own portfolio and begin chasing returns, making big bets, timing the market, and so on. These are all behaviors that have been proven time and time again to be detrimental to investment success.

When you share your risk profiles with each other and you have different opinions, listen up for irrationality on both your parts. Come to the table with a well-thought-out, reasonable case for your opinion, and think about not only your emotional risk capacity but your financial risk capacity as well. You want to be in a position of strength to have a better chance of winning your argument. But remember, it's not really about winning or losing, it's about coming to a compromise that you both feel good about. As we all know, compromise is not necessarily always easy or guaranteed—but it is possible.

If you are having problems coming to a compromise, it may be a good indication that working with an adviser would be beneficial. Another solution is for each of you to carve out a separate account for yourself and to keep an "ours" account, too. Keep in mind if you are going the yours, mine, and ours route, if you have been a nonworking spouse, make sure to take some of his as yours. Here, again, I implore you not to be a passive participant in this process. I can't tell you the number of times I have seen husbands invest very aggressively when they shouldn't have, and the wife is left saying, "If I only knew . . ."

DOES HE OR DOESN'T HE?

You may think your husband (or significant other) does not really want you involved in the decision making, but you would be surprised at how many people have told me that they are happy their spouse is now involved in the process. Often it's because their spouse's participation takes some of the pressure off. If something goes wrong, you have made the decisions together so one party is not all to blame. I remember one person saying to me how good it felt to have someone to discuss and bounce off ideas with instead of just getting a blank stare and the response "Whatever you think is fine."

We have spoken a lot about risk in this chapter. There is one more type of risk that affects many, many investors and that is procrastination. One of the greatest risks to your future is not to think about it or to pretend that you will think about it tomorrow. There is no time like the present, because just like in dieting we know that the "I will start on Monday" Monday never comes. But you, thankfully, have taken it upon yourself to read and to do the exercises. I want to congratulate you for doing the work.

The similarity between the work that you have done in these last four chapters and the work one does in successful dieting once again is uncanny. In weight loss if you do the up-front work of setting goals, seeing what you have to work with, choosing a diet plan that is right for you, and then sticking with it, you deserve to lose weight and you should expect to over time. It may not be the same weight loss each weigh-in, but you will have a high probability of reaching your goal in your (realistic) time frame.

If you don't do these steps nor do them correctly, do you really "deserve" to lose weight? You want to but do you deserve to? The exact same thing can be said about investing. There is no hidden secret to investment success. It is about setting goals, devising a plan of allocation and diversification, and implementing and adhering to that plan.

Asset allocation, used effectively and consistently, is a powerful tool for your investment success. Variety, balance, and moderation is your mantra. But an asset allocation is only good if it is executed upon. The specific investments or products to purchase to fill these asset classes are where I find people have the greatest challenge. It's no wonder—there are thousands and thousands of different products in the marketplace. Our goal in the next chapter is to help you make sense of the different product choices in order to make the best choices for your specific situation. Let's go shopping.

Review the investor types and select the risk profile that resembles you the most. Before you do any investing you must know what your personal risk profile is.

CHAPTER SUMMARY

1. The randomness associated with returns or the lack of pattern makes it very difficult for anyone to time the market perfectly.
2. This lack of predictability is one of the great arguments for multiasset class investing.
3. The goal of portfolio optimization is to create target portfolios that provide the greatest return for a given level of risk (or vice versa).
4. Your personal risk profile defines your asset allocation and is dependent on your financial risk capacity and your emotional risk tolerance.
5. To improve the risk-reward trade-off for your long-term investments you need to look at your strategy from a portfolio level, then an asset class level, and then finally a security level.
6. What you've learned:

5

GOING SHOPPING

Have you ever gotten a big box of chocolates with, say, thirty-two different pieces of candy? If you're like me, you'll begin to reach for one particular piece, then you'll pull back. Maybe another piece is better. But which one? Finally you pick one and ugh! It isn't what you thought it was. So you ponder a while longer and pick another. The first bite is heaven; the second bite is a disappointment. So you pick a third piece; it's pretty good but you are still not sure it's the best, and off you go and pick another and another and another in hope of finding the perfect chocolate. Pretty soon half (okay, for me, three-quarters) of the chocolates are gone. In disgust, you throw the box cover against the wall and out pops the paper that tells you which piece has what ingredients. "Ah," you think, "if only I knew the makeup and specific flavors of each piece beforehand, I would have selected the few pieces that would have given me the optimum tasting experience instead of the haphazard two thousand calorie experience."

How does this relate to personal finance? You got it: Investing is like a box of chocolates. You don't know what you get unless you know what you're getting. Profound, huh? The fact is, there are literally thousands of different investment products and choosing the ones that are right for you can seem overwhelming. Usually people end up investing some here and some there, mostly because it did really well last year or was on some top lists or some friend or colleague said it was a good investment. The end result: a portfolio that is not properly allocated based on your personal risk profile and goals.

I often hear people complaining during this step in the investment process that they "hate to shop." Who can blame them? They're stepping into this huge "investment supermarket" without knowing much about the products that are for sale. This often then leads to total confusion, indecision, and inaction.

This is unfortunate, because shopping the "investment supermarket" effectively makes your investment program come alive and gets you where you want to go. By the end of this chapter, investment shopping is going to be more than fun again. You will learn how to sort through the information available and make the choices that are best for you.

Before we hit that supermarket, though, we need to make sure we're all clear about something. I can't tell you how many times I ask people to tell me about their investments and they say, "I have an IRA" or "I'm in my company's 401(k) plan" or "I have an account at Charles Schwab." The problem here is that they're confusing their accounts with their investments. Accounts are like a piggy bank. Just as the piggy bank is nothing more than a container to hold pennies and nickels and dimes, investment accounts are merely the containers for holding your investments, whether those investments are stocks, bonds, mutual funds, and so on.

Besides cash, the most obvious things you can hold in these accounts is individual stocks and bonds. The benefit of outright ownership of individual stocks or bonds is that you know exactly what you own, for example: one thousand shares of General Electric stock, five hundred shares of Microsoft stock, and a $10,000 Treasury bond. But as we discussed earlier, there's nothing simple about figuring out which stocks and bonds to buy and, if you recall, I counseled you earlier not to even try to go that route. Instead, an investment product that packages a variety of stocks and/or bonds together, which does the selection process for you, may be a better choice.

With that in mind, the rest of this chapter is devoted to the different way individual stocks and bonds (as well as other investments) are packaged together.

DO YOU HAVE A PREPACKAGE PERSONALITY?

You are a candidate for prepackaged investment products if you answer no to the three T's—temperament, time, and training.

- Temperament: Are you going to stick to your buy-and-sell discipline when markets are acting crazy? Will you have the courage to buy as prices fall or to sell when they're going up?
- Time: Do you have the time to do the initial research and then the constant follow-up required to build and monitor a portfolio of stocks and bonds?
- Training: Do you have access to the resources, research, and overall knowledge that a professional investment manager has?

PACKAGED INVESTMENTS

There are six basic ways that investments are packaged:

1. Mutual funds
2. Separate (managed) accounts

3. Exchange-traded funds
4. Closed-end funds
5. Hedge funds
6. Variable annuities

A "mutual fund" essentially brings together lots of individual investors to pool their money and put it under the professional management of a portfolio manager. The managers then select the specific investments that they feel will produce the best performance to meet the stated objective of the respective fund. A given mutual fund may hold nothing but stocks while another holds nothing but bonds, and others may own a combination of stocks and bonds. With a mutual fund you don't own the underlying investments outright; instead you own shares of the respective fund. You buy these shares directly from the sponsoring mutual fund company at a price that is known as the net asset value (NAV). Mutual funds are often referred to as open-ended since the sponsoring mutual fund company can constantly create new shares of the fund. For more information on this and other unique features of mutual funds, see the appendix.

A more grown-up version of a mutual fund is the "separately managed account" (SMA). Like a mutual fund it is professionally managed, but an SMA is not a comingling of many investors' funds. The account is all yours. You own the shares of the stocks or the bonds outright. They usually have higher investment minimums than mutual funds, so the more sophisticated investor typically uses them.

A close relative of the mutual fund is the "exchange-traded fund" (ETF). It, too, holds a variety of stocks or bonds or both. ETFs are constructed to represent a specific index of the marketplace. The indexes can be broad-based, like the S&P 500, or be based on finer and more exotic slices of markets, such as nanotech. Indeed, broad-based ETFs look almost identical to index mutual funds. The only significant difference is that ETFs are traded on stock exchanges just like individual stocks. That means you can buy or sell an ETF anytime during the day that the exchange is trading. That's different from regular mutual funds, which can only be bought or sold once a day. Why that might make a difference will be explained as we get into more detail.

Another close cousin of the regular mutual fund is the "closed-end fund." Like regular mutual funds and ETFs, a closed-end fund can hold a variety of stocks or bonds or both. The difference is in the way a closed-end fund is priced and sold. They are far less common than regular mutual funds or ETFs, but they can be useful for certain investors, as we'll see later.

Next, we have the "hedge funds." There's been a lot written about hedge funds in the past few years because of the spectacular performance of a few of them as well as some of the unfortunate failures. Despite all the press, there still is plenty of confusion. Hedge funds, like mutual funds, are a mix of investments wrapped together. The difference is that hedge funds apply a variety of sophisticated and complex investing techniques and strategies to the underlying assets. Hedge funds have traditionally been the domain of the very wealthy. But more recently, there are newfangled packages being offered to the rest of us.

Last is the stepsister of all these packages—"variable annuities." Think of a variable annuity as the wrapping paper over a package. The wrapper of a variable annuity allows the earnings on the mutual funds or other investments that are inside the annuity to grow tax-deferred (like a 401(k)).

Each of the six packages (known in the finance world as investment vehicles) has its pros and cons, but the key benefit that is pervasive through all of the investment vehicles is professional management. You will find that the major differences among these packages lie in the way they are bought and sold, the way the portfolios are constructed or managed, and the underlying costs. But no matter the differences, what they hold underneath is very often the same.

As you go through this chapter, you may begin to feel overwhelmed. Don't be. You make these kinds of decisions every day. It's like choosing between frozen orange juice or a carton of juice or powdered concentrate: The ingredients are the same, but you choose one over the other because of some attribute. For example, you may choose frozen orange juice instead of a carton of orange juice because it is more convenient and keeps longer. So as you go through the descriptions of the various types of investment products, focus on the attributes that are most important to you.

MUTUAL FUNDS

Because mutual funds are such a huge and popular form of investing—and for good reasons—we'll spend most of the rest of the chapter taking a closer look at them. Additionally, we'll use mutual funds as a basis of comparison to the other "packages" or investment vehicles.

When you invest in a mutual fund you become a shareholder of that fund. The fund may own hundreds of different stocks (or bonds), but you don't own those stocks (or bonds). Instead, you own shares of the fund itself that represent a proportionate ownership of all the fund's holdings. Think of a mutual fund as a pie, and as a shareholder you own a piece of the pie. Your piece has all the same ingredients as everyone else's piece—but the size of your slice will differ because you invested more or less than other shareholders. Most funds allow you to begin investing with as little as a few thousand dollars (or hundreds or perhaps less if you commit to automatic monthly contributions), which means that you can attain a diversified portfolio for much less than you could if you had to buy individual stocks and bonds. That's the immense value of mutual funds: You can own a diversified portfolio without investing a small fortune and still have professional management watching over your investments.

Many people are familiar with the term "mutual fund," mostly because they're used heavily in 401(k) plans. But just as people confuse their investment accounts with their investments, they also confuse their mutual funds with the names of the companies that offer them. Too often when I ask people about what kind of mutual fund they have, they say something like "I have a Vanguard fund and a Fidelity fund." These are both very well-respected investment companies that each offer a hundred or so different funds. So to say you're in Vanguard or some other company doesn't really tell me anything about the specific fund, its underlying investments, and thus its risk-and-return profile. For example, is it a mid-cap value fund or perhaps an emerging-markets fund?

At the end of this chapter, when someone asks you what fund you own, you will be able to respond in a very specific and learned manner. Instead of saying, "I own a Vanguard fund," you will say, "I own the Vanguard S&P 500 fund, a large-cap index fund whose risk-and-return profile is similar to the overall market." Bravo!

The five general benefits to investing in a mutual fund:

- Professional management—portfolio manager
- Diversification—many different underlying investments
- Economies of scale—better acess to information, trading platforms, pricing, and so on than if you were doing it alone
- Liquidity—can get your money out daily
- Simplicity—it does the investing for you

THE MUTUAL FUND ZOO

There are literally hundreds of fund companies offering thousands of funds. The challenge with so many choices is that to the untrained eye (and sometimes the trained eye as well), the difference between all these funds isn't always obvious. Accordingly, you may be asking, if the differences between them are not necessarily so great, why are there more than eight thousand mutual funds? Well, the best way for me to answer that is to ask you a question: Why are there so many different brands of soda? The answer for both is the same: demand and good old American capitalism.

SHOULD I KEEP IT ALL IN THE FAMILY?

Fund companies that offer a whole host of different funds are called a fund family. Just because you like a fund from one fund family doesn't mean that you have to use only that fund family. There really is no great benefit in using only one fund company. In fact, investors often mistakenly believe that if they sell a fund and reinvest those proceeds in another fund from the same family they do not have a taxable event. The IRS may be giving them a call because they're flat wrong. Still, some people like to use the same fund family for simplicity and convenience. My point is that it is not necessary to use only one fund family, but it won't be tragic if you do (as long as the family is a quality shop).

So just as with soda, the best way to find the funds you will like best is to break them down by flavor (category) and then to compare within each category. There are five basic flavors (categories) of funds:

- Cash—money market funds
- Stocks—equity funds
- Bonds—bond funds
- Hybrids—funds that are a mixture of cash, stocks, and bonds
- Specialty funds—narrowly focused or sector funds

These are just the basic categories. Under each are lots of subcategories.

As we go into our discussion about the various types of funds the most important thing to remember is that your asset allocation and personal risk profile drive your choices among the various fund types. You may wind up with only a few kinds of funds or you may have a wide variety. It all depends on your personal objectives, risk tolerance, and your complexity quotient (more to come on that in Chapter 6).

MONEY MARKET FUNDS

If you recall, we discussed money market funds in Chapter 3, under liquid investments. As a quick summary, on the risk-and-return scale of mutual funds, money markets are the lowest. Two key things you want to pay attention to when comparing money market funds are their respective investments and expense ratios.

STOCK FUNDS

Recall our discussion in Chapter 3 about how stocks can be categorized in a variety of ways, such as by size (large, mid, or small cap), style (growth, core, or value), and nationality (U.S. or international). Each category has a distinct risk-and-return profile. Mutual funds that specialize in stocks—they're the majority of all mutual funds—tend to be characterized in the same way, that is, by the category of stocks they hold, such as U.S. Large Cap Value Fund.

Oh, if only it were that simple! There is a second way to categorize funds and that is by their investment objective. Stock funds tend to fall into one of four investment objectives:

- Aggressive growth
- Growth
- Growth and income
- Income

TYPICAL STOCK MUTUAL FUNDS OBJECTIVES

Aggressive growth funds have the objective of rapid growth and maximum capital appreciation. They often invest in the stocks of smaller emerging growth companies. Aggressive growth funds generally are at the highest end of the risk-reward scale.

Growth funds are looking for capital appreciation, but in a somewhat less volatile fashion than the aggressive growth funds. Thus they are more likely to invest in well-established larger companies believed to have good long-term growth potential.

Growth-and-income funds seek long-term growth of capital as well as current income. They tend to have a blend of growth and value stocks. Some funds stress one more than the other, but they all tend to have a lower risk profile than growth funds.

Equity income funds seek current income. They tend to invest in more value-oriented larger company stocks, because these are the companies that generally pay out the greatest dividends.

No need to stress because the investment objectives of the funds dictate the category(ies) of stocks they will own. We know from Chapter 3 that small-cap growth stocks tend to have a high risk-and-reward profile (that is, aggressive) and the key benefit of owning them is potential growth. Thus you can be fairly certain that the fund's objective is aggressive growth.

ACTIVE VERSUS PASSIVE

A portfolio manager pursuing one of those four investment objectives has to decide how to assemble and maintain a suitable portfolio of stocks to best accomplish the objective. There are two methodologies for achieving that goal: passive investing or active investing. It's like the difference in baking a cake from scratch or using a mix. Active investing is like baking from scratch. Everyone does it a little differently and the results vary: some cakes are great, some good, and some not so good. Passive investing is similar to baking a cake from a mix. No matter who bakes it, the ingredients are exactly the same and the cake tastes the same, whether it's really good or really bad.

Like baking a cake from a mix, passive investing is pretty straightforward. When you're searching for mutual funds for your investment portfolio you're almost certainly going to come across the term "index fund." That's basically a synonym for passive investing. An index fund is set up to duplicate the performance of a selected index. The most popular index funds are intended to mirror the performance of the S&P 500 index of large-cap stocks. If the fund performs as it should, it will go up by whatever amount the S&P 500 goes up in any given period of time. But it will also go down by whatever amount the S&P falls in any given period of time. Investing in an index fund means you will never beat the market, but it also means you will never underperform the market. Furthermore, certain people tend to be a fan of index funds because they tend to have lower expense ratios than actively managed funds.

Active investing is considerably more complicated. The only reason someone takes an active approach to investing is to beat the market, either gaining more than the market gains or falling less in a given period of time. Active fund managers use their own recipes based on the parameters of the respective funds to select the ingredients that they think will give them the best result. One common characteristic is that they tend to do a lot more buying and selling than do passive investors. They make their buy and sell decisions based on whatever their recipe tells them to do.

Active managers use different approaches to select investments for a fund's portfolio. Some use a "top-down" approach while others use a "bottom-up" approach. They may also use technical analysis or fundamental analysis in this process. Since you have wisely outsourced this to a professional manager, I will not eat up your time getting into the details of the various methodologies. If you had the time and the inclination, it's not too complicated to understand, it's just that it shouldn't be your major concern. You should be focused on determining if the "professional managers" embrace a process that is repeatable, predictable, and disciplined. The bottom line is this: Regardless of a portfolio manager's approach, we can say with certainty that some active investors beat the market and a few beat it by a significant amount. Other active investors fall short of the market, some by a significant amount.

Which of the two—active or passive—is the better approach? Unfortunately, there is no one right answer. The answer depends on your specific objectives as well as your tolerance for complexity. Passive investing seems to do a little better in areas that are very well researched and heavily traded, such as large-cap stocks. These markets are said to be very efficient because most of the information affecting stock prices is known by the public and priced into the securities. Active managers tend to do better in areas that are less researched and traded, including small-cap and foreign stocks. Not surprisingly, these are considered less-efficient markets because there isn't as much public information available about the various stocks, and an enterprising manager can discover something that others haven't yet seen that will affect a stock's price in the future. Also, in choppy (very volatile) markets like we experienced in 2008 and into 2009, active managers have more flexibility as to portfolio construction than their passive counterparts and thus have the potential to manage the risk-reward scenario more effectively.

BOND FUNDS

Open-ended bond funds are very similar in structure and operation to open-ended stock funds. The obvious difference is that they hold individual bonds instead of individual stocks. Thus they, too, can be actively or passively managed. There are far fewer bond index funds than there are stock index funds. But just like stock funds, there are a

BOND INDEX FUNDS

Most bond index funds track the Lehman Brothers U.S. Aggregate index. Thousands of individual bonds are represented in Lehman's bond index, some of which may be illiquid and infrequently traded. That makes it virtually impossible for a bond index fund manager to own the entire index. Bond index funds usually create portfolios whose characteristics resemble the overall index. This means that some bond index funds vary in composition. They also vary in fees, though they do tend to be lower than most actively managed bond funds.

huge variety of bond funds and you need to be sure you're comparing apples to apples when trying to choose among them.

As you will recall from Chapter 3, bonds also come in a different shapes and sizes, and thus with different risk-and-return profiles. There are three basic ways that bonds are segmented:

- Their credit quality (investment grade to junk)
- Their term to maturity (short, intermediate, and long term)
- Their taxability (taxable versus tax-free)

The same is true of bond funds, but instead of one bond determining the risk-return profile, it's hundreds of bonds. The issuers, the average credit qualities, and the maturities of the underlying bonds determine a bond fund's risk-return profile and taxability. Let's say a fund holds New York State muni bonds with an average maturity of five to seven years; it would then be an investment-grade (average credit quality), intermediate (average maturity), tax-free (interest on muni bonds is federally tax-free) bond fund.

It's important to note that because a bond fund is constantly buying and selling bonds as economic and market conditions change, a bond fund, unlike the bonds it holds, doesn't have a maturity date. In theory a bond fund can continue forever (it's just the underlying bonds that will change), so there is no scheduled date for payback of your principal. In essence, you get it when you redeem your shares in the respective fund.

Selecting one or more bond funds for your own investment portfolio doesn't have to be a nightmare if you keep in mind that you're looking for funds that are appropriate for your objectives, risk tolerance, time horizons, and your complexity quotient. In short, you want a bond fund or funds that work in your own asset allocation plan. Furthermore, just as with equity funds, there are a variety of strategies portfolio managers use to manage bond funds with similar investment objectives. And once again, no one way is the best.

I'm often asked why someone should own bond funds instead of individual bonds. That question usually arises because the person asking recalls that her parents, spouse, or another person of influence always owned individual bonds (and, in fact, most likely owned individual stocks as well). The answer is simple: professional management. The financial markets of today are not the markets of yesteryear. As we have seen for ourselves over these past few years, financial markets are much more complex, much larger, and much faster than we could have ever have imagined. In today's market, as individual investors we have had to become much more sophisticated and deliberate in our approach to investment management. Put simply, bond funds give us the professional management, economies of scale, and diversification that individual bonds do not.

Let's talk about professional management and scale. It would be

BONDS—MORE THAN JUST AN INCOME STREAM

In the past, investors typically owned bonds for one basic reason and that was income (yield). Usually, that income plus Social Security was able to fund their retirement (ten years or so). We, on the other hand, with possible twenty- or thirty-year retirements, hold bonds to take advantage of their income-producing capabilities as well, but also the potential for capital appreciation and perhaps more important for their diversification benefits. In other words, there's more to bonds than just their yield. This is a huge change in mind-set.

a daunting enough challenge to pick and choose among the thousands of bonds on the market (ranging from super-safe Treasury bonds to junk bonds of companies on the edge of failure), and their various maturities, from one year to more than thirty years. But add to that the difficulty of getting the best pricing for bonds and you have a recipe for lots and lots of work. Thus, having a professional manager make the selections and negotiate the pricing for you is often a more effective strategy.

HYBRID FUNDS

Stock mutual funds are by far the most popular type of mutual fund and bond funds are the second most popular. But there's a third kind of fund called a hybrid that is rapidly gaining in popularity. Hybrid funds hold a mixture of asset classes—mostly stocks and bonds, but occasionally others—all under one roof. They are increasingly marketed as a single-fund solution, the idea being that you only have to buy that one fund to solve all your financial needs. While that sounds appealing and it may work for some, it isn't for everyone. I'll tell you why after I explain a little more about them.

There are four basic kinds of hybrid funds being marketed these days, all with a specific focus. Some have been around for a while and others are newer to the marketplace. The ones that have been around for a while are balanced funds, growth-and-income funds, and global asset-allocation funds. The newer types of funds are often referred to as life-cycle funds. The difference between them is basically their allocation among the various asset classes.

FUND CATEGORY	GENERAL OVERVIEW	UNIQUE CHARACTERISTICS
Balanced funds	Own stocks, bonds, and cash and are designed to provide specific risk-and-return parameters.	Just because they're called balanced doesn't mean they have equal weightings of stocks, bonds, and cash. Rather, it means that over time the fund manager will try to keep the allocation to stocks, bonds, and cash steady in order to keep the risk profile the same over time.
Growth-and-income funds	They invest primarily in a portfolio of income-producing equity securities, including common stocks.	Income will fluctuate, and the investor should understand that it is only a part of the overall investment objective.
Global asset-allocation funds	They have the freedom to invest anywhere in the world in any publicly traded asset class.	Generally give their managers the most flexibility in allocation. Generally, the allocation is based on what the manager feels is appropriate for the current investment environments.
Life-cycle funds (or target funds)	Tend to have a broader defined spectrum of asset classes.	They typically don't hold the stocks and bonds themselves. Rather they are what we call a "fund of funds."

Two Flavors of Life-Cycle Funds Life-cycle funds come in two flavors—"risk based" and "age based." It is important to know the difference between the two flavors, because the risk-based fund requires some more action on your part.

Target-risk funds have been around for a while. These funds are usually split into three groups based on risk: aggressive, moderate, and conservative. The problem is that your risk tolerance usually changes over time and it is left up to you to determine when you should change your portfolio. For example, the fund you select when you're forty probably won't be appropriate when you're sixty-five.

Target-date funds were created to overcome this problem. Target-date funds are relatively new products. In 2000 there were twenty-three different funds; today there are approximately 300 funds with a steady stream of new market entries. Thus, the industry is just starting to analyze and rank them.

A target-date fund's allocation becomes more conservative as it gets closer to the target date. These are becoming more common in 401(k) plans. All you do is pick your estimated retirement year and forget about it. Over time the allocation will slowly change to a more conservative approach (one that looks for more of current income and some capital appreciation versus a high total return).

Some target-date funds are more conservative (or aggressive) than others. For example, at retirement some funds allocate up to 75 percent of assets to bonds, where the more aggressive funds could have a bond allocation as low as 50 percent at the end of their glide path (the expected change of asset allocation over time). In other words, funds with the same target date can have different risk profiles. Thus, it's important to look under the covers and ensure that the allocation and its respective glide path of a fund is in line with your personal risk profile. Furthermore, just as the risk can be different for funds with the same target date, so can the return. Obviously it's a matter of the allocation as with the risk, but it is also a matter of the underlying investment choices and fees. Deciding which one is right for you boils down to your comfort level with the overall risk profile of the fund.

The rating companies can help you to learn more about and compare the different funds.

Target-date funds are a good fit for people who have a bulk of their assets in retirement accounts and have typical retirement requirements. For those of you with more unique or complex needs and who are looking for help with determining a target asset allocation and the respective fund selections, you may be better off searching out the help of an experienced and well-informed adviser.

SPECIALTY FUNDS

Mutual funds that concentrate on a very narrow range of investments, such as technology stocks, gold stocks, or stocks from only a single sector or foreign country, are known as specialty funds. Because of that narrow focus—which is the same thing as saying "because of their lack of diversification"—specialty funds tend to be more volatile than broader-based mutual funds. Investors use them to make a bet on a specific sector of the market—for example, health care. If the investor has some deep knowledge of the sector in question and a sound reason for making that bet, then a specialty fund is an excellent instrument to accomplish that goal. But investors who turn to specialty funds when they're "hot"—that is, investors who are simply chasing performance without understanding the fundamentals underlying that performance—are making a big mistake. If you don't know what fueled the strong performance, you won't know when the fuel runs out and will be caught in a downdraft. And believe me, sooner or later the fuel always runs out.

I would be remiss if I did not mention one other category of funds that is getting a lot of attention lately—absolute return funds. The objective of an absolute return fund is to make money regardless of what the market does. For many of these funds, it is not so much a matter of beating the market as it is reducing the potential for losses in volatile markets. As you can imagine, that's easier said than done. These funds tend to have complex strategies and thus the overall philosophy and process of each fund can be quite different. The skill of the portfolio manager is critical to success. There are more and more absolute return funds being created every day, but because they've only been around for a relatively short time the jury is still out on how well they will perform. We'll talk a little more about them when we discuss hedge funds later in this chapter.

HOW MANY FUNDS DO I NEED?

Too often people who invest in mutual funds make the mistake of thinking that simply owning lots of funds, perhaps from different investment companies, means they have a diversified portfolio. Unfortunately, it doesn't necessarily work that way. Let's say you own three large-cap stock funds. Even though they're run by different people, distributed by different investment companies, and have different names, they often will hold very similar securities and have similar investment philosophies. So instead of getting more diversification you end up getting more of what you already have. A general rule of thumb is that most individuals can accomplish their goals and have a well-asset-allocated and diversified portfolio with between five and ten funds.

THE SIX C'S TO CHOOSING A MUTUAL FUND

As I mentioned earlier, there are literally thousands of funds to choose from and selecting the one right for you can feel daunting. But it

THE SIX C'S TO SELECTING THE RIGHT MUTUAL FUND FOR YOU

The Six C's are category, clarity, commitment, comparability, consistency, and cost.

1. *Category*: The underlying investments in the fund must be in line with your asset allocation.

2. *Clarity*: A mutual fund should have a clear buy-and-sell discipline.

3. *Commitment*: The fund managers should be committed to their stated process in different market cycles (see the appendix for a short discussion on style drift).

4. *Comparability*: Compare the fund's long-term track record (at least three years and preferably five years and more if available) against its benchmark and its peers.

5. *Consistency*: The manager or the management team in place currently is responsible for the past performance.

6. *Cost*: The expense ratio in line with its peers.

In other words, does the fund have a stated and utilized disciplined, systematic approach, which will enable you to get reliable results? (Now, "reliable" does not mean guaranteed or always positive. What it does mean is that you can have an expectation of how it should act in various market cycles.) These C's not only help you select the fund that is right for you, but they are also the criteria you use to monitor and determine when it is time to get out of a fund.

doesn't have to be that way because if you have dated you understand the process of selecting a mutual fund. Here's why. I think we can all agree that first impressions do not always ring true. Before we can be sure who a person is and what they are all about, we need to look under the covers, so to speak. You date to see if his "good behavior" is consistent and sustainable, you date to see how he reacts to various social situations and stressful situations, and you date to see if you have a stronger connection compared to other people you are dating. In other words, is he who he appeared to be, or did you just catch him on a good day?

We all know that finding the person who suits you the best takes time and energy. The same can be said for selecting the right mutual funds, but the good news is that unlike dating, there are services that do it for us. These services (Morningstar and Lipper, for example) rate funds based on their respective characteristics, which then will help you to narrow your selection to the mutual funds best for your situation.

If you'd rather not do the research, outsource the work to an adviser and work in partnership with him or her (or focus your attentions solely on index funds). Mostly I want you to realize that there is more to picking a mutual fund than seeing it on some list in a magazine or having a friend tell you that it's the best. If you do that, you'll probably wind up like so many people do—with a list of funds based on short-term performance, or a quality fund that is not in line with your specific needs and/or your risk tolerance.

So before you invest in any fund, make sure you look through the packaging to see what the portfolio is cooking up (investment objective), the recipe it is following (portfolio construction process), and the ingredients it is using (investment categories and the security selections). Make sure you are able to answer the following five questions:

1. What is the fund's investment objective?
2. What kinds of investments are permitted?
3. How does the fund's risk-adjusted return (over three, five, and ten years) compare to other similar funds (its peers)?
4. Is the same manager running the fund now who ran it for the past ten years or so?
5. What are the fund's costs and how do they compare with other similar funds?

If you don't know all the answers, no worries—because now you know what you don't know and the questions you should ask your adviser or the respective fund company, or you may need to reread the prospectus.

The most important aspect of these rating systems is that they are peer-based. So a five-star small-cap fund is not equivalent to a five-star large-cap fund.

Mutual Fund Rating Systems	
LIPPER	

Lipper is a peer-based numeric (5 to 1) ranking system that looks at consistent performance in respect to different time frames and respective classifications.

Top 20%	Lipper leaders
Next 20%	Rating of 2
Next 20%	Rating of 3
Next 20%	Rating of 4
Bottom 20%	Rating of 5

MORNINGSTAR

Morningstar, in contrast, is a peer-based rating system that ranks more according to risk as well as return. Funds must have at least a three-year track record to be included.

Top 10%	5 stars
Next 22.5%	4 stars
Middle 35%	3 stars
Next 22.5%	2 stars
Bottom 10%	1 star

FUND PROSPECTUS

Every mutual fund is required to provide you with a prospectus and it is chock-full of information. I'm not going to sugarcoat it: A prospectus is daunting. It's usually in very small print and the sentences are very long and lawyerly. However, a fund prospectus contains such important information that if you don't read it, you may be exposing yourself to potential harm. For simplicity's sake, we will focus on the "must-reads." Essentially you're reading the prospectus to find out four things:

Investment Objectives You can find key words in this section that will help you decide if a fund is trying to accomplish something you need in your portfolio, such as "income" or "capital appreciation" or "capital preservation."

Investment Strategies What you're looking for here is an explanation of the actual securities the fund uses to see if they match your goals and risk tolerance. Pay close attention especially to the paragraphs that have phrases like "may hold up to" or "are allowed to," because these limits may put the fund outside of your comfort zone.

Risk Factors Understanding the risk factors helps you to manage your expectations of what may happen in various market conditions.

Fees and Expenses Sales and management fees associated with a mutual fund must be clearly listed. The prospectus will also display the impact these fees and expenses would have on a hypothetical investment over time. For an explanation of the various fees and expenses associated with mutual funds, see the appendix.

WHAT'S IN A NAME?

A fund's name doesn't always tell you the whole story, although they are better now than they were in the past because of an SEC rule that requires a fund to have 80 percent of its holdings in the kind of investments implied by its name. But what about the other 20 percent? Herein lies the need for investigation and analysis because you could wind up buying something that is not really in line with your risk tolerance or investment objectives. Think of it as if you're picking a piece of cake. Two pieces may look the same from the outside, but the ingredients and the way the baker put them together can make a big difference in how those cakes taste and in their calorie count.

Notice that I didn't mention performance. Should you ignore it? Of course not. But looking at a fund's performance in isolation does not really tell you anything. You need to look at it from a relative perspective. What you want to know is how it did compared to funds with a similar objective, strategy, and risk factors. More important, you want to compare those performances not just over the last year, but over a period of many years. The best way to do this is to use one of the ranking or rating tools like Morningstar or Lipper, as we previously discussed. While it is true, as the fund prospectus is required to tell you, that past results do not guarantee future performance, the fact is that consistency over time is one of the best predictors we have for how a fund will perform in various market conditions. What you want to look for is that the fund, when compared to its peers, consistently performed in the top quartiles over time. It doesn't have to be number one, and in fact it doesn't have to be number two—you just want it to be in the game.

No matter how much I beg you to read the prospectus, I am a realist and know that some of you will just not do it. So, at the very, very least read through the fund's marketing materials looking for some of this same information. But keep in mind, it's like signing a contract without reading the fine print. As you read through those documents, I recommend highlighting the key words. If after doing that you still have questions, call the fund company or your adviser.

SEPARATELY MANAGED ACCOUNTS

Greater wealth often comes with greater complexity, such as unique tax situations, concentrated portfolios, and multiple investment accounts. Often this results in a need for a more customized approach than mutual funds can offer. When this is the case, investors often turn to "separately managed accounts," also known as SMAs.

As with mutual funds, SMAs come in wide variety of shapes and sizes. If you're inclined to go this direction you also need to open up the "package" to see what they hold, what their investment objective is, what the risk characteristics are, and, of course, what expenses are associated with it. There are three general reasons people would choose a separate account over a mutual fund: *tax efficiency, customization,* and *transparency*. Let's deal with each of those three separately.

- *Tax efficiency*: With mutual funds you own shares that represent a fractional interest in a variety of securities. With a separate account you own the variety of securities outright. This is an important difference, because it gives the portfolio manager flexibility to employ some specific tax-saving strategies that are generally not available in a mutual fund. Basically these strategies give you a degree of control over the timing and recognition of capital gains and losses.

- *Customization*: Unlike mutual funds, which are vast pools of money assembled from hundreds or thousands of investors, a separate account is a private account that contains only your money. That enables your portfolio manager to give full consideration to your specific needs and wants. For example, let's say you have a great distaste for companies that manufacture cigarettes. The portfolio manager of a separate account can be constrained in his security selection to ensure that you are not invested in stocks of companies that offend your morality. And if you have a high-ranking job in a company that offers stock and stock options as part of your compensation package, you probably want your portfolio manager to avoid your company stock since you already own lots of it within your compensation package. If you want to avoid certain

investments, just make sure that your separate account
gives you that discretion.

- *Transparency*: When you own a mutual fund you often
  don't know all of the stocks or bonds the fund holds. But
  if you have an SMA, you know precisely what you
  own, when a stock is bought or sold, and the respective
  prices.

Should you invest in a separately managed account? Not if you
have a smaller portfolio, because the minimum investment amount—
generally anywhere from $50,000 to $1 million or more—to open
such an account may restrict your ability to build a well-allocated
portfolio. Even at those lower minimum levels I would recommend
an SMA only if you have a deep desire to have as much control as possible without actually managing your money yourself. Keep in mind,
it needn't be one or the other. You could use an SMA for the bulk of
your core or strategic investments while using specialty mutual funds
(and/or other investment vehicles) to meet your more focused needs.

EXCHANGE-TRADED FUNDS

Exchange-traded funds are known colloquially as ETFs. There are
more than five hundred ETFs traded in the United States and the
number is growing every day.

Similar to shares of an index mutual fund, each share of an ETF
represents a partial ownership in an underlying portfolio of securities
intended to track a market index. Since an ETF, like a mutual fund,
is a package for the underlying securities, you may see the same (or
very similar) securities found in each respective package. For example,
the stocks that comprise an S&P index could be found in something

like the Vanguard 500 index fund and what is know as a SPDR (pro-
nounced spiders).

Generally, ETFs are replicas of broad, well-known indexes, like the
S&P 500, and are said to be passively managed. Recently, however, actively managed ETFs have been introduced into the U.S. marketplace
as well as an increasingly replica of narrow or obscure indexes (like an
index made up of companies that design microscopic products).

ETFs can generally be divided into four basic categories: *broad
based, fixed income, international*, and *sector.*

- *Broad-based ETFs* track a variety of indexes including
  those for growth and value stocks and small, mid-size, and
  large U.S. companies.
- *Fixed-income ETFs* track indexes for corporate and
  Treasury bonds.
- *International ETFs* track indexes for over a dozen individual foreign countries. as well as world regions (for
  example, Latin America) and broad-based global indexes.
- *Sector ETFs* track specific industries such as technology
  and health care.

ETFs that follow fairly narrow or obscure indexes tend to have very
few holdings or have a lot of their investment concentrated in only one
or two stocks. That's great if those stocks are going up, but very bad if
they're going down. In either case you don't have the diversification that
makes mutual funds and even other ETFs so attractive. Just as we discussed with specialty mutual funds that concentrate on a single industry, if you're an expert on that industry and understand what's
happening, fine. But if you're not an expert, the volatility of such narrow
ETFs can be very dangerous. If you are investing on your own, stick
with the broad-based indexes for either index mutual funds or ETFs.

The "ETF package" differs from the "mutual fund package" in four basic ways: where they are bought and sold, pricing, fees for buying and selling, and expense of owning. (For a refresher on these features for mutual funds, see the appendix.)

- *Where they are bought and sold*: ETFs are traded on stock exchanges just like stocks (not from the sponsor mutual fund company).
- *Pricing*: ETF prices fluctuate throughout the day depending on the supply and demand of the ETF (versus the NAV of a mutual fund, which is determined once a day)
- *Fees for buying and selling*: You pay a brokerage commission each time you buy or sell an ETF (but many mutual funds don't charge any fees for purchasing or selling the fund, although funds sold through financial advisers often do).
- *Expense of owning*: Since they are passively managed, the administration fees levied by ETFs tend to be lower than those imposed by actively managed mutual funds.

The benefits from the way ETFs are bought and sold and the way they are priced as compared to a mutual fund is pretty minimal for most of us. Only active traders who use such tools as short selling and limit orders will benefit to any great extent from the ability to buy or sell an ETF throughout the trading day.

The fees for buying and selling ETFs are something some of us need to pay attention to. If you're starting out with a small investment program and plan to put more money in each month, ETFs aren't for you. The purchase commissions would eat up too much of your investable assets. Better to stick with traditional mutual funds and particularly no-load funds. If, however, you're an active trader with access to a low-cost trading plan through a discount broker, the commissions won't be so painful.

Lastly, the costs of owning an ETF are something we must all pay attention to. Often ETFs are marketed as a low-cost alternative to mutual funds. But remember, with an actively managed fund you are paying for the fund manager's expertise. ETFs typically offer no such expertise. They just blindly reflect whatever is happening to the index they're supposed to duplicate. So when you look at ETF fees, it makes more sense to compare them to the fees charged for passively managed index funds. That's where you have to be careful. Different ETF sponsors charge different fees and not all of them are low cost. The bottom line is that to choose among ETFs that track the same index, select the one with the lowest expenses. Furthermore, not all ETF expense ratios are lower than their corresponding index mutual fund. For example, ETFs that give you broad exposure to foreign markets tend to have higher fees than you would pay for a similar index fund, while ETFs that track broad U.S. market indexes like the S&P 500 tend to be lower than similar index funds. Bond ETFs tend to charge about the same amount as bond index funds.

Part of the cost of owning an investment is the resulting tax on income. ETFs are no different, although they have a reputation for being tax-efficient, which means the way they are structured tends not to produce lots of taxable gains until you sell the shares (hopefully) at profit. But remember that ETFs also distribute the dividend and interest it earns as well as any capital gains from sales of securities, though it tends to be infrequent.

Furthermore, you should keep in mind that the tax-efficient reputation of ETFs depends on what you're comparing it against. Yes, ETFs are usually more tax-efficient than an actively managed mutual fund in which the manager is buying and selling stocks in an effort to get the best overall returns. But when you compare an ETF to an index mutual fund, the differences often aren't significant.

Become familiar with ETFs. They are becoming an increasingly common sight in today's investor's strategic and tactical portfolios. But just like mutual funds, they are not all the same; so make sure to look underneath the covers and see what lies beneath.

WHAT'S AN ETF?

If you've never heard of ETFs, don't feel bad, you're not alone. A recent survey of five hundred individual investors found that 38 percent of those surveyed didn't know what an ETF was, and that 53 percent did not know the difference between an ETF and a mutual fund.

CLOSED-END FUNDS

In our general discussion on open-ended mutual funds we mentioned that there are investment vehicles called closed-end funds as well. Closed-end funds aren't nearly as popular as open-ended funds. The assets in closed-end funds are less than 3 percent of the assets in open-ended funds and there are only about six hundred closed-end funds compared to more than eight thousand open-ended mutual funds. Needless to say, they are not the most common investment vehicle, but it's a good idea to have a general awareness of them.

They typically come in three basic flavors: funds investing in U.S. bonds and other debt instruments, funds investing mostly in U.S. stocks, and funds investing in foreign bonds or stocks. They tend to be actively managed, can use leverage, and thus typically have higher fees and increased taxes than passively managed investment vehicles. Furthermore, they tend to be used by investors looking for access to specialized markets.

Closed-end funds, like mutual funds, are "packages" that hold a portfolio of investments. So once again you have to look under the covers to see what is there and to understand the risk-and-return characteristics.

There are three major differences between open-ended and closed-end funds: the way they are created, the way they are bought and sold, and the cost of acquisition.

- *The way they are created*: Just like a stock, closed-end funds are formed with a fixed number of shares that are offered through an initial public offering (IPO).
- *The way they are bought and sold*: Also like a stock, closed-end fund shares are traded on an exchange.
- *The cost of acquisition*: You buy closed-end funds just like you buy stocks and ETFs—that is, through a broker—and you pay a commission.

Because closed-end funds are traded on exchanges the prices are determined by supply and demand, unlike mutual funds, whose NAVs represent the underlying prices of all the stocks they hold. Therefore, closed-end funds can sell at a discount or a premium to the value of the underlying securities. Also, because they are bought and sold on an exchange, closed-end funds can sometimes be considered less liquid than mutual funds since you need a willing buyer and a willing seller.

Due to the expansion and innovation of open-ended funds and ETFs, closed-end funds are not often seen in traditional investors' portfolios. Although they may get some renewed interest from retiring baby boomers since they tend to be one of the more higher-yielding investment vehicles.

Comparison Summary			
	MUTUAL FUNDS	ETFS	CLOSED-END FUNDS
The way they are created	Unlimited number of shares	Fixed number of shares	Fixed number of shares
The way they are bought and sold	From the fund company (or through an intermediary)	Traded on an exchange	Traded on an exchange
The costs of acquisition	Varies—could be none or could have a sales charge depending on the fund and the seller	Broker commissions	Broker commissions

HEDGE FUNDS

A hedge fund, like all other investment vehicles, is just a "package." The difference is that the package isn't as highly regulated by financial authorities (though as of this writing it's discussed that some sort of regulation is coming down the road), and is open only to supposedly "sophisticated investors" who can demonstrate they have sufficient assets to be clients of the fund. Furthermore, hedge funds are not very liquid, can increase the complexity of your tax situation, and use complex investment products and strategies that are not easily understood by the average or even above-average investor. The variations in strategies are so broad and complex that it can take a book or two to explain, but generally they fall into one of two very broad categories: (1) those whose objective is to create superior returns in any market condition, or (2) those whose objective is to create portfolios that are uncorrelated to the market so as to increase the diversification power of one's portfolio.

Over the last few years, hedge funds have become more mainstream through "knock-off" mutual funds. These funds are not invested exactly the same as traditional hedge funds, but they use a variety of hedge fund tactics, though they are limited to both the amount of leverage they can use and the ability to invest in thinly traded shares. In addition, these mutual funds tend to be more transparent, more liquid, and less expensive (though more expensive than traditional mutual funds) than their hedge fund counterparts.

The two most common "knockoffs," or pseudo–hedge funds, are long and short mutual funds and market-neutral mutual funds. The difference between these funds and "regular" mutual funds is that the fund manager uses both long and short positions. Long positions involve owning securities, which means that the investor's portfolio will benefit if the prices of the securities rise and will be negatively affected if they decline. On the other hand, short positions involve selling borrowed securities that later must be bought back and returned to their lenders. Shorting stocks may increase an investor's risk due to the potential for unlimited losses if prices continue to rise. For an example on how shorting works, see the appendix.

Market-neutral portfolios are achieved through a range of strategies. The simplest and best-known approach to market-neutral investing is to take long and short positions in stocks so that market exposure from the long positions is offset by the short positions. On the other hand, long-short funds invest in some stocks that the portfolio managers believe will go up in price as well as other stocks that they think will go down in price. This flexibility allows the opportunity for the funds to achieve positive results in both situations and thus their goal is to produce absolute, or consistently positive, returns regardless of market conditions (versus traditional mutual funds, whose objectives are to produce returns relative to those of a benchmark). In its simplest terms, market neutral matches the shorts with the longs where long-short does not.

Both of these types of funds are only as good as the strategy underlying them and the fund manager's execution of that strategy. Like any fund, the performance of a pseudo–hedge fund is not guaranteed. Statistically, even a very good manager will have periods of negative return. The key to understanding these funds is that the performance and the volatility are extremely dependent on the skill of the manager, so when selecting a fund, look for proven fund managers with established track records.

VARIABLE ANNUITIES

Before we get into the nitty-gritty, let's take just a minute to understand exactly what an annuity is. An annuity is nothing more than a contract between you and an insurance company that requires the insurer to make periodic payments to you, beginning either immediately or at some future date, in exchange for an up-front payment. This up-front payment can be the result of a series of purchases over time or a single purchase payment. Keep in mind, though, you do not have to do this exchange; it is an option, not an obligation. In fact, past history has shown that most annuity holders never surrender their principal for a series of payments.

Thus, there are two phases to the life cycle of an annuity: the accumulation phase and the distribution phase. The accumulation phase is what it sounds like. Your periodic deposits or lump sum will over time accumulate (earn) investment returns based on how you directed it to be invested. Then, if so desired, at some point in time you trade in the capital accumulated in your annuity in exchange for a stream of income from the insurance company that sponsors your annuity. That's the distribution phase. Typically, you have a variety of payment schemes to select from. For example, you may choose payments that last for your lifetime or for the lifetime of your spouse, whichever is longer, or a fixed period of time, say ten years, after which the payments cease. Obviously, the payment amount will be dependent upon the distribution scheme.

The accumulation phase is where one has the opportunity to invest in the markets through what is known as "subaccounts." Usually those subaccounts are mutual funds (but I am seeing separate accounts and ETFs as well).

Therefore, if mutual funds, separate accounts, and ETFs are packages, you can think of an annuity as the wrapping around a package. So why, you ask, do I need the annuity? Why not invest directly in the funds and forget the fancy wrapper? It is true that many of us don't need the wrapper. But for others it offers some specific attributes that can be very beneficial. As with most things in life, these extra benefits come with an extra cost, so it's important to understand what the trade-offs are. You should weigh the higher costs of variable annuities versus the benefits before you invest.

The three key attributes that make variable annuities attractive for certain people are tax-deferral, guarantees, and lifetime income.

- *Tax-deferral*: Money that you put into your plan accumulates or grows free of income and capital gain taxes.
- *Guarantees*: Guarantees vary by product but usually pertain to either a minimum earnings amount or a minimum value amount.
- *Lifetime income*: Just as it sounds, lifetime income is the ability to receive a payment stream over your lifetime.

Let's look at each of the three attributes of variable annuities a little more closely. Generally, tax deferral in the context of annuities means that you are not taxed on the growth until you receive payouts. Annuities were created (by the tax code) as a retirement savings vehicle, much like 401(k) plans and IRAs. They are designed to encourage long-term savings. Therefore if you take out money before age fifty-nine and a half you will be subject to a 10 percent penalty on the earnings, just as you would if you took money out of your IRA before age fifty-nine and a half.

DOUBLE DEFERRAL?

IRAs and annuities are both created by the tax code and are both account types that offer the same kind of tax-deferred growth. Therefore, you may hear people say that you should never use an annuity in an IRA because the IRA is already tax-deferred and thus you are not getting any added benefit. That's true, but.... The "but" is if you have a majority of your assets in an IRA and you want guarantees on performance, asset values, and/or income— certain annuities may offer that ability.

Arrays of guarantees exist in today's annuity products and are far too numerous for us to examine here. Typically, guarantees are good for people who have some concern or fear about the markets that prevents them from making rational investment decisions. Remember, though, guarantees are only as good as the company that offers them. So make sure you check the company's ratings; as with anything, the devil is in the details, and the more you know the details, the more you are giving yourself your own guarantee of peace of mind.

Lifetime income has a changing definition. In the past, to receive a lifetime income stream you had to annuitize or surrender the contract. Depending on the timing surrender, charges could be as high as 7 percent. But today insurance companies are offering ways to get cash out without annuitizing and without incurring any surrender charges. These are often referred to as "lifetime riders." Obviously, each contract is different, so read carefully.

Generally speaking, the above three attributes of annuities attract three types of investors:

- Those who have maxed out all their other opportunities for tax-deferred growth and still want more opportunities for tax-deferred growth.
- Those who are extremely fearful of the financial markets and are hurting themselves more by being completely out of the market and are looking for some guarantees.
- Those of modest means who want to know that they will have an income stream for life.

Annuities are not for everyone, but they are not as horrible as the press makes them seem. They just need to be used in the right way for the right people at the right time. Too often I see a wide disparity between what people think they are buying and what they are actually buying. If an annuity product is of interest to you, make sure you understand what you are actually buying and why it is appropriate for your specific situation.

WHICH PRODUCTS TO USE?

I am sure by now many of you are asking yourself the same question: "Should I use all the different types of investment vehicles? Some of them or one of them?" The answer, as with so much in financial planning, is not a clear yes or no. It depends on your personal needs, preferences, and desire for complexity. In Chapter 6 we will help you examine your preference and desire for complexity so that you can make the best choices for you.

AT THE VERY LEAST

Get familiar with the basic concepts and mechanics of mutual funds.

CHAPTER SUMMARY

1. There are a variety of investment vehicles in the marketplace today.
2. No matter what investment vehicle you choose, you must look through to the underlying investments. Know what you own.
3. There is more to selecting an investment than just short-term performance.
4. A prospectus can be your friend.
5. The investment vehicle(s) best for you is dependent on your personal needs, preferences, and desire for complexity.
6. What you've learned:

BANQUET OR SIMPLE SNACK?
IT'S YOUR CHOICE

When we "went shopping" in Chapter 5, we introduced a number of different investment products. Should you use all the different types of investment vehicles? Some of them? By now I am sure you can guess that the answer is an emphatic maybe.

There is not a general yes or no answer. It depends on your personal needs, preferences, and desire for complexity. Just like your asset allocation can be different from your friends, so, too, can be the way you choose to implement it. In fact, your asset allocation doesn't even have to be different and you still can implement it differently. The best products for you are the ones that you understand, can monitor, and that, more important, allow you to maintain a well-allocated, well-diversified portfolio that is in line with your goals and personal risk profile.

Some of you may have the time and the aptitude to be very involved in the creation of your portfolios and others may want to outsource as much as possible. Furthermore, some of your situations may be pretty typical and others have special or outstanding circumstances that require a more customized approach. This desire for involvement (or lack thereof) and need for customization drives what

I like to refer to as one's complexity quotient, or CQ. Your complexity quotient will help you determine which investment products are right for you.

DETERMINING YOUR COMPLEXITY QUOTIENT

I have found that investors' CQs typically fall into one of four distinct categories. And guess what? The categories have something to do with our diets (shocking, I know), and the different ways people approach food. I refer to the four basic ways people approach food as:

- Fast-Food Junkie
- Convenience Food Connoisseur
- Sophisticate
- Gourmand

APPROACHES TO FOOD	DESIRE FOR COMPLEXITY	TRAITS
Fast-food junkie	Low	Let's just say nutrition and quality are not high on your list. Quick and easy is your objective.
Convenience food connoisseur	Moderate	Concerned about quality but you don't really have the time or the aptitude to put a meal together.
Sophisticate	High	Likes to prepare, doesn't mind shopping around for the ingredients, and stays abreast of current trends. You take time preparing your food and, most.

		important, you make substitutions and replacements to a recipe to match your own specific preferences.
Gourmand	Very high	Well, you know the type.

The parallel to investor types is uncanny. Let's have a look.

FAST-FOOD JUNKIE INVESTOR

Approach:	Fast-food junkie investor (FFJI)
CQ level:	Low (minimal desire for complexity)
Investing traits:	You don't want a whole lot of detail or maintenance and you don't want to devote much time or effort. You just want to do it, get it over with, and be able to reach your goals with the least amount of effort on your part.

There are certain investors who do not look for the best or optimum experience out there. These people are the "fast-food junkie investors" (FFJI). They have the lowest CQ of all investors. The problem with this is the same thing that happened in the 2004 documentary film *Super Size Me*, in which Morgan Spurlock ate nothing but fast food for thirty days. The results were not the most favorable.

And that's the issue with being a fast-food junkie investor—you can do better. FFJI's typically invest exclusively in a S&P 500 index fund, a S&P 500 ETF, a balanced fund, a growth-and-income fund, or a global (or not) asset-allocation fund. The problem with investing only in an S&P 500 index fund or ETF is that you are only invested in the U.S. large-cap stock market and have no exposure to other asset classes. So most likely for your given level of risk, you are not getting the best return.

With a balanced or growth-and-income fund you are getting exposure usually to bonds and cash as well. To refresh your memory, the difference between the two is that growth-and-income portfolio managers tend to have more freedom in their allocation. So the question for you is this: Is this the most effective allocation based on your personal risk profile? Perhaps, but probably not. One size doesn't fit all. For example, if you're thirty years old, you'll have a very different asset allocation than your mother, who may be sixty years old. A balanced fund may be right for one of you, but the same fund wouldn't be right for both of you.

An asset-allocation fund typically has a broader allocation to asset classes than a balanced fund. All asset-allocation funds are not the same. Be sure to read a fund's investment policies, outlined in the prospectus, very carefully. Some have tremendous leeway in where they can go to search out returns, and others don't. The key problem that I see with these funds is that they may not always be in line with your overall personal risk profile. In other words, you may be taking on more (or less) risk than you are prepared or able to deal with. Again, one size does not fit all.

Look at your current portfolio. Are you a "fast-food investor"? If so, take a step back and review your choices. Sometimes things can be just too simple and with just a little more effort and focus you could have a plan that would greatly enhance your probability of success. Hopefully by this point in this book you are more aware and educated on investing fundamentals, and the decision to enhance your CQ is a no-brainer. These products have been around for a while and they used to be a good solution for one-stop shopping (as in multiasset class investing), but the next generation of multiple asset class funds has arrived that enhance the risk-and-reward quotient.

The bottom line is this: Ultimately, you'll want to devise a "healthier" plan for yourself and your future by adding some more "flavor" to your plan.

CONVENIENCE FOOD CONNOISSEUR INVESTOR

As you know, there is a big difference between fast food and convenience food. Convenience food is typically better quality but it does come prepackaged. Sure, with a little time and energy, your meals could have a taste more customized to your preferences, but then again, they're fine as they are. Convenience foods work for many of us, but if you have a restrictive diet or some other atypical need they may not be perfect for you.

Approach:	Convenience food connoisseur investor (CFCI)
CQ level:	Moderate
Investing traits:	Your needs are relatively simple, you want quality but you are not really interested in putting a lot of your time and effort into implementing your plan. Your desire for complexity is somewhat limited.

Let's look at your portfolio and see if your propensity is to be a CFCI. Can you answer yes to the following questions?

- Do you have a mishmash of investments?
- Have you accumulated some mutual funds here and there, perhaps based on a recommendation from a friend or a magazine article?

- Does your plan have no strategy?
- Is your life very hectic and you feel as if you have very limited time to focus on your needs?

If you answered yes to these questions, you most likely are a convenience food connoisseur investor. You most likely want to invest optimally, but don't have the time, temperament, and tools needed to truly implement (and maintain) an effective portfolio.

If you don't work with an adviser (or even if you do), life-cycle funds (or target funds) may be a good solution for you. As we discussed in Chapter 5, they tend to have a broader spectrum of asset classes (than balanced or growth-and-income funds), typically are a "fund of funds" that don't hold the stocks and bonds themselves, but invest in other mutual funds (typically stock and bond funds and perhaps alternatives). They come in two varieties—risk based and age based (which is the newer product of the two).

If a majority of your assets are in retirement accounts (or earmarked for retirement) your emotional capacity for risk is pretty much in line with your time horizons, your situation does not need a lot of customization, and you want it all done for you, then age-based target funds may be a good choice for you. Age-based funds' portfolios target the date of retirement and the asset allocations change over the years toward conservative as retirement nears. Just as important, the portfolio manager monitors the investments, makes changes, and rebalances as needed. But keep in mind that these funds do not factor in any investments you may have that are not in these funds, so you would need to allocate those yourself.

Risk-based funds are also an alternative, but remember that you have to change portfolios as your personal risk profile changes.

Now, if you are going to use these types of funds, use them correctly. Many people don't. What I mean here is that they invest in this type of fund plus other funds with different objectives that have performed well in the recent past. The problem with that is that your asset allocation is no longer "efficient." By adding the other funds, you may now be taking on more (or less) risk than you desire.

Certain commentators are not huge fans of these prepackaged funds, usually because some companies only use their own family of funds or put on an additional layer of fees, or because they do not agree with the asset allocation. That may be true, but I think the convenience of having a one-stop solution that is monitored, rebalanced, and changed over time outweighs the negatives. In fact, a 2006 JPMorgan Retirement Plan study showed that nearly 83 percent of participants who picked their own funds would have had more money if they invested in an asset-allocation type fund. Of course, if you "don't behave"—that is, allow greed or fear to overtake you—and don't stay invested, the benefits are moot.

For those of you who want a little more sophistication in your portfolios, have additional assets to invest outside of your 401(k) plans, and still want convenience and (just as important) minimal paperwork, you may find packaged programs such as nondiscretionary mutual fund advisory programs, or multidisciplinary accounts (MDAs), and multistrategy portfolios (MSPs), which use separate accounts of interest, to be an attractive option.

There are two key advantages to this type of account: First, if you are working with an adviser or you have set this on cruise control, you have someone to provide you with the discipline to stay the course and the focus to consistently monitor. Second is the way they are reported. Typically, if you had an allocation to five different funds, you would get five different brokerage statements. Now you get just one with (usually) a consolidated performance number that makes it easier for you to review results at the portfolio level.

Commentators do complain about the fees, but if you are not

going to do it on your own anyway and need the motivation and discipline provided by an adviser or an investment supermarket, the pros again may outweigh the cons. The particulars of each vary based on the firm providing the services, so do your own due diligence.

No matter how packaged a product is, it does not let you off the hook. You still need to understand what lies underneath the packaging, how it all works, how or why it is aligned with your goals, and what your expectations should be. What you are getting off the hook for is the selection, monitoring, and rebalancing process of the specific underlying investments—not your investment as a whole.

SOPHISTICATE INVESTOR

You have accumulated wealth and have a greater need for customization. The "common man's" solution does not always work for you

Approach:	Sophisticate investor
CQ level:	High
Investing traits:	But you still have no desire or intention to search out the different individual stocks, bonds, and alternatives. You want something a little more packaged, which allows for flexibility.

Have a look at your current portfolio. Can you answer yes to the following questions? If so, you probably are a sophisticate investor.

- Do you have concentrated positions?
- Is tax management very important to you?

- Do you have more assets than you will ever be able to spend?
- Do you currently own a variety of individual stocks and bonds, but are not sure what the overall allocation or performance is?

If you are a self-directed sophisticate, my major concern is your asset allocation. Too often, self-directed sophisticates pick investments, not portfolios, so make sure you go through the process of determining your personal risk profile and use portfolio optimization tools. Additionally, once you have your target allocation, make sure you use a consistent process to execute and monitor your plan. If you are interested in using alternatives, you may want to consider outsourcing the due diligence and diversification to a hedge "fund of funds" manager or hedge fund–like funds that come in a mutual fund format.

If you want the assistance of an adviser and have complex needs, the product choices and program types are numerous. Instead of the prepackaged nondiscretionary advisory accounts that we discussed earlier, your adviser may use programs that are more nondiscretionary, where you and the adviser create a customized asset-allocation model and implement it using a list of mutual funds or separate accounts or a combination thereof that have been prescreened and selected for inclusion by the firm's due-diligence team. The adviser remains responsible for the monitoring and rebalancing.

Furthermore, as a sophisticate, you may be open to using a variety of products, such as closed-end funds, structured products, and some more of the more aggressive alternative types of investments as well. Although you are using a wide range of products, they still are somewhat packaged in the sense that the respective solutions are professionally managed. Because of the advances in technology some firms are able to house a variety of different products in a single account platform. This is known as a UMA, or a unified managed account. UMA is an account innovation intended to eliminate the need to open multiple accounts. The ones that have predefined allocations and product selections are geared to investors with under $1 million, where the more custom ones are for those investors with assets in excess of $1 million.

GOURMAND INVESTOR

Finally, the gourmand investor. Basically, the more exotic, the better. A gourmand is obviously not reading this book, because she has very strong opinions of what to invest in and what not to invest in. They tend to take concentrated bets on a specific market segment and have the time, training, and temperament to manage their portfolio.

No matter what your CQ, I am compelled to be a nag. My advice is this: Do not buy anything you do not understand. By understanding, I mean that you have a clear perspective of how it works, the risks, the expected returns, liquidity restrictions, tax issues, pricing, and, most important, why it is the right solution for you and how it fits into your overall plan.

Understanding what your CQ is will help you determine your preferences of investment products. But whatever your CQ or the investment products that you utilize, the most important ingredients for achieving financial success are to have a vision of what you want, a plan to execute on that vision, and the discipline to stay the course.

AT THE VERY LEAST

Look over you existing portfolio and determine what your CQ is. If you don't see a coherent strategy, you may want to consider a more prepackaged solution. Keep in mind that just because you think you should be more involved in your portfolio construction doesn't mean that you really should be—it's a matter of time, tools, and temperament.

CHAPTER SUMMARY

1. Because of advances in technology it is getting easier to outsource the construction, monitoring, and rebalancing of portfolios.
2. A convenience food investor tends to be someone whose situation is typical and thus does not have special needs.
3. A sophisticate investor tends to be someone who requires some customization and advanced solutions.
4. Target-date funds are increasingly gaining popularity but are not all alike and due diligence is required before investing.
5. There is an alphabet soup of packaged accounts in the industry today—they differ by structure, products, discretion, investment dollar requirements, and so on.
6. What you've learned:

7

KEEPING UP

Hey, we all know the dirty secret of dieting. Losing the weight is the easy part. The hard part is keeping it off. I revisit that lesson nearly every day when I open my closet doors and see the range of sizes inside.

Keeping weight off is so difficult because we fall back into our old bad habits, often because of emotions. We eat because we're happy and we eat because we're sad. We even eat when we have no idea if we are happy or sad. Unfortunately, studies show that among successful weight losers, those who report emotional eating lose less weight and are more likely to regain.

But there's hope! Those dieters who are able to recognize their emotional triggers, come to terms with them, and adhere to their plan, lose weight and keep it off. The parallel to investing? Uncanny, once again.

As we've discussed throughout this book, most investors turn out to be their own worst enemy. And it isn't because we all are self-destructive. It's due to documented investor behavioral biases. These biases are potential stumbling blocks to managing your investments because they cause us to make irrational decisions (like investing in a fund just because it had great numbers last year). It's mostly psychological stuff, and tends to be rooted by two very powerful forces—fear and greed. These behaviors cause us to abandon the basic principles of sound investing and thus minimize our success.

These behaviors continually rear their ugly heads. It's human nature, after all. But just as with dieting, I have found that there are some pretty simple things we can do to keep from falling off our investment wagon by succumbing to fear or greed. There are two fundamental actions one can take:

- Have a discipline to your decision-making framework.
- Be able to recognize why we tend to make mistakes before we make them.

A discipline to your decision-making framework is exactly what we've been building over the last six chapters and it culminates in your portfolio review process. But, as we all know, emotions can bring any process down. So it is imperative that we understand and are able to recognize emotional triggers in the investment world and devise ways to overcome them. Therefore, in this chapter we will be discussing both the review process and the emotional triggers that can take you off course.

My first question for you is "Do you have a good portfolio review process?" If you are constantly looking at your investments or you never look at your investments, the answer is a definite no. If your answer is somewhere between the two, the answer is a definite maybe. I find that most people do not have a good portfolio review process in place simply because they do not know *why* they should be reviewing a portfolio and *what* they should be looking for.

Most people define their investing success in one of two ways:

- Beating the market
- Making money (meaning their portfolio did not lose money)

Now, if you think about what we learned in past chapters, you will recall your portfolio typically does not mirror the market. In fact, the term "beating the market" just makes my skin crawl. It's way overused and so misunderstood.

First, people define the the market differently and thus use different benchmarks of indexes as their measuring point. For instance, some people when referring to the market are referring to the S&P 500 index, some people to the Dow Jones Industrial Average, and so on. Each of these indexes has identifiable compositions with respective risk-and-return profiles—which may or may not be similar to your portfolio. The question you must ask yourself is "Are you comparing apples to apples?"

The point here is that the makeup of your overall portfolio is most likely different from the markets that people are referring to. Remember, asset allocation and diversification are about combining a group of asset classes that behave differently in different economic conditions in order for us to get the best return for a given risk level over the long term. So usually if you compare your portfolio to the market, you are comparing apples to oranges.

Second, if you define success as your portfolio only going up at each short-term measuring period, we know by now that you will surely be disappointed. There will be periods when your portfolio loses money because we do not avoid risk—we manage it.

The bottom line is this: Having "beating the market" or "positive returns" as your definition of success will most likely not lead you to success—more likely to disappointment. I am sorry to say that this disappointment typically leads us to a path of emotional and irrational behavior and, as a result, lackluster investment portfolio outcomes.

Therefore, I suggest you define success by being able to answer the following question with a confident yes: "Did my investments perform as would be expected in relation to my specific goals and objectives, my risk tolerance, the general market environment, and the specific market environment for the asset classes in which I am invested?"

This is a very different mind-set from beating the market or not losing money, and due to the nature of investing (that is, volatility), it is not always easy to hold on to, especially if you're the type to look at your portfolio values daily, weekly, or even monthly.

Instead, once you construct your portfolio you should go somewhere, do something fun, and not think about your portfolio again for at least six months. If you've chosen a more packaged approach to investing, you can even let it idle along for a full year before reevaluating it. Feel like you're slacking off? You're not. You're doing yourself a favor.

So let's fast-forward six months. If you're not comparing your portfolio to the market or you are not seeing if your portfolio went up or down, what should you be looking for? As we said earlier, what you want to determine is whether your investments are behaving as expected in terms of your specific goals and objectives, risk profile, the general market environment, and the specific market environment for those asset classes in which you are invested.

Therefore, before you look at anything, it's imperative that you have a sense of what "behaving as expected" looks like. You should refer back to the expected risk-and-return characteristics of your target asset allocation (the work that was done in Chapter 4 on portion control). You'll recall that risk is volatility of returns. So if your portfolio has an expected return of, say, 10 percent with a standard deviation of 15, you can generally (not always, but often) expect to see returns anywhere from -5 to $+25$ (depending on market conditions) in any given year, notwithstanding any very unusual circumstances (for example, 2008). If it's not in that range, deeper analysis is needed to determine if the problem is your allocation among the asset classes or the products within the asset classes or just the markets in general. Thus your goal is to determine if you should stay the course or make some changes to your portfolio.

If your CQ resembles that of a convenience food connoisseur investor and you use more of the prepackaged products (like a mutual fund advisory program or a target date fund), your advisers or the team running the portfolio will do this for you. If you are more of a sophisticate investor and you work with an adviser, he or she should do it for you and review it with you. But if you are self-directed, then you have some work to do. Regardless of your CQ and who has to do the work, the portfolio analysis process is the same. It is comprised of three steps:

- Step 1: Review of overall portfolio performance
- Step 2: Review by asset class
- Step 3: Review by individual investment product

In all three cases you are looking at the respective behaviors and comparing them to your expectations.

Now, just some words of caution before we discuss the portfolio analysis process in a little more depth. If someone else is analyzing it for you, you still need to be sure that you understand the how and the why of their process as well as if it's in line with your stated objectives and your personal risk profile. As you will recall from the previous chapters, markets, attitudes, financial capacity, and other aspects of your financial life change over time, and your investment approaches should change with them as well.

PORTFOLIO REVIEW PROCESS

The first step in the portfolio review process is from an overall portfolio viewpoint. Are the asset classes in line with the chosen target asset-allocation ranges? Because of market movements you may see some asset classes growing or shrinking beyond the optimal portion of your portfolio. For example, if your target allocation is 50 percent in stocks and 50 percent in bonds, and stocks just had a stellar year and bonds had a miserable year, your portfolio may now be 65 percent stocks and 35 percent bonds. Why should you care? Because now your portfolio is subject to greater risk or volatility than you are prepared for and desire. Unfortunately, while we may be cool with this as the markets continue to go up, we get into trouble when the markets start to come down. Typically what happens is that you get a little greedy and when markets start to drop you unexpectedly become fearful and irrational, selling too large a portion of your equities to go into something "safer." The concept of rebalancing is counterintuitive for some because you are going against current market conditions. It requires selling investments that have done well and investing more heavily in those that have underperformed. One of the best analogies I ever heard is that rebalancing is just like pruning an overgrown garden and planting new seedlings to keep the garden growing the way you want it to. Thus rebalancing is all about managing your risk, not about how green your garden can grow.

Most people should rebalance annually, but your specific portfolio makeup, objectives, and market movements may lead you to evaluate more frequently. As a rule of thumb, when your assets drift 5 percent or more away from your allocation ranges, you should consider rebalancing.

The second step in our review process is to see if each asset class performed as expected. This is accomplished by comparing the performance of the asset class to a specified benchmark or index. You should be somewhat familiar with the concept of an index from our discussion in Chapter 5 on index funds and ETFs. As you may recall, an index is a composite of securities designed to replicate the structure and performance of a specific segment or sector of the financial markets. These indexes are the standard measure of the respective market performance. You want to be on the lookout for extraordinary outcomes (either good or bad) of your respective asset classes compared to the market segment each represents for good news or bad news. The good news is that you picked great investment solutions for the respective asset class. Conversely, the bad news is that either you didn't pick such great solutions or that the investment solution is taking on more risk than you anticipated, perhaps by investing in securities outside that respective asset class. Fluctuations in either direction can throw off the balance of your portfolio and your original asset allocation, leaving you more at risk in the next market downturn. Thus, you should keep an eye out for investments that are performing both below and above your expectations. You should always keep in mind, though, that you can't count on the market to always behave the same way in the future as it has in the past. Performance is never guaranteed.

This leads us to the third and more intricate aspect of the portfolio review and that is to determine if the individual investment solutions performed in line with your expectations. The process that investment professionals undertake in the monitoring or review process of the individual investments is (or should be) very similar to the process or criteria used in the selection process. In other words, the Six C's we discussed in Chapter 5: category, clarity, commitment, comparability, consistency, and cost. The bottom line is that they are looking to see if the investment products are behaving as they said they would in light of market conditions and in relation to their peers. This is especially important when you use actively managed products rather than index funds or ETFs. ETFs or index funds shouldn't be acting any differently from each other and their market sector because they all are conceptually invested in the same underlying investments in the same proportion—that is, exactly like the index they are replicating. In actively managed funds a portfolio manager has discretion as to what, how much, and when he or she buys or sells the underlying securities. In other words, the manager controls the risk parameters. So what you are looking for is basically this: When compared to its peers and the market and in relation to its risk factors, did the fund earn an appropriate return? Was the manager's performance sufficient to justify the risk taken to get that return? Evaluating the return of an investment without regard to the risk taken offers very little insight into how an investment or portfolio has really performed.

Thus, you look to see if its behavior is consistent with past years and, most important, whether it's in line with its stated objectives. If its performance (as compared to its peers and its benchmark) is lower than in past years, don't panic. Investigate. Ask some questions. Did the portfolio manager change? Did its style drift without sufficient reason or proof that it made sense for a given management style or timing? If an investment does not perform as expected, investment professionals do not automatically get out of that investment. Usually, they will put it on a watch list and see if it corrects over the next few time periods. If it doesn't, get out. If it does, stay.

While we're talking about getting out of an investment, remember that just because a fund was number one last year doesn't mean that it will be number one next year. If you are constantly trying to have the number one fund, you will end up chasing returns and usually end up losing out. So, as mentioned earlier, you want to see your fund consistently perform in the top quartile (or two) of its peers, not necessarily number one (which would be nice, but not consistently realistic).

Whether this three-step process is done for you or you have to do it for yourself, there is one more step in the portfolio review process that only you can do, and that is to confirm that your personal risk profile has not changed since the last review. Things happen, time frames change, goals change, attitudes change, and as a result so does your financial and/or emotional capacity for risk. To show you what I mean, let's say that you have invested in a target risk portfolio and you choose an aggressive profile. Your retirement is coming up. Is your risk profile still aggressive or should it be scaled down to adjust to your changing circumstances? Remember, your plan is not a one-time event. It is as dynamic as you are.

I hope you can now understand that a review is much more than just looking at a performance number; it's about renewing your confidence and recommitting to the course that you are on. It's about risk, return, expectations, and your goals. Furthermore, I hope that you see if you don't do the work up front—that is, if you don't have a stated framework for constructing your portfolio—all you can do is look at a number, and sooner rather than later that number is going to disappoint, which usually leads to once again chasing returns, and as we have learned, chasing returns is a path with the least likelihood of success.

As we said earlier, it takes discipline and focus to ensure that your actions are rational. Avoid making snap decisions about your investments and acting on them. Instead, step back, take a deep breath, and ask yourself if you're being rational or if you're letting your emotions get the best of you. Before you take action, think about these questions:

- Are you using faulty reasoning to make your decision? For example, do you think to yourself if it's down it will keep going down?
- Are you underestimating the range of potential outcomes of your decision—that is, are you too focused on the upside potential and do not give a similar thought to the downside?
- Are you overreacting or underreacting to events in the markets? Experiencing greed or fear?
- Do you have unrealistic expectations? Are you comparing performance numbers to all-time highs instead of to long-term averages?
- Does your decision have long-term consequences and have you identified those consequences? Is it okay if you won't be able to reach your goals?

Obviously, we can justify anything, so it isn't always the easiest task to determine if we are acting irrationally. To help you think about your past behaviors so you can be more aware about your future behaviors, let's have a look at these five women. See if you have behaved similarly in the past. (Since 2008 was so extreme, let's think about your behaviors prior to then. But also as you are reading have a think about how your experiences of 2008 will or will not affect your behavior going forward.)

HEADLINE HANNAH

In the late 1990s Headline Hannah put a large portion of her investment portfolio into technology stocks and mutual funds that concentrated on tech issues. It seemed like the thing to do, as everyone else was doing it and Hannah felt she, too, had to participate. Of course, we all know now that the tech bubble eventually burst. Hannah, along with hundreds of thousands of other investors, was left with a substantially smaller portfolio.

As life went on, Hannah started to get back on track, saving diligently and investing in a more diversified array of mutual funds and stocks. But just when things seemed to be going so well, the stock market took an unexplained drop of more than 10 percent. Hannah, though, was determined that she wouldn't get caught flat-footed again. She wanted to know what was happening before she made any decisions about her portfolio. So she dutifully tuned in to the cable business news stations to get educated. What she saw, though, really frightened her. One after another the "experts" who were interviewed warned that the market was in real trouble, things were going to get a lot worse, the Dow might drop 30 percent or more. There was a tremendous amount of cash going into money market funds instead of being invested in the market. That was all Hannah had to hear. She immediately went online and began selling her stock funds and moving the money to the safety of a money market account.

Well, some of those doom-and-gloom scenarios in fact did come true. But it only lasted a very short while and after that little hiccup the market began recovering and went on over the next few years to hit one new record after another. Hannah, unfortunately, missed most of that ride. After first succumbing to the greed of the tech bubble, Hannah had fallen prey to the fears that were stirred up by what was actually not a very significant drop in the market. If only she had kept her money as allocated originally and rebalanced annually, she would have saved herself a lot of pain and a lot of money.

I'm happy to report that Hannah persevered. Initially she couldn't stop berating herself for being "bad." But after having a good think, she realized that what was in the past was the past. She couldn't undo

BEAR MARKET BOUNCES BACK

During 2008 and into 2009 I am sure you felt that the market would never recover. As of this writing, we have to wait and see, but if we look back historically, we see what comes down often comes up again. In the last seventy-five years (that is, 1934 to 2008), the S&P 500 stock index has suffered total return losses of at least 20 percent in four different years; the most recent was 2008's 37.0 percent decline. In the year after the three previous 20 percent plus tumbles, the index gained an average of plus 32 percent. (Source: BTN Research.)

what she had already done. Instead, she realized that everyone has different levels of risk tolerance and investment objectives. She learned some very valuable lessons about her own risk tolerance and how to tame it. But the real lesson here is that it is never too late to get on the right track. You just have to empower yourself to recommit to your plan.

Are you like Hannah? Can you answer yes to these questions?

- Do you want to invest in a specific sector or stock that has been getting a lot of media attention?
- Do you hear about a hot investment or manager and just have to get in on the action?

If so, have a play account. When we're dieting and feel deprived, we end up misbehaving. In fact, researchers at Stanford University say that what many investors fear the most is not the risk of a loss per se, but the risk that they may do poorly relative to their peers. That means that even though investments may be particularly risky, investors tend to cluster around these opportunities to avoid being the only one in the neighborhood to miss out on the "next best thing." The solution? Give yourself certain small "cheats" as part of your weight management program. Do the same thing in your investment portfolio by allocating a small sum that you can play with. Buy a stock that intrigues you, do a little market timing if you want to try your hand at that. If you make money, great. If you lose it all, *c'est la vie.* You're scratching the itch without putting your long-term goals at risk.

Engaging an adviser may be worth looking into as well. A good adviser helps to keep you disciplined, focused on your plan, and not chasing the next best thing.

OBSESSIVE OLIVIA

Olivia is something of a compulsive. She never sends an e-mail without checking that every word is spelled correctly. She reconciles her checkbook and checking account each day. She keeps meticulous files all year long so she can do her income taxes easily. And she checks the value of her investment portfolio almost every day. Poor Olivia.

Olivia is like a dieter who weighs herself every day. You know how that works. If you've lost a little, you get to have a snack as a reward. If you've gained a little, you go on a binge to assuage your guilt. Weighing every day taxes your emotions and results in shortsighted decisions.

Checking your investments every day can lead to the same behavior. Investors who obsess over their portfolio's value tend to over- or underreact to market conditions that typically result in less than optimum results. If the balance is going down, they fall victim to the temptation to sell before it all disappears. If one asset class is moving up, they're tempted to sell other classes and chase the gains. The pros call this market timing and they know how difficult it is to do successfully. Most people wind up getting out too early and getting back in too late. In fact, a recent study by Dalbar, a financial services market research firm, shows that market timers actually lose money instead of making money. Examining the flows into and out of mutual funds for twenty years (1985–2004), the Dalbar study of investor behavior found that market timers in stock mutual funds lost 3.7 percent per year on average while the S&P 500 was growing by an average annualized return of 11.9 percent during that same time.

Are you like Olivia? Can you answer yes to these questions?

- Do you want to divest out of underperforming asset classes into assets classes that have outperformed in recent months?
- When you become nervous about the market environment, do you want to move completely into cash or make another drastic change?

If so, you have to go cold turkey. Forget the password to your online accounts and do not open your statements. Just relax for at least six months (I would say a year, but in this day and age of identity theft, it is always a good idea to take a peek to be sure the balance makes sense). If this is just too extreme, you may want to "detox from your balance checking habit" in stages. First, see if you can go for a week, then two weeks, then a month, then two months, and so on until it's time to do a semiannual or annual review.

You may also want to consider working with an adviser whose business model includes semiannual reviews with his or her clients. This way you know that at a prespecified time you will be reviewing your portfolio and making any changes as needed. Over time, hopefully you will see that if the portfolio was constructed effectively to begin with the changes will be limited in nature.

ANCHORED ANNIE

Anchored Annie is a stubborn one. She has a number in her head and won't let go of it. Annie is five feet five and is big-boned. Once in college she was able to get her weight down to one hundred and twenty pounds. In her mind that number is the measure of success. It's what she thinks she should weigh.

Is that target realistic? For her body type, her lifestyle, and her health, it is not. For one thing, she set that target twenty years ago, she was only able to maintain that weight for a week or so, and she had to starve herself to do that. But Anchored Annie just won't let go. She ends up sabotaging her diet success over and over again because she is anchored to a number that is not real.

Unfortunately for Anchored Annie, she carries this behavior over to her investing. Too often she ends up confusing investment returns as the goal rather than as the means to achieve her bigger financial goals. Annie is stuck in the past. She keeps having flashbacks to the days when her portfolio returned 15 percent in a year. When she sees returns of just 8 percent a year she worries that she's doing something wrong. As a result she ends up chasing returns, taking on more risk than is appropriate, and minimizing her success.

Can Anchored Annie be cured? Yes. As with Hannah and Olivia, Annie needs to get back to basics and pay attention to her plan. Will an 8 percent return, which is perfectly healthy for almost any investor, get her to her long-range goals? If the answer is yes, then she should sit back, relax, and tell herself that performance alone is not a goal.

Are you like Annie? Can you answer yes to these questions?

- Are you fixated on a previous all-time-high market or stock value that is no longer relevant?
- Are you a corporate executive who will not diversify your employer stock until it reaches a specific number?

If so, well, get real. Review your target allocation and its respective risk-and-return parameters. If you must hold on to some corporate stock because you really, really, really know the price is going to come back, only hold so much that a 20 percent drop in the value will not put your long-term must-have goals at risk.

If you have a concentrated position, you may want to engage an adviser. There are more sophisticated strategies that you can employ to let you participate in some of the potential upside while protecting you on the downside.

INDECISIVE IRIS

Choice is good. Too much choice, not so good. Confronted by too many choices, most of us find ourselves confused and unable to decide. Confusion in the face of overwhelming choices is one of the most common barriers to investment success that I see. Given too many choices, people wind up making no choices. That's the story of Iris.

Every time Iris thought she needed to start investing, she would begin to second-guess what she was doing: "Should I invest in stocks or is there something better out there that I don't know about? Is this mutual fund better than that mutual fund? Should I buy Treasury bonds or muni bonds?" The questions kept coming and Iris simply couldn't reach a conclusion. Only after she talked to a financial adviser did she realize that building an investment program isn't about finding the single best-performing asset. Instead, it's about building a framework of investments based on her goals and time frames, understanding her CQ, coming to terms with her personal risk profile, and searching not for the best but for what will fulfill her needs.

Are you like Iris? Can you answer yes to these questions?

- Do you have cash sitting idle because you can't decide what to do?
- Do you not invest because you fear that you will do more harm than good?

If so (besides reading this book) you may want to engage an adviser to help you sort out the choices and make a decision that is best for your situation. Remember, nothing is guaranteed, but you have a greater probability of success if you make an educated decision based on your goals and your personal risk profile. If you don't have the assets to get the attention of an adviser, use one of the "prepackaged" products that is in line with your risk profile.

The bottom line is that none of us are perfect. We all make mistakes. But hopefully by being aware of the more common "misbehaviors," and putting mechanisms, processes, and people in place to help manage these behaviors, we will all reach the success that we deserve.

The lesson surrounding portfolio reviews is a familiar one: Have a consistent process, use a disciplined approach, and have realistic expectations. But most important, remember that a portfolio review is much more than a performance number or "beating the market." It is a time to see if you are progressing toward your goals in a way that is comfortable for you. A review in essence is looking at your life, your goals, the markets, and your portfolio to see that they are all aligned.

Try to always keep this in mind: If your portfolio is providing a return over time that will allow you to reach your financial goals while maintaining an acceptable level of risk, then it is on track, no matter what the broad stock indexes are doing. If you can meet your personal investment goals, who cares how well the market or anybody else is doing?

AT THE VERY LEAST

Designate one day per year as your own personal financial fitness day. Choose a day you'll be able to remember and that will be the same each year (Martin Luther King, Jr., Day, Columbus Day, your birthday, whatever), and on which you'll be able to set aside at least one full hour to yourself. On this day, you'll review your financial plan and adjust accordingly.

CHAPTER SUMMARY

1. Review your portfolio at least annually.
2. A portfolio review is a four-step process.
3. A portfolio review answers the questions:

   - Did my investments perform as would be expected in relation to my specific goals and objectives, my risk tolerance, the general market environment, and the

specific market environment for the asset classes in
which I am invested?

- Does my portfolio need to meet a changing personal
  risk profile?

4. Rebalance when an asset class is greater than 5 percent
   outside of its high and low ranges.

5. Be aware of the more common "misbehaviors" and have
   mechanisms, processes, and people in place to help manage
   these behaviors.

6. What you've learned:

8

PROTECTING YOURSELF FROM SABOTAGE

Have you ever noticed that almost every book or article on dieting has a section on "protecting yourself from sabotage"? The reason, well, you can sum it up in one word and that is "life." Here's what I mean. You work so hard to lose a few pounds and then—whoops!—life gets in the way. A party, a stressful day, or a bad case of PMS and, *bam*, you scarf up an extra two thousand calories without even realizing it. It's almost guaranteed: If you don't take precautions against these events, the chances of succeeding at your diet plummet.

Fortunately, there are steps you can take to stay on track. Going to a party? If you head out to the party hungry you're putting a stick of dynamite under your diet plan. Instead, nutritionists recommend that you eat a small healthy meal an hour before you leave for the party in order to protect yourself against the evils of the buffet table.

If you distill all the advice from dieting experts, you'll see that what they're really trying to do is get you to ask yourself the following questions:

- What are the kinds of events that could tempt me to forget my dieting goals?

- How likely is it that the various kinds of events will indeed persuade me to go off my diet? Even if it's "just this once"?
- How serious will the damage be if I succumb to the temptation?
- How serious am I about protecting myself against this kind of event?

Experience has shown that a successful weight-loss plan depends on your ability to recognize the obstacles, understand how likely you are to succumb to them, and devise ways to minimize the impact.

Well, that same thing is true of your investment portfolio. You can have the best plan in place, but life often gets in the way. Life in this case is one or more of the five D's:

- Disability
- Dementia
- Death
- Destruction
- Divorce

Wait, I don't want to frighten you! I admit these aren't the most pleasant subjects to be reading about, but remember, the focus of the chapter is on ways to protect you. If you put off dealing with these subjects, chances are one or more of them is going to catch up to you and the resulting damage will be much worse than if you had done some planning. The fact is, even doing nothing is, in effect, having a plan. Just not a very good one. For example, by not taking precautions for the possibility of your early demise, you are more than likely "planning" to condemn your kids to a severely reduced lifestyle and perhaps even no chance of affording a decent college education. Further, if you don't make plans, somebody—too often the government—will wind up doing it for you! That's why I prefer to think about this chapter as empowering, not depressing. It's about making sure that you and your families live the best life possible even during times of stress.

I could write separate books on planning for each of the five D's. Since I'm only writing a chapter, my goal here is to build your awareness and perhaps raise some concerns. This chapter, then, will serve as a solid overview that will give you the knowledge you need to move forward with planning as well as the urgency to get on with it. We all underestimate the probability of these events or think none of them will ever happen to us. Oh, if it were only so. But it isn't.

DO I REALLY NEED INSURANCE?

Four questions you should be asking yourself:

- What would the impact be if something was to happen and I was not insured?
- What is the likelihood of a life-changing event occurring?
- What portion of the impact do I want to protect?
- Am I able to self-insure or do I need to buy protection?

When thinking about impacts, don't focus only on your current life but on your long-term goals as well. For example, if you were to get disabled or die, you may currently have enough assets to live your life today, but will not have enough to fund your children's education, and so on.

THE FIRST D: DISABILITY

We're starting our discussion of the five D's with disability because very few people realize that the chances of becoming disabled are greater than dying prematurely. In fact, it has been reported that by age forty-two, it is four times more likely that you will become seriously disabled than that you will die during your working years. The problem is that no matter how careful you are about staying healthy— eating well, exercising, driving carefully—accidents and illness do happen and there is nothing you can do to prevent them.

AGE AT BEGINNING OF DISABILITY	LIKELIHOOD OF LONG-TERM DISABILITY SOMETIME BEFORE AGE 65
30	1 in 3
40	3 in 10
50	5 in 22
60	1 in 10

SOURCE: 1985 Commissioners' Disability Individual Table A.

According to the American Council of Life Insurers, the majority of long-term disabilities are because of illnesses, such as cancer and heart disease. Worse yet (according to the National Underwriter Company), men have a 43 percent chance of becoming seriously disabled during their working years and women (yes, you know what's coming) have a higher chance (54 percent) of becoming disabled during their working years.

The chart below describes how long your disability would last depending on your age when you became disabled. As you can see, one of the biggest misconceptions out there is that disability only happens when you are old. Notice that the duration for all is more than three years. We aren't talking about missing work for six weeks or so, which would probably be covered by your health insurance and sick days. We're talking about serious downtime.

AGE AT BEGINNING OF DISABILITY	DURATION
30	3 years, 1 month
40	3 years, 11 months
50	4 years, 2 months
60	4 years, 6 months

The question you face is this: If something were to happen to you today that would not allow you to work for an extended period of time, do you have enough assets to cover your living expenses for that period without putting your long-term goals at risk? Being able to meet your long-term goals is an important caveat. You may be able to cover your expenses for a long time by selling your house and cashing out your IRA, but that would be a disaster for your future. Therefore, it would be safe to say that if you haven't won the lottery, received a very large inheritance, earned a tremendous amount of income, saved most of your income, or married into big money, the answer to the above question is almost certainly no. In fact, according to the National Association of Insurance Commissioners, 56 percent of Americans claim they would be unable to pay their bills to meet their expenses if they were to become disabled and could not work for a year or longer. Yet less than 40 percent of Americans own any type of long-term disability insurance.

Your ability to work and earn income is one of your greatest assets, so the first thing I want you to do if you are under the age of fifty and working is to consider buying a long-term disability insurance policy. If you don't work and have a working partner (or if you both work), make sure to have this discussion about disability with him or her. As we go through the discussion we will refer to "you," but keep in mind it applies to you and your working partner.

You can think of a disability insurance policy as a long-term income replacement tool. You may be able to buy such a policy through your employer, but in this day and age your job can be eliminated at the flick of a switch. If you have an employer-sponsored disability insurance policy, check to see if it's "portable," which means you can take it with you when you leave. If it isn't, you should consider getting your own policy from an insurance company.

If you have an employer plan, you need to know what it covers. Does it cover your base salary only or does it include bonuses? Is there a monthly cap? Just because you have an employer-sponsored plan doesn't mean that you may not need a private policy as well. Take a good look at what you have or, more important, don't have. And don't confuse a long-term disability policy with a long-term care policy. They're totally different. We'll discuss long-term care policies later.

To develop an estimate of how much disability insurance (that is, income replacement) you need, go back to Chapter 2 where we determined how much you spend each month and what your balance sheet looks like. The question is: "If I could not work for an extended period of time, do I have enough savings to cover my current needs and not destroy my future goals?" In essence, you need to determine how much of your net assets you are able and willing to put at risk. Obviously the more risk you are able to absorb, the less insurance you will need. I have found that most want to—and need to—put the minimal amount at risk and therefore need to cover a maximum amount of income. A very common provision in disability policies is to cover 60 percent of after-tax wages. If you need more coverage you can get it, albeit at a higher price. No plan will cover all of your salary for fear you will have no incentive to get back to work.

You may be thinking that if you get disabled Social Security or workers' compensation will cover you. Maybe. Even if you qualify under the strict definitions for Social Security (more than half who apply for disability payments under Social Security are denied coverage), chances are the benefits may not be sufficient even to support the most frugal standard of living. To receive workers' comp you have to be "lucky" enough that your disability results from a workplace condition or accident and as we said earlier, the stats show that most disabilities stem from illness, not accidents.

No matter where you buy your policy, you need to pay attention to four things beyond the amount of income replacement you will receive:

- Definitions
- Time frames
- Types
- Cost

Each of these has its own costs and trade-offs. Like most things in life, the more you get, the more you pay.

Definitions Disability means different things to different people. For you, disability means what your policy says it means. Your policy can define disability as a condition that prevents you from doing the work in which you specialize or it can mean a condition that prevents you from doing any work, even flipping hamburgers. The policies usually state what they mean in terms of "own occupation" or "any occupation." Too many people looking for bargain prices on disability insurance make the mistake of choosing an "any occupation" policy. If you aren't sure about the definitions in your own policy, ask. And keep asking until it's clear.

Time Frames When investigating a long-term disability policy, you will probably hear the term "waiting period." The waiting period is the length of time you must be disabled before your policy begins to pay benefits. Typically the waiting period is ninety days, but you can buy policies with shorter or longer waiting periods. Ask yourself, "How long can I go without a paycheck without putting my goals at risk?" Generally, the longer the waiting period, the lower the premium.

If you have an employer-sponsored plan, be sure to find out how much short-term disability coverage you have. There's no reason to pay a premium for a long-term disability policy with a waiting period of, say, sixty days when you have short-term coverage for six months.

Disability policies also offer different "benefit periods"—that is, the length of time they pay you benefits. The most common benefit periods are two years, five years, and until retirement age, generally specified as sixty-five years old. Obviously the longer the period you choose, the higher the premium.

Types There are two major types of individual long-term disability insurance, "noncancelable" and "guaranteed renewable." Under a non-cancelable policy, your premiums are fixed and cannot be changed. As long as the premiums are paid, the policy cannot be canceled. With a guaranteed renewable policy the premiums can rise, but only if the change affects an entire class of policyholders. You'll usually find that initial premiums for guaranteed renewable policies are less expensive than noncancelable policies.

Cost We've already seen that the definitions, time frames, and types of policies determine the cost. But there are other factors that go into calculating the premium, including your age, your occupation, your health history, your gender, and whether you want extra kinds of coverage (called riders). A very general rule of thumb is that you can expect to pay approximately 1 percent to 3 percent of your annual income for a quality disability insurance plan.

You may be thinking, "Ugh, another expense; I'll just take the risk." But instead of thinking about disability insurance as just an expense, I would like you to ponder the question someone once asked me: "You are offered two identical jobs, the only difference being that one pays you $100,000 a year while you work, but nothing if you suffer a long-term disability, while the other pays you $98,000 a year while you're working and $60,000 a year (free of income tax) if you suffer a

---

THE SHORT AND LONG OF IT

Short-term disability insurance, also known as sick leave, kicks in as soon as you're unable to work due to an illness, injury, or the birth of a child. Most employers provide some type of coverage, ranging from just a few days to as much as one year. Five states require employers to provide short-term disability. Hawaii, New Jersey, New York, and Rhode Island mandate that most employers provide twenty-six weeks of coverage. In California, employers are obligated to offer fifty-two weeks.

Long-term disability insurance kicks in once your short-term disability benefits run out. Unfortunately, there are no state laws that require employers to provide long-term disability, but it's estimated that half of all midsized to large firms do provide at least some insurance.

long-term disability. Which one would you choose?" I've found that many people have a psychological hang-up about insurance. They put way too much weight on what is being taken away from them (the premium) and way too little weight on what they're getting (peace of mind).

The bottom line is that disability insurance is too often overlooked even though it is critical to your long-term financial success.

THE SECOND D: DEMENTIA

I'm using dementia—Alzheimer's or other forms—as a generic example of the kinds of things that can result in a deterioration in your physical or mental health that prevents you from performing the ordinary tasks of life, such as bathing, dressing, eating, getting from a bed to a chair, remaining continent, using a toilet, and walking unaided. You don't need constant skilled medical care, but you do need some form of care providers. In short, you need "long-term care," whether it is delivered at home or in a nursing home.

Unfortunately, studies have shown that women face a greater likelihood than men of needing long-term care, mostly because our life expectancies are longer and we typically are the ones who are the caregivers. In fact, one study, by Genworth Financial, found that women were 60 percent more likely than men to enter a nursing home at some point in their lives and may experience large financial sacrifices in their roles as America's predominant unpaid care providers.

The profile of people who buy long-term care insurance has changed dramatically over the last twenty years. The average customer used to be in his or her seventies. Today many purchasers are still working and in their fifties. And that's good. More than 40 percent of

Americans receiving long-term care are under age sixty-five. You should consider long-term care insurance in your fifties if you have a chronic condition like diabetes that could prove incapacitating over time or a history of serious illness in your family. Otherwise, begin at about age sixty to assess whether you need long-term care coverage, and, if so, buy a policy by age sixty-five. If you buy later than age seventy, the policy will likely be too expensive or you may not pass the medical tests needed to qualify.

There is some debate about who should have long-term care insurance. A good way to think about it is in terms of asset protection of legacy and freedom of choice. We all know long-term care is very expensive, so without insurance it is possible that a person can spend all her assets and destroy the legacy she wanted to leave her children. Thus, long-term care makes sense for anyone who has accumulated assets, planned for a comfortable retirement, and is concerned about leaving a legacy. What's more, you may not be concerned about protecting your legacy but your children may be. What I am going to say may sound cold and ludicrous, but when adult children have to choose between spending your money on your maintenance and making sure that a legacy will exist for them—the choice is not always as expected. I know, your kids would never be like this, but believe me it happens. The other aspect is freedom of choice. Once your assets are spent, you are at the mercy of the government. You may want to stay in your home with some aides, but for costs' sake the government wants you in a nursing home. So are you willing to give up some freedom to spend today to have freedom to choose tomorrow? Only you can answer that question.

A special note for those of you in the "sandwich generation": If your parents do not have an estate to protect but you want to ensure that they get the best possible care, you may want to consider purchasing long-term care insurance for them to protect your own assets from being depleted because you pay for their care.

The best long-term care policy has a reasonable deductible, covers a wide range of care options (that is, is flexible), guarantees a sufficient financial benefit, and has some sort of inflation protection. As with any insurance product, read the policy carefully and understand what you are buying. Items to look out for: type of care, conditions covered, maximum daily benefit (amount and calculation), cap amounts, benefit period, eligibility, elimination period, inflation adjustments, and other options available. Pay close attention to when your premiums could be increased and what the company's past history has been.

If you live beyond age sixty-five, there is a good chance you will need some long-term care services at some point, and the likelihood of needing care increases as you age. More than anything when you think about the cost of long-term care, think about the emotional and financial cost to you and your family without it.

THE THIRD D: DEATH

Death and taxes. They're both certain, but at least you know when your taxes are due. Life insurance is intended to provide the future for others that you want to provide for them if you live. In other words, it's not about you, it's about them. You may already have some kind of life insurance, but don't skip this section. You may very well have the wrong life insurance or you may need to update your policy.

Many people find discussions of life insurance both depressing and confusing. It's depressing for obvious reasons and confusing due to the tremendous variety of life insurance policies available. But the bottom line is this: Start with the most basic insurance and then choose the options you want to add. The best place to start assessing your life insurance needs is to ask yourself what you want a policy to do. There are three basic answers:

- Protect lifestyle
- Provide liquidity
- Create a legacy

Lifestyle doesn't mean only your lifestyle today. Instead, think about what would happen to your family's overall lifestyle if you (or your spouse or significant other) were to die tomorrow. Would your kids still be able to go to an excellent college? Would your elderly parents have to hire a nurse or other assistant to do things that you now do for them? Would your death and the loss of your income jeopardize your spouse's plans for retirement? The basic formula for determining your life insurance need to "protect lifestyle" is to determine if your savings (and other cash flows) will be enough to cover your family's lifestyle today and tomorrow. If not, then what amount (lump sum) would it take today to ensure that that would happen? It's difficult to apply a rule of thumb because people may have other sources of income, no kids or many kids, heavy debts or no debts. But if your situation is pretty average, you can think in very general terms of a life insurance benefit between five and ten times your annual salary.

You will want a life insurance policy to provide liquidity if you're in a closely held business with a buyout option or if you have a sizable estate that will require your survivors to pay substantial estate taxes upon your demise. A life insurance policy under these circumstances is intended to ensure that your survivors won't have to sell your assets to meet these unique costs. Finally, an insurance policy can be used to provide a legacy to your loved ones or a charity. This is sometime referred to as a "leveraged legacy," because you generally (at death) get more out than you put in. We will talk more about this in Chapter 10.

POLICY PRIMER

If you've done any life insurance shopping at all, you know how confusing the huge array of different policies can be. But don't worry. It all boils down to two numbers: two and three. By that I mean there are really just *two* types of insurance, term and permanent, and then just three types of permanent insurance.

Term insurance provides protection for a specific period of time and generally pays a benefit only if you die during the term in which the policy is in effect. The insurance coverage ends when the term of the policy expires. Term periods typically range from one year to thirty years, with twenty years being the most common term. In contrast, permanent insurance does not expire as long as the premiums are paid. Term policies tend to be used for lifestyle and short-term needs while the permanent policies are more suitable for liquidity and legacy. Most people who choose term insurance are

---

RENEWABLE TERM

When purchasing a term policy, look to see if is "guaranteed renewable"—that is, you can renew your policy without a physical exam. If something happens that changes your insurance profile—an accident or illness—you don't want to be in a position in which you need life insurance the most but can't get it. With guaranteed renewable insurance you are assured you can obtain coverage even though the premiums increase every year. Guaranteed renewable term insurance is very inexpensive in the early years, but very expensive in the later years.

younger, concerned about current cash flow, and do not need an additional source to grow assets tax-deferred. (I'm assuming if you are in this category you're already making the smart move of maxing out your 401(k) plan and/or your IRAs.) Typically, term insurance has substantially lower premiums that allow you to purchase sufficient coverage to protect your survivors against loss of income. The premiums are lower because it's just "pure insurance," while permanent insurance polices tend to offer some additional benefits.

Permanent policies offer a savings or investment component combined with the insurance coverage. The savings or investment component is often known as the "cash value." The way the premiums are paid and the way the cash value is invested differentiate the types of permanent insurance. The cash value is "tax-deferred," that is, the growth from the investments are not taxed currently, just as gains in IRA or 401(k) plans are not taxed immediately.

Term or Permanent		
	TERM	**PERMANENT**
Length of Coverage	A specified term, typically 20 years	Until age 100 or later, as long as premiums are paid
Premiums	Based on your age and health, but typically lower than those of permanent insurance	Initially higher than term premiums, but often level for life
Cash Value	None	Accumulates over time on a tax-deferred basis
Key Advantage	Typically offers the highest death benefit for the lowest cost	Offers lifelong protection and tax-deferred savings

Now that you understand the difference between term and permanent insurance, let's look at the three types of permanent insurance: whole life, universal life, and variable life. The basic difference among them is premium flexibility and investment control. These policies are also known as cash value policies, because of the possible buildup of the tax-deferred investment account. But keep in mind that the first and foremost reason to buy life insurance is the death benefit. If this is not your main goal, then some other investment may be more appropriate. Also remember that permanent insurance is meant for the long term. Depending on the policy, your premiums over the first two to ten years may basically be paying fees, not building significant cash value.

On the next page is a summary of the different features of the three kinds of permanent policies, which we'll discuss in more detail. Don't worry so much about the terminology. The most important thing to note is this: As we move toward the right in the chart, there is more flexibility in how we can manage our insurance policies, both from a premium and an investment point of view, but you are shifting much of the investment risk from the insurance company to yourself.

The cost of life insurance can vary greatly, depending on how much you buy, the type of policy you choose, the underwriter's practices, your age and health, and other factors. But it all comes down to this: You're going to be charged a premium that reflects the insurance company's best estimate of how big a risk you are. Before you purchase any insurance policy, be sure that you are looking at illustrations that reflect your personal situation. Furthermore, look at the investment return assumptions. If they are too good to be true, they probably are. I have seen many proposals that have a 12 to 15 percent growth rate on the investment component, which results in

a low premium, only to find that the investments never achieve that
level and the insured winds up paying more than they expected to
keep the policy in force. So the name of the game here is reasonable-
ness.

Permanent Policies		
	WHOLE LIFE	**UNIVERSAL LIFE**	**VARIABLE**
Premium	Level premiums	Flexible premium adjustable life	Typically flexible
Death benefits	Fixed and guaranteed	Guaranteed as long as premiums are sufficient to sustain death benefit.	Adjustable based on the performance of the investment portion of the policy
Investment control	Insurance company— usually have a minimum guaranteed rate of interest	Insurance company—more diversified than whole life	You
Cash surrender value	Guaranteed	Guaranteed	Not guaranteed

Because of the increase in volatility we have seen in the financial
markets over the past few years, it may be a good idea to review your
universal or variable policy to be sure it is behaving as you expected. A
review may lead you to exchange your old policy for a new one. Generally speaking, there are five typical reasons why someone would
exchange their policies. They are as follows:

- The policy is not performing up to your expectations.
- Your needs have changed.
- You are concerned about the insurance carrier.
- Your health status has greatly improved, qualifying you for a preferred underwriting status.
- You will not want to use the accumulated cash value.

Notice I used the word "exchange" instead of "cash out." In many cases it makes sense to exchange a policy rather than to cash in a current cash value life insurance policy outright and purchase a new one. The main benefit of exchanging is to avoid incurring an income tax liability on the cash value's growth (that is, cash value in excess of premiums paid into the policy). If you rolled that cash value into a new policy, you are not subject to current taxes according to (don't be scared!) section 1035 of the Internal Revenue Code. Thus, you will hear many advisers say, "You should 1035" or "Do a 1035 exchange."

Remember that while you are rolling over cash value, you are not rolling over the commission and expenses paid on that old policy. As a result, new fees and expenses are likely to consume the first year's investment returns. So don't change just for the sake of changing policies. You should only change if your needs have changed, not just your adviser.

The bottom line is, unfortunately, most of us know that the death of a loved one is one of the hardest things to deal with. If you are someone whom people depend on financially and have not properly planned, shame on you. You are leaving them not only a tremendous burden but also most likely bitter feelings as well. Is that really what you want as your legacy?

SECOND-TO-DIE LIFE INSURANCE

If you have done some estate planning, you may have a policy known as a second-to-die policy. With second-to-die, no death benefit is paid until both spouses are deceased. Second-to-die policies are commonly used to pay estate taxes and other expenses due at the death of the second spouse. These types of policies are generally available under any type of permanent life insurance. Other than the fact that two people are insured under one policy, the policy characteristics remain the same.

THE FOURTH D: DESTRUCTION

We are all too aware that hurricanes, fires, and floods have become part of the daily news coverage. Unfortunately, these catastrophic events are not under our control and cannot be accurately predicted. When thinking about these types of events you should ask yourself three key questions:

- How likely is an event?
- How much damage would it inflict on you and your property?
- How much can you afford to lose?

In the fall of 2007 there were some spectacular wildfires in Southern California. Regretfully, California's insurance commissioner estimated that 90 percent of the people affected by the wildfires were underinsured. A 2006 survey by an insurance services firm

(Marshall & Swift / Boeckh) estimates that 58 percent of homeowners are underinsured nationwide.

For most of us, our home is our most valuable asset. With that in mind, I must ask the following four questions:

- Are your policies up-to-date and adequate to cover your potential losses?
- Are the policy's payouts in line with what it would take to actually replace your home and its possessions?
- Do you have any "property" that may need special attention?
- Have you reviewed your policies within the last three years?

Now, in order for you to be able to answer those questions, you should get out a copy of your policy and review the declarations page and the coverage sections. My point here is this: Don't wait until you have a claim to learn your policy's limits. The time to make these adjustments is now. It's too easy in the chaos of living to put off investing in your coverage, but it's too late once a disaster strikes. Too often I hear of stories about people who thought they were covered for disasters but weren't. Typically this happens with floods and earthquakes. So look to see which "perils" (causes of loss) are covered and which aren't. Don't assume anything.

Another area that surprises people is the amount they receive in a payout. It's often much less than they expected. To prevent that ugly surprise, look right now at your declarations page to see if it says "replacement cost" or "actual cash value." Replacement cost policies give you more protection than actual cash value coverage. The difference is depreciation (subtracting an amount for wear and tear). Thus, the actual cash value amount most likely would be much lower than the replacement price of a new item. Let's say you have a couch that is fifteen years old. To buy a brand-new couch will cost $3,000, but you will only get, say, $50 from your insurance company if the couch is destroyed, because the company deducts wear and tear. Another caveat: There is no set formula for calculating depreciation and different companies use different formulas for different things. Therefore replacement is the way to go. But buyers beware! True guaranteed replacement policies are pretty rare these days. Instead, insurers cap the payouts at 100 percent to 150 percent of the amount for which the home is insured. You may want to be sure that you have the highest cap you can afford.

Now, here's the big question: Since you have purchased the policy, have you added a room or made substantial home improvements? Home additions and major kitchen or bath remodeling projects can add significant value to your home, which may not be covered by your current policy. Here's a little exercise to help you determine what it would cost to replace your house and all your personal possessions within it. Look at new construction in your neighborhood and add at least 10 to 20 percent. (Rebuilding a property tends to cost more than building a new home.) Is it in line with your policy limits on the declarations page? Yes? Great! No? Call your agent today!

Now get out your inventory of your personal property.

What, you don't have one?

Now's the time to make one. Many insurance companies provide you with "household inventory" schedules and the Insurance Information Institute has helpful free software that can help you make a home inventory at www.knowyourstuff.org. Take a leisurely stroll through your house. If you already have an inventory, see if there are any recent large purchases, such as furniture or appliances, that aren't on the list. Once your inventory is complete, estimate the value of those items. Is it in line with your policy? Be sure to identify "special" items like expensive jewelry, furs, cameras, or a coin, stamp, or sports-card collection. Look to see if those special items are insured through a "scheduled personal property endorsement" or a separate "personal articles floater."

If you have not already, you may want to consider videotaping all your possessions. Remember to open all the doors and drawers of your furniture and verbally describe the major items. Another good suggestion is to put serial numbers on your property. And be sure to store copies of your policy and inventory outside the home so that in case of the ultimate disaster, all the paperwork won't be gone along with your house.

I can hear you screaming, *"Who has the time to do all this?"* Believe me, you need to find the time. Your investment of time now will be minuscule compared to the time that you will have to put in if a catastrophe occurs.

If you have accumulated some wealth, you may want to add one more bit of coverage to your insurance: an umbrella policy. An umbrella policy provides protection against events that might otherwise exceed your various coverages. If someone were to slip and fall on your property or a tree on your property fell onto the sidewalk just as someone was walking by, you can be held legally liable. You're covered, of course, under the liability section of your homeowner's policy. But the typical homeowner's policy covers you only to a maximum of $500,000. What if the victim sues and wins a jury verdict awarding him more than $500,000? The horrible truth is that you would have to pay that yourself unless you have an umbrella policy.

An umbrella policy sits atop your auto and homeowner's liability policies to provide extra protection. It is relatively inexpensive with a $1 million umbrella policy usually costing about $200 to $300 per year. When purchasing a policy, it's important to think about your situation today as well as tomorrow. For example, will your kids be entering the dreaded teenage years and be behind the wheel? Will there be parties at your house (even though they promise there won't)? Will you be getting a trampoline to replace the swing set? You can also get umbrella protection for incidents that occur off premises. If you're planning to start traveling a lot, you should investigate such a policy.

If you already have an umbrella policy but recently inherited some money or got some other windfall, review your umbrella to be sure it offers the level of protection you need.

Typical umbrella policies require you to have homeowner's and auto liability insurance equal to the amount of your deductible. It's a good idea to obtain your umbrella liability, homeowner's, and automobile policies from the same company. Not only is it probably more cost-effective, but it can also reduce paperwork and bureaucracy if, heaven forbid, you have to file a claim. Umbrellas don't cover everything. If you own a business, a personal policy probably won't apply. Most umbrellas don't cover punitive damages or intentional acts of damage. But no matter, this type of insurance is not that expensive for the security or peace of mind it can give you. These types of policies are greatly underutilized by the American public. It is worth your time to understand what they are and if they are appropriate for your situation.

As always, if you have any questions about your policy, call your agent. Sooner rather than later. If you don't get a satisfactory response, it may be time to look for another agent. While insurance agents will help determine the kind of coverage you can buy, it is ultimately your responsibility to know what the policy covers.

The bottom line is that our homes tend to be one of our largest assets; if we can't control Mother Nature, at least we can control the financial hardship she may lay on us. Furthermore, we live in a litigious society and umbrella insurance can be a key part of protecting your assets over and above what are normal insurance levels. You've worked so hard to accumulate your assets; it would be a shame to see them slip away by someone slipping on a banana peel on your patio.

SELECTING AN INSURANCE COMPANY

With any type of insurance, research the company that is offering the policy. Generally you want a company with strong financials and that has experience offering the type of insurance you are looking to purchase. To check an insurance company's rating, check www.moodys.com, www.standardandpoors.com, or www.ambest.com.

THE FIFTH D: DIVORCE

You know the joke: You've been dieting for years and haven't lost a pound. Then suddenly you lost a hundred and eighty pounds . . . by divorcing your husband! Unfortunately, divorce is no joke, especially when it comes to financial sabotage.

In this section we'll be looking at three different scenarios:

- Before marriage
- During marriage
- After marriage

This can get very complicated because there are different laws in different states governing marital bliss and its absence. This is not do-it-yourself stuff. You definitely need professional help in getting out of a marriage. I'm just providing the basic information you need to be informed so that you can work more efficiently with your adviser when dealing with asset protection during a divorce.

A long time ago people married young, before they had time to build a career or accumulate assets. No longer. Not only are people getting married for the first time much later, they're also getting married more times period. Later first marriages and lots of second and third marriages mean people are coming to the altar with more kids and assets than ever before.

I know the idea of protecting your assets when you enter into a marriage isn't very romantic, but it is a "must-do" before you say "I do." It's hard to imagine (unless you already have been there and done that) that this person you are so in love with today can cause you financial havoc later on. But it happens more often than you think. I recently had dinner with a few friends from various parts of the country. All three were recently divorced and complaining about how their husbands had raked them over the coals. Half their assets had just disappeared in one quick swoop. If I closed my eyes, I could have sworn I was sitting at the table with men!

The point is, if you have significantly more assets than your intended, or you want to protect the assets you already have for your current children, then you need to be familiar with prenuptial agreements. Prenups can be complicated and vary from state to state, so we will touch only on the basic guidelines.

PRENUPS

So what is this thing called a prenuptial agreement? In its most basic terms a prenup is a contract that lays out the distribution of both marital and separate assets, spousal support in the event of divorce, and inheritance rights in the event of death. Typically, prenuptial agreements do not control issues like child custody, child support, or visitation. For a prenup to be valid, you both must fully disclose your assets and debts; it must be fair and signing it must be voluntary and not under duress.

To understand prenups is to understand the difference between marital and separate property. Generally speaking, marital property includes all assets acquired during a marriage. Separate property includes all assets acquired prior to the marriage in addition to gifts and inheritances during the marriage. At the time of divorce (generally), the owner retains separate property, and marital property is divided between the spouses. I'm oversimplifying the definitions, because they vary from state to state (and judge to judge), but the overall concept is the same. The purpose of a prenuptial agreement is to supersede, where possible, state laws that apply to dissolutions of marital property.

If your intended comes to you with a prenup, know what you are signing. Understand how it would affect you today, tomorrow, and in retirement. I know this is a difficult subject to discuss amid the emotions of love. You sort of feel as if you're planning your divorce before you've even gotten fitted for your wedding dress. But as with all the other topics in this chapter, better to endure a little discomfort now than to suffer grievous losses later. If you want to have a prenup, find an attorney who specializes in the field. Hopefully you live in a town that's big enough to provide business for two prenup attorneys, because your intended needs to develop his own using different legal counsel. Don't engage any lawyer who claims he can handle prenuptial agreements for you both. That's a built-in conflict of interest that sets you up to lose in a court fight during a divorce.

Even if you decide you don't want a prenup, you still need to have "the money conversation." You have to understand your intended's financial goals and values and he has to understand yours. It goes without saying, financial surprises are not very good for marriages.

POSTNUPS

Okay, you didn't have this book when you got married and as a consequence you don't have a prenup. But you want one. What to do?

First, change the name. You're married, so you can't really have a prenup. What you want is a postnup! It's really the same thing, just created after the wedding instead of before. Don't laugh; they're becoming increasingly acceptable. As with a prenup, a postnup can be utilized to compensate, as well as to waive or limit, benefits flowing from a marriage, especially if your business is on the verge of going public, or you became a successful hedge fund manager, or you just received a large inheritance. You might also want a postnup if your spouse is doing things with which you don't agree but you want to remain married. It may be something as potentially lucrative as a risky business deal, or as potentially destructive as an addiction. We're also seeing more postnups in situations in which one partner gives up a career to raise a family. Under those circumstances the postnup is used to state an alimony amount in case of divorce sufficient to reimburse you for the interruption of your career and lost pension. Couples who have created postnups often say that it is not the easiest process to go through, but a little (okay, a lot of) discomfort today can bring you much greater comfort tomorrow.

PREDIVORCE WORK

Then comes the sad day when you realize it just isn't working. You want a divorce. Before delivering the bad news to hubby, you have to do a few other things. First, update the balance sheet you prepared in Chapter 2 (what you own versus what you owe), and your income statements. In other words, get organized. Know what you have and, more important, think about what you will be losing. For example, are you a nonworking spouse and covered under your husband's health insurance?

Additionally, it is a good idea to check your credit rating. Creditors don't care that your soon-to-be ex-husband was the only one who used the card or the car. Joint debts are your debts. Each person is liable for the full amount of debt until the balance is paid. If you don't have your own credit history, you may want to start to create one. A simple way is to get department store or gasoline credit cards and use them. Pay the bill on time.

You also need to do a little research to determine how the property laws in your state are applied. Is it a community property state or equitable distribution state? Community property is observed in the following states: Arizona, California, Idaho, Louisiana, Nevada, New Mexico, Texas, Washington, and Wisconsin. In its simplest terms, community property means a fifty-fifty split. The husband and wife are deemed to equally own all property and income acquired by either one of them during the marriage.

In an equitable distribution state, assets are distributed in an equitable, but not necessarily equal, manner. The courts determine a fair, reasonable, and equitable distribution, which may be more than or less than 50 percent of any asset to either party. There are no set rules for determining who receives what or how much, but a variety of factors like the length of the marriage, standard of living, and health are taken into account by the court.

The next step is to get some referrals to a matrimonial law attorney. Ask your accountant, estate attorney, financial adviser, friends, and family. A cautionary note on friends and family: Keep in mind that each person's situation is different, so don't assume that what your friends needed or got is what you will need or get. You do not know what goes on behind closed doors. On the outside their situation may look very similar to yours, but on the inside it may be very different. If you do not have anyone to go to, a good place to start your search would be the American Academy of Matrimonial Lawyers at www.aaml.org and the American Bar Association at www.abanet.org.

As you start negotiating, understand the impact of your choices.

For example, many women tend to want to keep the home. That's understandable. But if you keep the house and he keeps the investment account, will you have enough cash flow to pay upkeep and expenses? If you sell the house, would you owe much larger capital gain taxes than he would from the sale of the investment account? My point is that you can't take things on surface value, and only focus on the here and now—you need to think long term as well.

DISTURBING STATS

According to a study by the National Marriage Project at Rutgers University, a woman's standard of living usually drops by 27 percent after a divorce, while a man's standard of living actually increases by 10 percent. Part of the problem is that women are more likely to be unaware of the family's financial status, making it difficult to negotiate a proper settlement.

Retirement Assets in Divorce One of the key areas of focus for you should be retirement savings. Thus, you must add the word "QDRO" (qualified domestic relations order) to your vocabulary. I say this because qualified retirement plans (that is, pensions, 401(k)s, 403(b)s, and so on) have special rules that you should be aware of. If you don't educate yourself, you may be leaving yourself vulnerable to unnecessary, unwanted, and costly taxes and penalties. The QDRO is a document with very specific language that allows for your soon-to-be ex-spouse to receive a designated percentage of your qualified plan account balance or benefit payments. If you are like many couples in America today, your retirement plans are one of your biggest assets, so it is imperative you work with experts. When interviewing attorneys find out how much experience they have with QDROs. You want all the i's dotted and the t's crossed, especially if you are self-employed or work for a small business that doesn't have model QDRO forms.

Notice how we didn't mention IRAs in our discussion of QDROs? You don't need a QDRO to split up your IRA accounts, but you still need to be very careful and make sure that you have the right language in your divorce agreement to ensure that it is a tax-free transfer.

AFTER THE DIVORCE

Once the divorce decree is issued, you'll discover the unhappy truth: A woman's work really is never done. There are many "to-dos" as a result of a divorce to ensure that things happen the way you want them to. Some have to do with your current situation and many have to do with your estate planning. Too many people forget to do these tasks and that can result in problems down the road. Among the simplest and easiest to forget: changing beneficiary designations on various investment accounts and life insurance policies.

The following is a list of questions to get your thought process started—it is not all-inclusive:

- Have you changed your will to reflect your new situation or is your former husband still a beneficiary? What about your living trust?
- Have you ever given your former husband a power of attorney (right to act on your behalf in legal and financial matters)? Is that power of attorney still valid? Should it be?
- Is your former husband the decision maker for your health-care directives? If something were to happen to you, is he really the person you want making the decision

to pull the plug (it might help to remember that his alimony payments stop when you die!)?

- Did you have any joint credit cards? Are they canceled? You are liable to the company for any amounts charged on the card whether or not you made the purchase. Do you really want to keep paying for the gym membership he never uses?
- How are your bank accounts and investment accounts titled? Are they "transfer on death" or "payable on death" with your ex-husband as the payee? Many people forget to change the designation on these accounts especially if their control over them did not change as a result of the divorce.

So far in this divorce section we have focused on your marriage. But many people I speak with are not as concerned with the state of their marriages as they are with their children's marriage (or potential marriage) and the best ways to protect their legacy in case of a child's divorce. This is a very valid concern and has to be approached with delicate forethought. We'll visit that topic in Chapter 10.

IGNORANCE IS NOT BLISS

If you don't protect yourself from sabotage, you end up a victim, a victim who says, "I should have, could have, would have. . . ." Ignorance in this case is far from bliss; it is financial suicide. So instead, be a person of strength. Know what you are up against and have the right tools in place. Don't assume that your spouse or significant other has everything under control. Ask questions, write things down, be a partner in your financial life. So much of our conversation these days is focused on managing investment risk that the five D's are often forgotten or put on the back burner. But your investment plan means nothing if your "risks of life" are not managed or protected well. Don't let yourself be a victim—you have the power not to be.

AT THE VERY LEAST

Review your current insurance coverages to ensure that they are aligned with your life goals.

CHAPTER SUMMARY

1. Your plan is only as good as how well you manage "life risks." Don't fall into the trap of thinking, "It's never going to happen to me."
2. Disability is more probable than death at various ages.
3. Your life insurance needs change as your life progresses.
4. Long-term care not only gives you freedom of choice, it also protects your assets.
5. Umbrella policies are highly underused.
6. What you've learned:

THE BUDDY SYSTEM

Dieting can be tough work and we can all use some guidance and support. I am sure, then, that you will not be surprised to hear that most people have the best chance of success with weight-loss programs when they have a support system that wasn't emotionally connected to them, because it helps them stay motivated by fostering accountability, self-confidence, and a realistic perspective. Funny, those are the exact same ingredients that I have found lie at the heart of investment success, and that is why I believe a majority of people should work with a financial adviser.

You may be tempted to skip this chapter if you're already working with an adviser. I urge you not to—this chapter will help you to determine if you are working with the best adviser for you.

Before you hire any kind of adviser (whether a diet counselor or a financial adviser), you must make sure that you are in the proper state of mind to be part of a relationship. If not, most likely you will not follow through with the program and will end up wasting your time and money. To get a sense of how you feel about working with a financial adviser, you may want to ask yourself three important questions:

- Are you ready to make the commitment to your program?
- Are you willing to accept help from others to achieve your goals?
- Are you willing to expose your vulnerabilities to another person?

Before you say yes, you are in an "adviser state of mind," let's delve a little deeper with the first question: Are you ready to make the commitment to your program? I'm really asking you if you are ready to make choices and possibly very hard ones at that. I'm asking, if need be, can you sacrifice something today for tomorrow? Now, I really hate putting it that way, because for many the word "sacrifice" equals deprivation, when it really doesn't have to. As we saw earlier, it's all how you look at it. I strongly suggest you focus instead on what you are going to get in the long term versus what you need to change (perhaps give up) in the short term.

The next question: Are you willing to accept help from others to achieve your goals? This isn't usually a big problem for women. As a general rule, women tend to be more open to help from others than men. But we are not all alike. So if you are the type who is much more self-directed, you must determine if you can share control.

Lastly, vulnerabilities. Think hard about this one. It is easier said than done. The best way to explain to you what I mean is to share with you my personal experiences with diet counselors. I can't tell you how many times I've made appointments with nutritionists or weight counselors only to cancel the appointment. I would always rationalize by telling myself I was too busy at work, I didn't want to spend the money, I knew what to do and I just had to do it, or (my personal favorite) I was bloated, so I needed to wait until I wasn't so swollen. But the reality was that I was embarrassed to get on a scale and have someone else, even a professional, see how much I weighed.

I see this same thing happening over and over again with people and their investments. So many people avoid going to an adviser because they think they should have saved more or invested better and are embarrassed to tell a financial professional how poorly they have done. Others convince themselves that starting an investment program means they will never be able to shop again. I even know people with MBAs who are ashamed to seek help because they think they should be more knowledgeable and/or be able to do it all themselves.

So you see, wealth success, like weight-loss success, can only be achieved if one starts the process in the right state of mind. Only once you're sure you have the correct mind-set can you begin to select an adviser who is right for you. It's important to realize that not every investment adviser is going to be right for you, and similarly, you're not going to be right for every investment adviser. The key to the right adviser-client relationship is to find a person and company that blends well with three key aspects of your overall personality:

- Your investment style
- Your communication style
- Your financial lifestyle

Throughout this chapter, you will find various questions to ask an adviser to determine if that adviser is the right person for you. At the end of the chapter you will find a summary table.

One word of caution before we get into the particulars of selecting an adviser: Hiring a financial adviser is not a substitute for taking charge of your own financial future. Your adviser will complement, not replace, your own responsibilities. After all, it's your money and your future. You don't have to be a financial genius, but you must be a willing participant.

> ## DO YOU NOT HAVE THE RIGHT "STATE OF MIND"?
>
> If you're not ready, willing, and able to expose your investments and, more important, your fears, hopes, and dreams about money to an adviser, you have three choices. The first is to do nothing. But you know that's not a responsible choice. The second is to do it yourself. That may work for you as long as you have the time, training, and the right temperament to stay committed. The third is to find a "one-stop shopping" investment solution like a target age-based fund for your retirement savings.

SELECTING A FINANCIAL ADVISER

Too often people seem overwhelmed by the process of selecting a financial adviser. Mostly it's a question of trust. They aren't certain to whom they should trust their financial future, and who can blame them? We hear story after story in the news of advisers who were just plain bad people. Unfortunately, the news doesn't cover the adviser who helped a client out during a divorce, or found a nursing home for the aged parent or took them car shopping, or just did what many advisers are doing every day, which is helping people reach their life goals. Too often the media makes advisers out to be the enemies of investors. In truth, the vast majority are trustworthy and knowledgeable professionals. The bad ones can only take advantage of people who aren't aware and involved in their own investment plans or are overcome with greed. You may not recognize a bad adviser immediately, but that bad adviser will very quickly recognize a client they can take advantage of. If you're interested in and conversant about their process and your portfolio, the bad guys don't want you as a client.

The most important single criterion for selecting an adviser is to avoid the "product pushers." The difference between a real adviser and a product pusher is obvious: An adviser talks about your needs; the product pusher doesn't care about your needs and only wants to sell you whatever it is he sells. An adviser has a defined process to analyze your specific situation and determine a product mix that best fits your needs. That process should be easy to discern in your conversation with a prospective adviser. A product pusher, in comparison, spends his time trying to convince you that you need his product. The conversation is all about why you should buy his product, not about your needs and goals. So if in your first meeting he does all the talking—run for the hills.

STARTING THE SEARCH
FOR AN ADVISER

The best way to find an adviser is through a referral from another professional or a current client of the adviser. Your CPA or attorney should have a small circle of advisers with whom they work closely. I recommend that you start your search there. They should give you at least two names from which to choose. And don't just take the names on face value. Ask questions to get a sense of why they believe these are the right advisers for you.

Here are four basic questions that you might pose to your CPA or attorney:

- How long have you worked with the advisers you're recommending?

- Why do you think these advisers are high quality?
- Why do you think these are the best advisers for me?
- Do you have any formal or informal compensation agreement with these advisers?

You're looking for advisers who work with clients who are just like you. And don't get freaked if the answer to that last question is yes. Many lawyers and CPAs work regularly with financial advisers. That's how they get to know the best ones. As long as the answers to the first three questions make sense to you, the fact that your attorney or CPA has some kind of business relationship with a financial adviser usually doesn't pose a problem. You may not even have to ask the fourth question—your CPA or attorney should be forthcoming with that fact.

If you don't have a CPA or an attorney, trade organizations or networking groups may also be a good hunting ground for an adviser, especially if you are in a specialized or niche business. For example, let's say you own an air-conditioning servicing company. Wouldn't it be nice to work with an adviser who truly understands the seasonality of your cash flows? Of course, just because someone shows up at a networking meeting does not mean that she specializes in that field, so you need to do be an inquisitive shopper.

You can, of course, also get referrals to possible advisers from friends, family, and coworkers. That's the route that most people seem to take and they typically seek out one of three kinds of people to ask for referrals: the wealthiest person they know, the most investment-savvy person they know, or a close friend or family member.

Those aren't necessarily the best sources. First, the wealthiest person you know may have very different needs and goals than you have and thus have an adviser who might not be best for you. Second, the savviest investor you know may be taking a lot more risk or using some exotic techniques that aren't best for you. Finally, recommendations from any friend or family member might be fine unless their situation is different from yours.

For all those reasons I suggest instead to get a referral from someone who looks like you. Not physically but financially. A person about the same age as you, with about the same income and the same family circumstances, will probably have similar needs and goals. If she's found an adviser she feels is well suited to her needs, chances are he may be a good fit for you, too. It helps, of course, if the person you're asking has worked with her adviser for three years or more.

One question I often hear is whether a person should use a friend or a family member not for a recommendation but as the actual adviser. My answer: It depends. You need to think about how comfortable you would be divulging some of your most intimate life details to that person. Furthermore, a big part of an adviser's role is to protect you from your emotional self. Will you listen to your brother's advice and not think he's being judgmental? Will you treat your friend with the same respect you would any other professional, keeping appointments, doing what you promised to do, and not take advantage of the relationship by, for example, not paying her customary market rates? And if your investments decline in value, will you be able to figure out whether it's your cousin's fault or just the nature of the markets? And if you aren't happy in the relationship, will you be able to fire your sister without your mother getting mad at you?

THE DUE DILIGENCE PROCESS

Now that you have a list of names for some prospective advisers, make appointments for the initial interviews. You should go prepared with a list of questions. Professional investors call this fact-finding mission "due diligence," which means you owe it to yourself to discover the good, the bad, and the ugly about something before investing in it. In your case, you want to know what your prospective advisers know, how they work, how they get paid, and, most important, how they communicate. An adviser may be a great technician, but if he or she can't communicate the how, what, and why of a potential investment and/or process in easy-to-understand English, you're not going to be able to follow that advice over the long term.

One of the most confusing aspects of choosing a financial adviser is figuring out who's what. There are a variety of different titles that advisers give themselves: wealth manager, wealth adviser, financial consultant, financial adviser, financial planner, and retirement specialist, among others. Unfortunately, there is no threshold of experience, educational requirements, or certification standards for a person to hold herself out as an adviser under any of those titles. Therefore, just recall what we learned about mutual funds: It isn't what they call themselves that's important, it's what lies underneath. In other words, it's the *who*, the *how*, the *why*, and the *what* that matter most:

- Who are they?
- How do they do what they do?
- Why do they do it that way?
- What do they charge to do it?

Your first meeting with an adviser should be a conversation, not a presentation. In other words, you should be talking just as much as the adviser—you both should be asking and answering questions at this meeting. Just as much as you want to make sure that an adviser is the right fit for you, he should want to make sure that you are a good fit for his business model. Therefore, you should both ask questions about each other's attitudes, life and financial experiences, expectations, and definition of success. It has been my experience that the best (most effective) relationships between adviser and client occur when there is an alignment of attitudes and values.

THE WHO

I can't overestimate the importance of an alignment in attitudes and values. I believe that one of the more common mistakes people make in selecting an adviser is to ignore the adviser's style or personality. And, in fact, many commentators will say performance is what you're after, not a sparkling personality. I disagree completely. Sure, performance is important, but you can get similar performance among a wide range of advisers. Still, you may only feel comfortable sharing your intimate personal and financial information with a select few of those advisers. Remember that you are partners in the wealth management process and you need to feel comfortable asking lots of questions and getting understandable answers. It's important to have an adviser who talks *to* you, not *at* you.

If you are already working with an adviser, are you a good match? Does she have the patience, personality, and professionalism that you require? Advisers often unconsciously give important signals about how they view their clients. The following are some signs that you and your adviser may not be well aligned:

- Your adviser gets a little impatient if asked to explain a concept more than once.
- He keeps looking at his watch.
- She never answers your questions completely or perhaps directly.
- He does not make eye contact.
- She uses arcane financial terms versus plain English.
- He answers phone calls, e-mails, or texts during your meetings.

If you are a married (or have a significant other) there is an additional sign—and it is one of my pet peeves. The sign is: All comments or questions are directed at your spouse.

Advisers often talk about "my client and his wife." Unfortunately, we women bear some responsibility for that because we often defer to our male counterparts on financial affairs. But we shouldn't, and our advisers shouldn't think of us as afterthoughts. If you hear your adviser say something that puts you in a subordinate role, your first thought should be, "Why did he or she say that? Is it because I appear uninterested in our financial affairs?" If that's the case, you have no one to blame but yourself. But if you're taking an active role alongside your partner in your financial plans, it's inexcusable to be treated as some sort of second-class citizen. If you don't get the attention and respect you deserve, it may be time to find another adviser. The smart advisers don't engage in that kind of behavior because they know that the facts of life say that most women will outlive men and one day you may be a sole client rather than a partner.

THE HOW AND WHY

As you know, in reality a sparkling personality is not enough. Your adviser does not have to be the life of the party but he does have to be someone you feel comfortable with and he must have a clearly defined and easily articulated process. This process should be able to take you step by step through the investment experience—how to define your goals, develop your asset allocation, select the proper investments for the allocation, and review and monitor your situation. (In regards to monitoring your situation, he should be able to convey in a clear-cut way the methods he will use and the frequency of measuring and reporting your progress. This should include an annual meeting—or more—to bring you up-to-date and inquire about any questions or concerns you may have.)

One useful tool to gain some insight into how an adviser or an investment advisory firm operates is to visit the firm's Web site. The best firms maintain Web sites that are excellent sources of information, including statements of their investment philosophy and the range of services they offer as well as answers to such important questions as, does the firm believe in asset allocation? Is it focused on "knocking the lights out" (trying the get the biggest return without taking into consideration risk) or is it more concerned with protecting clients' assets in a down market? In other words, does the firm adjust its risk profile to meet yours or do you have to adjust yours to meet the firm's? You may also learn whether the firm prefers specific types of investments.

THE WHAT

In addition to an adviser's attitudes, values, investment philosophy, and methodology, there are five fundamental areas of questioning you should do in your due diligence process:

- Experience
- Client profile
- Communications
- Disciplinary actions
- Fees

Experience First, how long has the adviser been in the business of financial advice? It's best for you if an adviser has at least five years of experience because during that time she's likely to have experienced both up markets and down markets. Everyone is a great adviser in bull markets; it's the bear markets that are really the litmus test of an adviser's ability. While five years is a minimum, you don't necessarily want to sign up with someone who has forty-plus years of experience. You also have to consider that an adviser with forty years of experience may retire sometime in the next five or so years and then you'll have to repeat the entire search process again.

If your investable assets are less than about $250,000, you'll be somewhat limited in your choice of advisers. The most experienced and successful advisers generally set minimum amounts for the accounts they handle. So you may wind up with someone who has less than five years of experience. That's okay, if he or she has the necessary support system. You may want to ask the following series of questions:

- Is he or she part of a team?
- Does he or she have a mentor in the firm?
- Does someone more senior oversee his or her decisions?
- Is he or she passionate about his or her work?
- Whom does he or she go to with questions?

If a "new" adviser is a complete solo act, that may not be your best choice. Someone with less than five years of experience still has a lot to learn, and to pretend otherwise is not good for her or her clients. And by the way, don't be fooled by gray hair or other signs of seniority. Often financial advisers are pursuing a second career after retiring or leaving some other industry. That's okay as long as they're up-front about their experience level. Indeed, someone who has worked in the same industry as you might have particularly valuable insights even though she doesn't have years of experience in personal finance. My point is that you should not assume anything. Be an inquiring mind.

Furthermore, don't assume that you will always be meeting with the "big cheese." It's important to understand with whom you will be directly working. Many advisory firms have teams. On those teams the senior person often focuses his or her time on generating new clients while perhaps less senior relationship managers or more analytical senior managers will be designated to work with clients like you. These may be—indeed, they usually are—people with very good advisory skills. Some of them, however, may not have the best marketing skills. So before you sign the dotted line, understand the roles and responsibilities of each specific team member. In other words, find out exactly who will be doing what.

In order for a financial adviser to sell securities she has to have one or more licenses. But many of the best advisers don't stop with the required licenses; they go for advanced education and accreditation under such acronyms as CFP, CFA, CIMA, and CHFC, among others. Having these designations does not guarantee that an adviser will produce better results for you, but it should tell you that the adviser is dedicated to the field, has met a certain set of educational and experience standards, and, more important, is committed to continually keeping abreast of current trends and expanding his or her knowledge base. It is a good idea to ask any adviser what he or she does about continuing education.

Total years of experience are one thing. Experience with the firm is another. I say this because there are a few advisers who are serial firm switchers. People change firms for a variety of reasons—better support or better management, for example—but there are a few who keep changing to "cash out" as often as possible. When an adviser changes from one large firm to another, he gets an up-front payment for the potential new business that he is going to bring to that firm. A red flag should be raised when you see an adviser change firms every three or four years without really having a compelling reason. If the person you're interviewing as your potential adviser has switched

CREDENTIAL ALPHABET SOUP

- *CFP or Certified Financial Planner.* This designation is awarded to people who have completed an approved course of study (sponsored by the Certified Financial Planner Board of Standards), passed a rigorous exam on financial planning, and met certain other educational, work experience, and ethical requirements.

- *ChFC or Chartered Financial Consultants.* A ChFC certificate is awarded to people who have completed a designated course of study and passed the exams on personal finance (sponsored by The American College). Many times their practice has an insurance focus.

- *CPA or Certified Public Accountant.* A CPA certification tells us that a person has passed a stringent examination on accounting and tax preparation, but it does not indicate training in other areas of personal finance. CPAs who specialized in that area many times have a Personal Finance Specialist, or PFS, designation that is offered by the American Institute of Certified Public Accountant.

- *CLU or Chartered Life Underwriter.* People with a CLU certification have completed coursework and taken exams regarding life insurance (sponsored by The American College). They do not necessarily have training in investments.

- *CFA or Chartered Financial Analyst.* A CFA has completed coursework and taken very rigorous exams (sponsored by the CFA Institute) specifically focused on global investment and portfolio management.

- *CIMA or Certified Investment Management Analyst.* A CIMA has completed coursework and passed an exam (sponsored by the Investment Management Consultants Association) whose focus is investment consulting.

firms often, ask why. Listen for an answer that is about how his clients benefited from the moves, not how he benefited.

Now, as we know, the recent financial crisis threw the financial services industry into a tailspin that resulted in a tremendous amount of adviser movement. Much of this movement was understandable, so if an adviser changed firms during that time, you may want to take it with a grain of salt. But still question him or her and understand his or her reasoning for switching firms.

Client Profile When searching for an adviser, one of the most important questions you can ask is "Who is your typical client?" You want to work with someone who is familiar with your wealth size, planning needs, and lifestyle. You don't want to be the biggest fish in the pond nor the smallest. For example, if you have $25 million and almost everyone else in the adviser's practice has less than $5 million, the adviser probably won't have a lot of experience with portfolios as large as yours. Conversely, if you have under $5 million and most clients have $20 million, you may not get the attention that you want or deserve.

Furthermore, if you have specific needs, you want to make sure that the adviser has had experience in that area. For example, if you have a special-needs child, you would want to work with someone who has a good working knowledge of the specific planning aspects required. Or if you are a small-business owner or a corporate executive, you will want an adviser with the expertise to maximize your success. Thus you want to ask a potential adviser about her areas of specialization and market niches. Obviously, no one can know everything, so you also want to ask about the expert resources available on staff or in the adviser's "virtual network."

Additionally, you want to know how many clients your adviser serves. The answer to this question may give you good insight into the adviser's practice. The days of an adviser having two thousand clients are going by the wayside with the concept of the constant buying-and-selling type of (transactional) broker. So if you hear that an adviser—the person, not the team—has more than five hundred clients, you might wonder if that adviser will have time to service your needs. Generally speaking, if you are a million-dollar client, your adviser should have no more than two hundred clients. If you are investing more than $10 million, make sure your adviser has fewer than one hundred clients. Obviously, a firm that uses a team approach can work efficiently with more clients.

Communications We all know how important communication is to a relationship, and when you are interviewing advisers, you want to have a clear understanding about the person-to-person, phone, e-mail, and snail-mail communications. How often should you expect to get documents, phone calls, or e-mails from your adviser? Don't assume anything. Think about what you need and expect—and see if it is feasible for the adviser. For instance, some people want a phone call from their advisers if the market goes down more than 10 percent. Others don't want to be bothered. Some want to speak every week; some only at the annual review. There is no general right answer. You want to make sure your communication needs match what your adviser is offering.

Disciplinary Actions One of the most important questions you should ask a potential adviser is "Have you ever been publicly disciplined for any unlawful or unethical actions in your professional career?" Most people just aren't comfortable posing that kind of question directly. Still, you need to know the answer, and there are ways other than asking directly to find it. There are four typical types of client complaints: churning, unsuitable investments, overconcentration, and material omissions or misrepresentations. Churning means that an adviser keeps buying and selling investments with the intent to increase his commissions. Unsuitable investments are those that are not in line with a client's risk tolerance, risk capacity, or investment needs. Concentration is putting too much of a client's money in a single or just a few investments that produce outsize commissions for the adviser. And misrepresentation or material omissions are not telling the client the truth and the whole truth. You'll be less likely to run into these kinds of problems if you steer away from the product pushers.

Nevertheless, it doesn't hurt to be cautious. Do some background research by going to the Financial Industry Regulatory Authority (FINRA). FINRA was created in July 2007 through the consolidation of the National Association of Security Dealers (NASD) and the member regulation, enforcement, and arbitration functions of the New York Stock Exchange. You many want to check out www.finra brokercheck.org or call toll-free at (800) 289-9999 to learn about any compliance records and complaints. Information about certain investment adviser firms is available through the SEC's Investment Adviser Public Disclosure (IAPD) program at (800) 732-0330. You may also obtain information about brokerage firms, individual brokers, and investment adviser firms, as well as information on individual investment advisers, through your state securities regulator. You can find out how to get in touch with your state's securities regulator through the North American Securities Administrators Association, Inc., on their Web site, www.nasaa.org. Don't be surprised if the adviser you're interviewing has had one or two complaints lodged against him or her. Financial advisers sometimes become the target of complaints from investors who are looking for someone else to blame for their own mistakes. What you don't want to see is a lengthy history of complaints.

Fees Advisers get paid in any of several ways—a flat fee, commissions, a percentage of assets under management, or hourly, for example. No one way is the best way and often it will be a combination of two or more ways. For example, you may pay a flat fee to have a financial plan prepared, your investments may fall under an "assets under management" fee (the average is between 1 percent to 2 percent) while your insurance pays commissions (varies by type). It all varies by adviser and products. The message here is for your adviser to be very transparent and clear on how she charges and that you have a good understanding of what you are getting for that fee. You want to avoid situations in which you pay twice. That can happen, for example, if you pay an hourly fee to an adviser who is also collecting a commission at the same time on products she advises you to buy. That isn't common, but it does happen. Get a written statement explaining how your adviser is paid and if you at any point suspect that your adviser isn't being up-front about fees or is having trouble explaining how she gets paid, it's time to find another adviser. Remember, if you work effectively with your adviser, your fee is not only for investment products, it's for having a guide and a partner to help you increase the probability of meeting your life goals over the long term.

Can you do it yourself with no-load funds or ETFs and pay the minimum amount of fees possible? Of course you can. But will you? Remember the three T's from Chapter 3—temperament, time, and training.

Have you noticed anything? I did not suggest you ask about their performance or track record. Hopefully by now you are not surprised by this and understand that it is not a question that can be answered with one simple number. An adviser has many clients with different needs, different risk tolerances, different portfolios, and thus different returns. There is not one performance number and no guarantees of

---

THREE T'S REMINDER

Temperament: Are you going to stick to your discipline when markets are acting crazy? Will you have the courage to buy as prices fall or to sell when they're going up?

Time: Do you have the time to do the initial research and then the constant follow-up required to build and monitor a portfolio of stocks and bonds? Do you want to take a three-week vacation and not have to worry about what's happening to your portfolio?

Training: Do you have access to the resources, research, and overall knowledge that a professional investment manager has? Are you truly up for the task?

---

future performance. Don't fall into the trap of chasing returns. You should only be concerned with what your specific goals and targets are. Many times when you are disappointed with the performance it is because your expectations were not managed correctly.

WHOM TO TRUST

The process of hiring and working with an adviser shouldn't be something that causes you anxiety. There is a tremendous amount of negative commentary about fees in the media—some warranted and some not. Don't think everyone is out to overcharge you and rip you off. Now that you have read this book, you are more equipped than ever to work with an adviser because you have a clear understanding of what you want and a broad understanding of how you have to go about planning for and implementing a strategy to maximize your potential for success. In other words, you are an educated consumer.

Therefore, the answer to the question of whom to trust is simple—trust yourself, as long as you do the work, keep your greed in check, and remember this: If something sounds too good to be true, it is!

As you do your work and meet with potential advisers, bring a list of written questions so that you can stay focused, and take notes so you can compare answers from different advisers. Also, don't be freaked out if an adviser asks you to either send them in advance or bring with you your balance sheet, investment statements, tax returns, and other documents. Some advisers like to use them during the interviewing process to reduce or be more targeted with their questioning. If you don't feel comfortable, let the adviser know that you would rather chat first, but that you are prepared to share all your information upon engagement.

That leads me to a question I hear very often: Shouldn't I use several advisers to make sure that I don't put all my eggs in one basket? Ten years ago I might have said yes, because investment management was transactional in nature and advisers traded individual stocks and bonds and only sold other investment products manufactured by the companies they worked for. Today, because the investment management approach is more consultative (asset allocation) than transactional and advisers have access to a multitude of different investment managers (versus only proprietary) through what is known as open architecture, I believe that you can have the best success working with one overall adviser. Think of it this way: If you were to go to a doctor, would you only give him or her access to half of your body?

Please don't misunderstand what I mean by working with one overall adviser. I am referring to the cases where an adviser practices asset allocation and uses a variety of investment tools and solutions, not (with a capital N) an adviser who actually (supposedly) runs money and in only one specific way (à la Bernie Madoff).

BREAKING UP IS HARD TO DO

So far we have been discussing hiring an adviser. But we all know relationships can go bad. So when should you fire your adviser? The answers, not surprisingly, are very similar to when you would end a personal relationship. Just as with personal relationships, many times problems stem from a breakdown in communication. Just as your significant other cannot read your mind, neither can your adviser. So if you are unhappy, bring it to his or her attention and see if you can work it out. If not, it's time to move on. The following are some of the more common reasons that advisers and their clients "break up":

- *You grow over time but she doesn't.* You may have started with someone early in your career when your situation was pretty simple, but over time your situation has gotten much more complicated and you need more complex solutions and advice that is outside of her expertise.
- *He's just not that into you.* This is the opposite of the situation we just cited. You may have started with your adviser early in his career and over the years the profile of his client has changed and you no longer fit within the business model and tend to be an afterthought.
- *She never calls or takes you for granted.* You never hear from your adviser; she doesn't return your phone calls promptly; she doesn't follow through. Whatever. When you do hear from her, she talks in a language that you don't understand, or seems annoyed that you are bothering her. If there are repeated administrative problems, she doesn't take ownership for it (even if it was out of her control), and does

nothing to resolve the problem and doesn't recognize the inconvenience it may have caused you.

- *He overpromises and underdelivers.* One of the most important jobs of an adviser is to manage expectations and help you to understand the volatility of the markets. Advisers who promise too much are the ones who disappoint when things are beyond their control. It's important to understand the difference between unanticipated market fluctuations versus the financial adviser doing something wrong.
- *She doesn't listen.* Need I say more? As we know, there is a huge difference between hearing and listening. Hearing is "to perceive sound with the ear," whereas listening is "to consider with thoughtful focused attention."
- *He breaks the bond of trust.* No explanation needed.

TEN SIGNS THAT YOUR ADVISER IS "JUST NOT THAT INTO YOU"

1. He doesn't call you back in a timely fashion.
2. She doesn't make an effort to meet with you at least annually.
3. He doesn't check in when market conditions are distressing.
4. She intimidates you or talks "over your head."
5. He doesn't listen.
6. She doesn't understand you.
7. He only calls when he wants something.
8. She can't explain where she's been or what she's done.
9. He doesn't put you first.
10. She's too good to be true.

Most people stay with an adviser they are not happy with because they don't know who to go to next. But with the help of this chapter, hopefully you now know how to go about finding someone who will be the best fit for you. Your adviser is a very important partner in your life, and generally speaking, the more you are into them, the more you will be into being a partner in your finances and the greater probability for your success.

What most people want and need in a financial adviser is simple: someone who is responsible, accountable, and predictable. This can only happen if an adviser has integrity, experience, and knowledge, and, most important, an energy and passion for the work of helping you reach your goals. By following these basic suggestions, you can find a suitable adviser to keep you on the road to financial stability and independence. But always remember this: Your adviser is your financial partner, not your parent. An adviser is your guide, not your caretaker. You are ultimately responsible for your own success.

Summary of Questions	
SITUATION	**QUESTIONS TO ASK AN ADVISER**
All—want to find out: • Who they are, for example, do they have the patience, personality, and professionalism that you require? • How do they do what they do? • Why do they do it that way? • What do they charge to do it?	• How long have you been in the financial advisory business? • How many firms have you been with and why? • What do you do about continuing education? • Who is your typical client? • Do you specialize in my specific need? • What expert resources are available on staff or in your "virtual network"?

Summary of Questions	
SITUATION	**QUESTIONS TO ASK AN ADVISER**
	• How many clients do you serve? • What is your communication style and process? How often should I expect to get documents, phone calls, or e-mails from you? • Have you ever been reprimanded and why? • What is your fee structure?
Adviser new in the business—want to find out: • What is their support system?	• Are you part of a team? • Do you have a mentor in the firm? • Does someone more senior oversee your decisions? • Are you passionate about your work? • Who do you go to with questions?
Asking a CPA for an adviser referral—want to find out: • Why do they believe this is the right fit for you?	• How long have you worked with the advisers you're recommending? • Why do you think these advisers are high quality? • Why do you think that these are the best advisers for me? • Do you have any formal or informal compensation agreement with these advisers?

AT THE VERY LEAST

If you are currently using an adviser, have a think about your relationship. Are you getting the service that is right for you?

If you are not currently using an adviser, think about if you have the time, temperament, and training to do it on your own.

CHAPTER SUMMARY

1. An adviser can foster accountability, self-confidence, and a realistic perspective.
2. Before you engage any adviser, you must ensure that you have the proper state of mind to be in such a relationship.
3. Hiring a financial adviser is not a substitute for taking charge of your own financial future. Your adviser will complement, not replace, your own responsibilities.
4. The five fundamental areas of questioning you should do in your due diligence processes are experience, client profile, communications, disciplinary actions, and fees.
5. Advisers should be up-front and have a transparent fee structure.
6. What you've learned:

PASSING IT ON

Remember playing Telephone when we were kids, where we would whisper a short message into the ear of the person sitting next to us, and that person would pass it on to the person next to him or her, and so on down the line? Finally, the last person to hear the message would say it out loud. Seldom did the message arrive in its original form. In fact, it was usually so garbled that it evoked fits of uncontrollable laughter. But besides providing great amusement, the game showed how easily information can become corrupted by bad communication.

The same can be said about passing on your wealth to your heirs and passing on good money skills to your children. Both can be corrupted by bad communication.

Passing on your wealth to your children in the best manner possible takes some work on your part. Not only does it take careful thought and consideration, in some cases it takes a little (okay, a lot) of courage to share your plans with your family. I say this because when it comes to estate planning, "fair" does not always mean an even split.

The estate-planning conversation can be difficult and fraught with emotion, but it is a conversation you must have. Any pain that may be involved with estate-planning discussions is often significantly less than the pain felt by family members whose spouses or parents ignored discussions and failed to implement planning strategies. Parents many times delay this discussion because of the unpleasant overtones connected with growing old and dying. Adult children may not mention estate planning to avoid appearing greedy or as if they are trying to "take over."

I know these types of conversations may be the last things you want to think about. Who really wants to talk about death? But in reality, estate planning is a conversation about the living. It is about making sure that the people (and pets, too!) you love will benefit in the future as you see fit from your life's successes. The best estate plans are communicated in advance to heirs.

DON'T BE A STATISTIC

- 51 percent of parents and 41 percent of adult children haven't talked about the location of assets because they "haven't gotten around to it."
- 39 percent of married late boomers have no will.
- 37 percent of adult children would not be able to find their parents' critical documents to settle their estate and 28 percent wouldn't know what to do or whom to contact.

Source: MainStay Investments.

ESTATE PLANNING

Our aversion to talking about our certain, though hopefully far away, death is the single biggest hurdle we encounter when it comes to devising an estate plan. And yes, we *all* need an estate plan, even if our assets are limited. It may be something as simple as a beneficiary designation, or a simple will, or it may consist of multiple trusts and bequests that you need the help of an estate lawyer to decipher. But without an estate plan, guess what? In most states it will be some cranky bureaucrats who will decide who gets what part of your estate. Do you really want to let that happen to the loved ones you leave behind?

It's never too early to have an estate plan, but it's also never too late. When you get yours set up, you'll want to review it at least every five years and certainly every time some major event occurs in your life: marriage, kids, divorce, or illness. I have seen too many people forget to update their will after a divorce and end up leaving assets to someone they definitely didn't want to have them and shortchanging those to whom they truly wanted to bequeath something.

The basics of estate planning are pretty straightforward, although some plans can become extremely complicated. In its simplest form, an estate plan should have two purposes. The first and most important purpose of an estate plan is to make sure that your assets get distributed as you desire. The secondary purpose is to distribute these assets in the most tax-efficient manner. (This chapter is based on the estate tax scheme that was in place in 2009. For 2010 there is no federal estate tax unless Congress takes some action. It is anticipated that there will be an estate tax in the future. Be advised, though, that the exemption and tax rate amounts may be different from those highlighted in this chapter.)

When we talk about the distribution of your assets, your estate plan should answer four questions:

- Who
- What
- When
- How

WHO

On the surface, the "who" question is pretty simple: To whom do you want your assets to go to? Recall that in Chapter 1 when we discussed goal setting we determined that your money could go to one of four places: you, your family, a charity (or charities), or the government. That remains the case at death. Your assets can go to you in the sense that they are used to pay debts you may owe, including funeral expenses. And the remainder can be distributed among heirs, charities, and the government in various ways. Most people desire to leave the greatest possible amount to their heirs (and/or charity) and the least amount possible to the government. Others make a conscious effort to spend their last dollar on their last day and leave little or nothing to anyone. Any combination is fine, as long as it's what you want and what you intended. There's nothing wrong with dying broke as long as it is an intentional act and you spend that last dollar the day you die and not ten years before your death. Keep in mind, typically this type of plan will only work if you are a clairvoyant.

If you are married you need to think about a plan that assumes your partner dies first. This is particularly important for women, who tend to outlive men. It's even more important for women who are second or third wives. I've heard too many stories about second wives unable to maintain their lifestyles or whose children were inadvertently left very little because a negligent husband didn't prepare a proper estate plan. And, by the way, don't believe him (or her, in some cases) when you hear, "Don't worry, I took care of it." That "don't worry" is closely akin to our own promise to "start my diet Monday." Too often the plan is in his head or the planning was done in fits and starts, but the finalized document wasn't signed and thus is useless. You should insist on understanding what exists and how the assets are going to pass. I suggest you and your spouse meet with the estate attorney and get familiar with the plan. It may be beneficial as well to bring along your financial adviser so you can be sure that you and your spouse's investment assets are titled according to the plan as well as to be an informed resource for you in your time of need. Don't be afraid to ask questions or say, "I do not understand, please review it." If the attorney speaks solely in lawyer jargon and cannot talk to you in plain English, you might want to seek an attorney who can. I can't stress enough that you should never feel bad about not understanding or posing questions to an expert until you feel completely comfortable and knowledgeable about your plan. It's an estate planner's duty to lay out your plan in a clear, concise, and comprehensible manner. Your responsibility, on the other hand, is to let him or her know when you are not clear or comfortable about something. He or she can't read your mind. If your significant other is in the meeting as well and asks a question you don't understand, don't let your partner just say, "Don't worry, I'll explain it to you when we get home." Rather, insist on the expert answering your questions, because too often "when we get home" means never (because your partner might not understand it either). You are a partner in this plan and deserve to understand everything before you sign on any dotted line.

WHAT

The "what" question is pretty obvious. It's whatever you have. But who gets what is not always such an obvious choice, especially when one child has more wealth than another or when one child is a spendthrift. You must consider the needs of each of your heirs as well as their willingness and ability to manage a particular asset. What you may find is that "fair" is not always "equal." For example, I know a couple with two grown children, a son and a daughter. The son is very successful in his own right and the daughter did not choose a high-paying career, but works hard. The parents want to ensure that their daughter will be able to maintain a certain standard of living, so they plan to split their assets unevenly, with approximately a third going to their son and two-thirds to their daughter.

The balance-sheet exercise you did in Chapter 2 should give you a good overview of what you own that would be distributed on your death. Also, be sure to include any life insurance policies that you own. The value of the policy is included in your estate unless it is in an irrevocable life insurance trust, which we'll talk about later.

WHEN

The "when" question is a lot tougher than the who and the what, mostly because few of us know the date of our death far in advance. Think of "when" as one or more of three choices:

- Before death
- Immediately after death
- Sometime later after death

People may want to give assets away before they die because of the potential tax savings as well as the emotional advantages of giving away assets while still alive in the form of gifts. That's why I always told my father he should do that, not for my benefit, of course, but so he could have the ultimate delight of watching one of his pride and joys spend his money. I'm kidding, of course (but not really). Seriously, though, giving away money before you die not only reduces the size of your current estate, but also keeps it from growing inside your estate (it will grow, instead, in the hands of the giftee) to the point that your heirs could wind up paying more in estate taxes. The second "when" is pretty obvious. You die, your will is read and approved, and your assets distributed. The "sometime later" part of "when" relates mostly to the use of trusts to set certain conditions an heir must meet to lay claim to the assets you leave them. It may be simply attaining a certain age, say twenty-one, or your terms may require an heir to obtain a college degree or achieve some other goal you set. Usually it is the age, the maturity, and the financial sophistication of your heirs that are the driving forces behind these decisions. This is especially important for those of you who have young children and/or grandchildren or spendthrift spouses. Many times the question that is posed to you is this, "How much control, if any, do you want from the grave?"

HOW

The final question, "how," is determined by the who, what, and when. You have two choices: pass your assets outright, or set up methods that allow you to maintain some sort of control over the assets. As explained earlier, the usual form of maintaining control after death is through a trust. There are many kinds of trusts and the provisions of those trusts can vary widely. The trust area is very specialized and you should work with someone whose primary business is estate and trust work rather than an attorney who dabbles in this area.

So to summarize the decisions you must make about the disposition of your assets:

- Who: You, heirs, charity, government
- What: Net assets
- When: During life, at death, at a later date
- How: Outright or maintain some control

WHO OWNS WHAT

Before you can develop any estate plan you must know how the property in your (and your spouse's) estate (bank accounts, investment accounts, real estate, and so on) is titled and accordingly owned and thus passed on (see the appendix for explanations of the different types of ownership). Don't be overwhelmed by the different names of the types of co-ownership, just focus on who gets what upon the death of you or your partner. For estate-planning purposes you need to be able to answer two questions:

- What happens to the property if I die?
- What happens to the property when my co-owner dies?

In other words, does it automatically go to the other owner or a beneficiary of your choice? Too often, I see people taking the titling decision too lightly. Do not do so! The titling decision requires forethought and focus. You should always take into consideration with whom you may wind up sharing ownership of an asset, if your co-owner were to die first. It is possible, for example, that you wind up owning property with your child's spouse (because your child passed) and he or she may act in ways you never expected. Who knew your son-in-law had a shoe fetish and he was dipping into your investment account and buying closets full of Jimmy Choos?

Additionally, often in the case of married couples in which only one spouse worked, the ownership of assets can be out of whack with the working spouse holding everything in his or her name. Therefore, often one of the first items "to do" when creating your estate plan is to make sure that there are enough assets in both names to fund the estate tax exemption amounts. Sometimes you may hear this being referred to as "equalizing your estates." Keep in mind that "equalizing your estate" does not necessarily always mean that each of the respective spouses owns all of the property fifty-fifty, rather that the ownership is structured in such a way that you are able to achieve your estate-planning goals in the most tax-efficient manner.

ESTATE TAX MINIMIZATION

Once you determine the who, what, when, and how, you want to make sure that it is done in the most tax-efficient manner. The tax I am referring to here is the federal estate tax.

Federal estate tax is a separate tax system from the personal income tax system. The estate tax, in essence, is a tax on your right to transfer property at your death. A federal estate tax in some form or other has been around since 1916. But don't worry, the high exemptions in place today ($3.5 million for 2009) ensure that the vast majority of estates are not subject to estate tax. It is estimated that only approximately 2 percent of deaths result in an estate tax. So we will touch upon it briefly. (Again, please note that exemption amounts may change as tax laws change.)

The federal estate tax only applies to net estates that are greater than the estate tax exemption amount. This means you can pass (at death) up to that amount to your heirs free of estate taxation regardless of whether you are married or not. Everybody has his or her own exemption amount. So if you are married, you and your husband each have your own estate and thus your own exemption amount.

CALCULATING ESTATE TAXES

A $3.5 million dollar estate may sound like a bigger estate than yours, but a word of caution: your estate may be larger than you think. Especially for those of you who have appreciated residences, life insurance policies (not held in trust), retirement plans, jewelry, art collections, and so on. If your net assets are in excess of these amounts you will most likely owe an estate tax. To illustrate this, let's examine a simple example. In the chart below, you will find the financial profile of Jane, who is single.

Market value of assets (a)	$5 million
Life insurance (a)	$1 million
Mortgage and other loans (b)	($2 million)
Net estate (a − b) = (c)	**$4 million**
Estate tax exemption (d)	($3.5 million)
Net taxable estate (c − d) = (e)	**$500,000**
Tax rate (f)	45%
Estate tax (e × f) = (g)	**$225,000**
Net after tax (e − g) (h)	$275,000
Total inheritance (d + h)	**$3,775,000**

As you can see, Jane's net estate is greater than the exemption amount of $3.5 million. Therefore, she will not be able to pass her entire estate of $4 million to her niece estate tax free—the amount in excess of the exemption amount ($500,000) will be subject to estate tax. So (assuming the tax rate is 45 percent) instead of inheriting the entire $500,000 her niece will get the net after-tax amount. In this example it would be $275,000 net after-tax. Therefore the total that her niece is to receive out of the $4 million is the sum of the exemption amount and the net after-tax amount ($3.5 million + $275K).

If Jane was married and instead of passing her assets to her niece she passed them on to her husband, the entire $4 million dollars would be passed on to him. Why the difference? Because transfers between spouses are subject to what is known as the "unlimited marital deduction." Generally, you can transfer any or all of your assets to your spouse, if he or she is a U.S. citizen, without incurring any estate tax.

You may be thinking, "If my goal is to transfer assets in the most 'tax-efficient' manner, then I should just pass everything to my spouse so I won't have to pay an estate tax." Sounds simple, doesn't it? So why, you may ask, do people say that estate planning is so complex? Two reasons: first, because leaving all your money to your spouse may not align with your desires (about who, what, when, and how), and second, because it isn't always the most tax-efficient way to transfer wealth. (To see what I mean, check out the example of our married couple, Lucy and Ricky, in the appendix.)

LIFETIME GIFTING

You can get around some of the estate tax provisions by giving away money prior to your death, but remember that gifts can be subject to the "gift tax." Don't worry, there is an exemption for the gift tax, too. It allows you to give away or gift up to $1 million of taxable gifts to whomever you choose during your life without owing any federal gift tax. Obviously, you only want to make large gifts to your heirs if you have more than enough assets to support your lifestyle until your passing.

A gifting program may also be useful if you are in a second marriage or have a significant other who is not the parent of your children. I say this because gifts to these children during your life may provide some piece of mind (on all parts). For some families tensions between a second spouse and children from a first marriage arise due to concern over whether there is going to be "anything left."

GIFTS THAT ARE NOT TAXING

There are ways to gift that do not generate a current gift tax. The four most common are:

- Annual exclusion gifting
- 529 plans
- Medical and educational expenses
- Lifetime exemption

Annual Exclusion Gifting A person can give away up to $13,000 each to as many individuals as desired each year without incurring any gift tax. The IRS adjusts this amount based on inflation, but only in increments of $1,000. To get the biggest bang out of your buck, instead of just giving cash away, give away assets that have a good potential for growth. In essence, that allows you to transfer the potential growth on that asset free of estate taxes as well. Check out the appendix to see how this works (mathematically) by comparing two different giftors (Laverne and Shirley) who own the same amount and type of assets but gift differently.

529 Plans The second rule also relates to the annual exclusion ($13,000) of gifts but here only if the gift is placed into a 529 plan. A 529 plan is a tax-deferred college saving vehicle named after the section of the IRS code that created them. These plans are particularly effective estate-planning tools because they allow a donor to give away in one year an amount equal to five years of regular gift tax exclusions. That means you could contribute $65,000 ($13,000 × 5) to a 529 plan in one year. If you're married, your spouse can give an equal amount. Thus a couple can contribute $130,000 in one year to a 529 plan gift and estate tax free. Think of it this way: You want to help fund your grandchild's future college education and want to maximize the tax-deferred growth benefits of a 529 plan. Let's say your grandchild is going to start college in seven years. Which account do you think would most likely have the largest balance when he is ready to start college: one in which $60,000 grows for seven years tax-deferred or one in which you deposit $13,000 per year for five years? Barring any extreme market events, because of the power of compounding, the answer, generally, is the former account.

Another benefit of 529 plans is that the values of the accounts are not includable in your estate, even though you could make changes to the beneficiaries, allocations, and so on up until your last breath. An important footnote to 529 plans: Don't worry, if your grandchild decides not to go to college, someone else will be able to use the funds for college, perhaps even yourself! (Hey, in 2007 a ninety-five-year-old woman graduated from the University of Kansas!) You may want to check out the Web site www.collegesavings.com for a listing and commentary on the various 529 plans available.

Medical and Educational Expenses This is a very simple and, unfortunately, very underutilized way to gift assets to someone tax-free. If you make payments on behalf of another directly to a medical provider or educational institution, the payments are not considered taxable transfers, no matter how much and no matter what other gifts you have made. Say it costs $6,000 to send your grandson to nursery school. If you write the check out directly to the school (instead of giving your kids a check that they deposit and, in turn, write their own check to the school), you will still be able to gift the $13,000 annual exclusion amount to the child's parents without any tax consequence. But if you write the check out to one of the parents, you will only be able to give that parent an additional $7,000 that year tax-free.

Lifetime Exemption People who have large estates may want to make larger gifts to their friends and family than the ones just mentioned. The IRS allows you to gift a total of $1 million over your lifetime without incurring any gift tax. Upon your death, that million dollars (plus any growth on those assets) will not be included as part of your estate since you have given it away and no longer own it. But keep in mind that what the IRS giveth, it usually take away—meaning that upon your death, your estate tax exemption is reduced by your lifetime exemption gifts. For example, if the estate tax exemption amount is $3.5 million and you utilized your lifetime exemption amount of $1 million, upon your passing your estate tax exemption amount will be reduced to $2.5 million.

TWO SECRETS OF ESTATE TAX MINIMIZATION

Estate tax minimization is all about the numbers. No matter what the actual numbers are, the two key "secrets" to estate tax minimization are: (1) Take advantage of each person's exemption amounts, and (2) take advantage of gifting strategies to transfer assets during life to heirs without incurring any gift tax as well as reducing the value of your estate for estate tax purposes.

As you go through this process, you may find that some of your estate goals may contradict one another. For example, you want to minimize your estate tax today (so you would have to gift or transfer assets to your children), but you want to maintain complete control over your assets (which does not a gift make). You can't maintain complete control of those assets and not have them included in your estate. It just doesn't work that way. So you need to decide which one—estate tax minimization or control—is more important. You are the only one who can answer that question and there is no right answer. What is right for you may not be right for me. What I am saying is that goal planning for your estate plan is all about choices and trade-offs, both from a financial and emotional standpoint. It seems that even in death we can't have it all.

ESTATE-PLANNING DOCUMENTS

Now you're ready to put a plan on paper. Remember, without a plan your documents are most likely flawed, and without the documents, your plan will not be executed. A plan without necessary documents is like a rowboat without oars. You'll just be drifting aimlessly rather than getting where you want to go. Remember also that your estate attorney's job is to create the documents for you (not to remind you time and time again to sign them)—your job is to make sure that they are signed, sealed, and delivered. Too often, documents are left in a drawer to be executed "soon."

If you never get around to creating and executing your plan, a default plan will be provided for you by your state. As we mentioned earlier, every state has what is known as "intestate succession statutes" and these provide for the distribution of your estate to your spouse and relatives in a specific order (in most states, the surviving spouse receives one-third of the estate with the balance of the assets equally divided among the surviving children). Instead, wouldn't you rather have a plan that best fits your needs and those of your family?

Unfortunately, most people will tell you that they know they need an estate plan, yet only one in four people who need a will actually has one. Are you one of them?

Let's imagine that your spouse is going to pass before you. Therefore, you are the one who will have to deal with all the issues, fights, and complications at your spouse's death. So if I were you, and I didn't have an executed plan, or I had an old plan that hadn't been updated for years, I would get the ball rolling as soon as possible. As I said, a plan is only as good as the documents that are incorporated and executed in it, and I've heard too many stories about people who procrastinated—"I'll do it when we get back from vacation or when work slows down"—and events overtook them.

We'll start with the simplest documents and work our way up the complexity scale. Keep in mind, though, that just because your estate is not large enough to be subject to tax doesn't mean you don't need documents to ensure that your assets pass to your heirs in the exact way you desire. Furthermore, make sure that the people who need to know where your documents are and whom your advisers are know this information.

ESSENTIAL INCAPACITY DOCUMENTS

The next few documents we will discuss are must-haves for everyone to have in order, no ifs, ands, or buts! These documents are typically implemented during the estate planning process, but they apply mostly during your life. They give the directives in the event you are incapacitated and can't act on your own behalf. Incapacity documents can sometimes create a lot of confusion because people tend to call the same documents different names and different states have somewhat different documents. Don't get caught up in the names, but instead pay attention to what they are intended to accomplish. The first two deal with health-related problems and the last one deals with financial matters. Check with your specific state to be clear on what documents it requires for these situations. Also, a reminder: These directives are not part of your will. Wills are usually looked at after death.

Again, these documents are to be looked when you are living but incapacitated. The three documents are:

- Health-care proxy
- Living will
- Durable power of attorney

The first two of these documents allow you to set out your wishes for medical care: a health-care proxy and a living will. I urge you to prepare both. In some states, the living will and the health-care proxy are combined into a single form, often called an advance health-care directive.

With a health-care proxy, also known as a durable power of attorney for health care, you are appointing a person (a proxy) to step into your shoes to make decisions about your health-care treatment in the event that you are unable to provide informed consent. This only comes into effect when you become unable to speak for yourself. You do not have to be terminally ill; you only need to be unable to communicate your wishes due to a temporary or permanent illness or injury. Until then, you continue to be in charge of making your own health-care decisions. The proxy can be revoked and you always have the right while you are competent to sign a new health-care proxy.

If you don't have this document, your state law will decide who will make these decisions on your behalf. It may be a doctor, family members, or hospital administrators. Are their beliefs and feelings going to be exactly the same as yours?

The second document, a living will, allows you to state whether you want your life prolonged if you are suffering from a terminal illness or if you're permanently unconscious. In general, a living will indicates whether you want certain treatments withheld or withdrawn if they are only prolonging the dying process or if there is no hope of recovery.

Discuss your choices with your physician and give a copy of the documents to your "stand-in" (whomever you have chosen to follow through on your wishes) and other family members. It's worse than a bummer if you have done all this work and no one knows these documents exist and you are treated in a way you never would have wanted.

The third document, the durable power of attorney for property, is another document you should consider having. This document allows you to designate a person to act for you and handle financial matters should you be unable or perhaps unavailable to do so. (You can't pay your electric bill if you are unconscious.)

I am sure you will agree that the person you select to "stand in your shoes" from a medical and/or financial perspective must be someone who:

- You trust
- Knows you well and understands your preferences
- Can make educated decisions
- Will honor your wishes

Please, make these documents a priority. Studies have shown that although the majority of people believe having some form of advance directives is a good idea, most people have not actually developed advance directives for themselves. Many people state that they want their family to make health-care decisions; however, less than half of these people have ever discussed the issue and their specific desires with family members.

In many cases, you can obtain forms from your health-care provider. Forms are also readily available online. You may want to make an appointment with your doctor to be sure you are aware of the implications of your choices. These documents should be reviewed every few years or so. If you do change them, make sure the appropriate parties have the new forms.

The bottom line is that I know thinking about these directives can be frightening and hopefully they will never be needed. But without them you risk subjecting those you love (including yourself) to incredible amounts of grief and suffering.

Incapacity Documents	
INCAPACITY DOCUMENT	DESCRIPTION
Health-care proxy	Appoints a person (a proxy) to step into your shoes to make decisions about your health-care treatment in the event that you are unable to provide informed consent
Living will	Indicates whether you want certain treatments withheld or withdrawn if they are only prolonging the dying process or if there is no hope of recovery
Durable power of attorney	Allows you to designate a person to act for you and handle financial matters should you be unable or perhaps unavailable to do so

WILLS

Almost everyone needs a will, especially if you own property or have minor children. In its most basic terms a will is a legal document that instructs how and to whom your property will be distributed upon death, who will be the guardians of minors and/or incapacitated heirs, who will and how to pay your debts and expenses, what trusts are to be created, and who will manage the process of winding up your affairs (generally known as the executor or executrix). Obviously the financial knowledge of the person chosen to manage this process should be aligned with the complexity of the estate. For more complex estates, some people choose their lawyer, financial adviser, or, more and more frequently, a corporate trustee (or a combination thereof). People with smaller and simpler estates generally choose their spouse, a family member, or a close friend. But keep in mind that very little in this world is simple or easy.

Once a will is created, it is not set in stone. It is revocable, which means it can be changed in any way you wish and as often as you wish up until your death, at which time it takes effect. A will should be

SELECTING EXECUTORS AND/OR TRUSTEES

An executor or trustee is the one who carries out the directives in the estate and/or trust. This role can involve investment selection and management, tax return preparation, legal negotiations, distribution management, administration, and so on. Many people when naming someone to this role believe that that person will feel much honored to be chosen. If truth be told, for many named executors or trustees it is not an honor but a burden. Why? Instead of telling you, ask yourself these three questions:

- Does the person you have selected have the *time* to take on this responsibility?
- Does the person you have selected have the *temperament* to deal with all the family issues and emotions?
- Does the person you have selected have the expertise and specific *training* to do all this?

Often the answer is no, and thus you may want to seek out the assistance of a corporate trustee. Your estate-planning attorney, accountant, or financial adviser should be able to provide a referral to one.

updated to reflect your changing life situations, including your changing tax status or changing tax laws. It should have some flexibility built into it. One mistake a lot of people make is to assume that if their spouse has a will, they don't need one. Wrong! You must have your own. If you outlive your partner, obviously it doesn't matter. But what happens if you die first or if you die together in an airplane crash, or if you're both involved in an automobile accident that kills your spouse instantly but you linger for a few days before passing away? Bad news! Because, if you remember, if you didn't have a will, who gets what will be determined by that cranky bureaucrat, and your heirs may end up paying more estate taxes than need be.

As you are creating or reviewing your will, it is extremely important to check whether or not a beneficiary has been designated for a specific account and how your various assets are titled. Beneficiary designations and titling override what your will says. For example, your IRA beneficiary may be your husband, so if you leave your IRA to your son in your will, he won't receive it; the beneficiary is your husband, not your son. When it comes to titling property, as we discussed earlier, there are a variety of ways to do it and each has its own ramifications regarding how or whom the property will be passed on to at the owner's death. Don't just think you know how it is titled; find out for sure how.

People often overlook personal property like china, jewelry, or camera equipment when preparing a will. These items may not be your most financially valuable assets, but many times they have deep emotional value for your heirs. I have seen sisters never speak again because of a rope of pearls or a set of china. That's why you should consider making a list of your personal property designating whom you wish to get what (and I think it's nice to add why you choose that specific piece for that specific person—for example, "Jane gets the pearls because when she was young and I was getting dressed for an evening out she would always want to put the pearls on and dance around my bedroom"), then sign and date it. I like to call this an "I love you letter." In financial terms, it is known as a "personal property memorandum."

When you hear the word "will," you will also often hear the word "probate." Probate is a court procedure in which a judge authenticates your will and officially transfers those assets that pass through your will to your stated beneficiaries. Going through probate usually entails legal and probate fees, as well as time. Depending on your state and the complexity of your estate, probate can cost as much as 10 percent of the value of your estate and can take up to a few years to complete. For most people it costs between 2 percent and 7 percent of the estate's value and takes about a year. Be aware that in probate your affairs may become public record. You can go on to www.trutv.com and see the wills of Michael Jackson, JFK Jr., John Lennon, and even Marilyn Monroe. Even if you are not sufficiently famous (or infamous) to have your will posted on www.trutv.com, your neighbors and business associates (or enemies) can obtain a copy of your will because it is a public record. Because of that lack of privacy, as well as the costs and time taken up by probate, many people are turning to a revocable living trust as an alternative to (really in addition to) a will.

Before we move on to discuss living trusts, I feel compelled to stand on my soapbox for a minute and plead to parents with minor children who have not yet created a will. Shame on you! If you and your spouse die without a will, your child's destiny will be in the hands of the state. I know that guardianship is a very hard decision and possibly a contentious one, but you owe it to your children to make it. Furthermore, if you have minor children make sure you review and update the guardianship decision as situations change. Named guardians may move out of state, get sick, pass on, or experience adverse changes in their financial conditions. They may have been the right choice earlier, but not now.

And speaking of minor children, keep in mind that most simple wills leave assets to the other spouse with the children as the contingent beneficiary. This is usually not a problem, especially if you have a small estate. But a problem arises if unfortunately you both die at the same time. Your assets are left to your children in guardianship and that usually ends at age eighteen. You need to ask yourself: Do I

DOES YOUR WILL NEED AN UPDATE?

Once they make a will, many people will put it in a safe-deposit box or leave a copy with their attorney and forget about it. However, there are many reasons to review and update your will and other estate-planning documents. Below is a checklist of events that may prompt you to do so.

_____ The individuals you have named are deceased

_____ New people should be named in your will (for example, birth, adoption)

_____ Divorce or marriage

_____ Moving across state lines

_____ Change in guardians, personal representatives, or trustees

_____ Children reach the age of eighteen

_____ A substantial increase or decrease in the value of your estate

_____ The acquisition or disposition of a significant asset

_____ Retirement

_____ It's been five years

want my children to get a lump sum of assets upon turning eighteen? Will they be mature enough to live responsibly with perhaps a large sum of money? Or would they be more likely to take off on a motorcycle and travel through Europe? This same problem arises when you gift assets directly to young children. Thus, if you have significant assets (don't forget the life insurance) you may want to consider using a trust (or trusts) as well.

REVOCABLE LIVING TRUSTS

A revocable living trust (aka family trust) is in many ways similar to a will. For instance, it becomes irrevocable at death and includes the details and instructions for how you want your estate to be handled at your death. But it has very distinct differences as well. First, in addition to the distribution of property at death, a revocable living trust (RLT) also deals with the ownership of property during one's lifetime. Thus it is a plan that is in effect **both** during your lifetime **and** at your death. During life it is revocable, meaning you can change it. It only becomes irrevocable on your death. The key benefit of a RLT is that the property that is held by the trust does not go through probate, and thus avoids the costs and time eaten up by that process.

In a will you name an executor. In a revocable living trust you name a trustee. It is very common that during your life you (and your spouse) are the trustee(s) and that at death (or incapacity) you have someone named to take your place. Just as we discussed in the will section, your successor trustee should be someone who can step into your shoes. It is important that their financial sophistication be in line with your financial situation. That is why many people choose an institution as a trustee (or co-trustee). The benefit of naming a successor trustee can also be very helpful in the event of an awful disability leaving you incapacitated. If something were to happen, the successor trustee can step into your shoes immediately and keep the assets growing without any court fights or disputes.

Just as you had to make sure with your will that your beneficiary designations and property titling were in line with your wishes, an RLT requires the same thing as well as an extra step. This extra step is known as "funding." In its simplest terms, to fund an RLT you are transferring the "ownership" of the assets from you to the trust. You can think of the trust as a big manila envelope that holds all your assets in one organized place. What you have does not change, where the accounts are doesn't change, it's just the name that changes. For example, accounts in the name of Alan and Robin Jones would now be held as "Alan and Robin Jones, Trustees of the Jones Family Trust, dated 1/1/01." Because you are the trustees of the trust, you still have control over your property after the transfer. Generally speaking you can still buy, sell, borrow, or transfer your property as you so desire.

But buyers beware! Too, too often, I see people creating the trust but never getting around to transferring the property as intended (there are revocable living trusts known as standby trusts that will be funded at a certain event such as incapacity), and so all they accomplished was to incur extra legal fees. During life, no great biggie. But at death it could be a big deal. That is why most trusts have what is known as a "pour over will" provision, which means that assets that have not been titled as a trust asset (and thus are not in the trust) will pour into your will and be distributed according to your wishes as outlined in your will and not by the wishes of your state. Of course, assets that pass through your will are subject to probate.

I also see frequent misunderstandings about tax benefits. An important thing to note about a revocable living trust when compared to a will is that the trust does not have estate tax minimization preferences. Both the trust and a will can have the identical provisions that may help to minimize one's estate tax exposure. What you are saving is really on probate and perhaps administrative fees (since with a trust your assets tend to be more organized). Another misunderstanding is that a trust can be used to avoid income taxes. Sorry, no. Since it is a revocable trust you are treated as the owner of the property and must report all trust income on your personal income tax (just like you would if you had not set up a trust).

The bottom line is that a revocable living trust can be a good idea, but it is not always necessary. Work with a financial adviser and estate attorney to ensure that a trust is for you, based on your lifestyle, family situation, occupation, domicile, age, and goals.

IRREVOCABLE TRUSTS

For the more sophisticated and larger estates, there is a variety of irrevocable trust structures to consider. Irrevocable trusts, unlike revocable trusts, are binding and cannot be changed without court intervention (but don't freak—because you can build flexibility into the trust documents). Many trusts are created by provisions in your will or living trust and therefore come into play upon your death, but depending on your personal wealth and situation, irrevocable trusts are created during your lifetime as well.

These can be complex structures, so obviously the goal is not to make you a trust expert. But I do want you to be familiar with the terms and the very basic way in which they work. We will focus on the three common irrevocable trusts:

- Credit shelter trusts
- Irrevocable life insurance trusts
- Generation-skipping trusts

Remember, if you are younger or do not have significant assets yet, you may be the beneficiary of these trusts, so don't skip this section.

TRUSTING PEOPLE

In any trust, whether revocable or irrevocable, there are four main characters:

- *Grantor*: Creator of the trust
- *Trustee*: Designated person(s) and/or organization who carries out the wishes expressed in the terms of the trust as well as the administration of the trust
- *Income beneficiary*: Designated person(s) and/or organization(s) who are entitled to receive the income generated by the trust assets
- *Remaindermen*: Designated person(s) or organization(s) who have a future interest in the trust assets

---

Credit Shelter Trusts If you are part of a married couple with a significant estate and have heirs, you should be aware of a credit shelter trust. It is called the credit shelter trust because it "shelters" your assets from estate tax up to the exemption amount. The purpose of this trust structure is to ensure that both you and your spouse's estate tax exemption amounts are used effectively, and thus they usually are discussed in conjunction with estate tax minimization.

By now you know that the financial services industry never calls anything by one name. Credit shelter trusts are also known as bypass trusts and B trusts. It is called a bypass trust because it "bypasses" estate taxation when the surviving spouse dies.

Depending on the size of your estate, this can save thousands of dollars in estate taxes. (See the second Lucy and Ricky example, "Married Couples with Larger Estates," in the appendix.) In addition, with a credit shelter trust your heirs do not get those assets outright (do you really want your twenty-five-year-old to have unrestricted access to those dollars?) and your spouse can have (limited) access to those funds as well. So in addition to the tax savings, one of the key selling points of a credit shelter trust is the control that it gives one from the grave. That sounds ominous, doesn't it? But it isn't, really. All it means is that the person who creates the trust (grantor) has a say over how the surviving spouse uses the assets and where those assets go after the surviving spouse's death. Why would that be important? Well, think of it this way: You were the major breadwinner (or it's your family's money), you pass away, leave the money to your husband, and your husband remarries. Will he and his new wife become spendthrifts and spend everything so nothing is left for your kids? Will the new wife convince him to leave everything to her with the "promise" that she will take care of the kids and your kids wind up getting nothing? I know these are extreme examples, but it happens!

Thus, a credit shelter trust protects a portion of the first spouse's legacy for heirs other than the spouse.

Irrevocable Life Insurance Trust Life insurance proceeds are included in your estate. Life insurance proceeds can be sufficient to put someone who didn't think they were subject to the estate tax into a taxable position. To avoid having life insurance in your estate, you may set up an irrevocable life insurance trust that owns the life insurance policies. Since you don't own the insurance yourself, it's not part of your (or your spouse's) taxable estate, and therefore is not subject to estate taxes. The trust is named the beneficiary of the insurance, and collects the proceeds upon your death and distributes those assets according to trust provisions.

Many people think life insurance is an ugly word. But in estate planning it can really be helpful because of two words—"liquidity" and "legacy." Let's look at a very simple example for liquidity. Let's say your parents have passed away and their estate consists only of a very expensive house, which results in an estate tax due of, say, $500,000. How are you going to pay that tax? Sell the garage? My point is that many times estates consist of assets that are not easily turned into cash and the estate tax may cause a forced sale or some other unfortunate situation.

Also, life insurance can be used to create a legacy for an heir. For example, let's say you are in your golden years and are living with a significant other. In case you go first, you want to ensure your partner's financial security, but you also want to leave a majority of your assets to your children. Or let's say you want to leave some significant assets to a charity, without greatly affecting your children's potential inheritance. In other words, in certain situations you can leverage a small portion of your estate to create a greater legacy for your heirs. For some of you, it's at least worth investigating.

GENERATION-SKIPPING TRUST

Years ago, people would give or leave property to their grandchildren instead of their children in order to keep the property out of their children's taxable estates, and in essence avoid estate taxation upon the child's demise (when they would pass those assets to their children). Well, that wasn't very popular with the government and as a result Congress enacted the generation-skipping tax (GST) on lifetime or death gifts that skip a generation. The tax is in addition to the estate tax. There is a $3.5 million exemption per person (as the law stood in 2009). Big estates that want to pass on big assets to grandkids (as well as future generations) without incurring further estate or generation-skipping taxes tend to use a trust that is funded with assets up to the GST exemption amount. Trusts like these that are intended to last from generation to generation to generation are frequently referred to as dynasty trusts.

These three trusts—credit shelter, irrevocable life insurance, and generation skipping trusts—were the more typical types of trusts in the past. But families and people's situations these days are not necessary typical. Life in the twenty-first century is incredibly diverse and that includes how we live. People are living in alternative lifestyles, with or without permanent or long-term partners, and in blended families. Consequently, the "typical" estate-planning tools may not be sufficient to carry out one's wishes. Thus, alternative estate plans for the more nontraditional family or household require careful planning. Let's look at a few different situations.

SPECIAL CONSIDERATIONS
FOR SECOND MARRIAGES

You both come to the marriage with assets and children. With assets and children come complexity. When one spouse dies, what does the surviving spouse get versus the passing spouse's kids from the previous marriage? I am sure I do not have to tell you that not thinking about these things in advance is a recipe for disaster and unintended results.

Too often I see people set up simple wills in which the assets go to each respective spouse upon the passing of the other, with the implied assumption that each will take care of each other's children. Unfortunately, no matter what promises are made to preserve your legacy for your children, all bets are off after you die. This is especially important if there is a significant age difference or life expectancy among the spouses.

In addition to the credit shelter trust, spouses in second marriages often use a qualified terminable interest property (or QTIP) trust for assets in excess of the estate tax exemption amounts. To make a long story short, upon the death of the first spouse, a trust is formed in which the survivor spouse receives the income at least annually from the trust assets. Then, on the survivor's death, the remaining assets go as directed by the first spouse. The main purpose of the QTIP trust is not tax savings, but rather to allow for asset control and peace of mind for you, your children, and your current spouse. A QTIP is also used in first marriages in which there is concern that a spouse may not be able to manage assets in the future and you would like an independent trustee to help manage the assets. An independent trustee is also

Summary Chart of Trusts	
TRUST TYPE	DESCRIPTION
Revocable living trust (RLT)	Used to avoid probate, assign a trustee in case of incapacitation, and provide for the distribution of your property upon death
Credit shelter trust (CST)	Used to shelter assets that are not left to spouse from estate tax as well as provide for some "control from the grave"
Irrevocable life insurance trust (ILIT)	Used to protect the proceeds from life insurance from estate tax
Generation-skipping trust (GST)	Used to protect assets from estate tax across generations
Qualified terminal interest property (QTIP) trust	Used to provide assets to surviving spouse, but controls who receives the assets upon spouse's passing

a good idea with second marriages so that there is a third party who looks at the trust for the benefit of both the wife and the kids.

No matter how loving your adult children are to your second spouse, and vice versa, if they feel that their inheritance is in jeopardy, it can become very ugly, both before and after you die.

SPECIAL CONSIDERATIONS FOR UNMARRIED OR NONTRADITIONAL COUPLES

Estate planning is especially critical for an unmarried couple. If there isn't a plan, the surviving partner may wind up with bubkes because the assets will be distributed as specified in state statute, usually to blood relatives, not unmarried partners. If you're in that kind of relationship, you must have a carefully prepared and executed plan, especially if one partner has significantly more wealth than the other and that wealth is what is used to support your joint lifestyle.

Life partners should also pay special attention to personal property. If you don't, and your documents are not in order, imagine the emotional toll when others come in and take your partner's antique clock that has been a big centerpiece of your home.

If there are potential conflicts of interest or contentious relationships with children or if the wealth status of the partners is not equal, it usually is a good idea to seek separate counsel. It adds a level of protection and validity.

Another very important aspect of estate planning that unmarried partners have to pay particularly close attention to are the documents that drive your health-care and financial directives. The basic question you need to answer is this: If you become disabled or incapacitated, who will make the decisions for you? Typically if there are no directives, the default is next of kin. Is that what you want? For instance, let's say you and your partner have had the "pull the plug" conversation and you know each other's wishes but you never got around to writing them down or discussing them with your children or parents. Something happens and the decision needs to be made: pull or not? Your children or parents are emphatic about keeping the plug in and your partner keeps telling them that you wanted the plug out. Who wins? Next of kin. Who loses? You. This isn't the life you would have chosen.

SPECIAL CONSIDERATIONS FOR THE NEWLY DIVORCED

For many recently divorced people, the last person to whom they want to leave any assets to is the ex. Yet all too often this is what happens and the cause can be summed up in one word—procrastination.

By the time a divorce is finished you're burned out, sick of lawyers, and sick of thinking about financial matters. But if you just bear a little more discomfort, you will gain a tremendous amount of comfort in return.

First you need to develop a plan. You will need new wills and trusts as well as health-care directives and powers of attorney (you don't seriously want your ex to have the power to pull the plug, do you?). You also need to make sure you change beneficiary designations on your retirement accounts, life insurance policies, and annuities, as well as change any titling of accounts.

Remember: Beneficiary designations and titling will trump the will or state rules. This is a "must-do," not a "nice to have."

Since we are discussing divorce, I would be remiss if I didn't mention an often-heard concern: how to protect your legacy if your child gets divorced. Obviously, prenuptial agreements can be useful, but not always possible. In those instances, one of the best ways to protect your legacy is by using irrevocable trusts. The key is to ensure that gifts or inheritances given to your child aren't comingled with your children's other "marital assets" and/or that the distributions are not necessarily certain. There are a variety of ways to use trusts (or trust provisions) to accomplish this. This is a very valid concern and with a little work today you can get peace of mind without even getting the "outlaw" to sign anything.

SPECIAL CONSIDERATIONS FOR SINGLES

Singles tend to be the worst about having an estate plan in place, especially if they don't have children. But you still have assets and you still have to make smart and thoughtful decisions about the "what-ifs." Stuff happens and you may become incapacitated or disabled and need people to make financial as well as health decisions for you. Don't you want to have a say about the who and what? If nothing else, please be sure you at least have health-care directives and powers of attorneys in place.

Be careful whom you name as beneficiary. I often see singles naming their minor niece or nephew as the beneficiary on their account. They assume the kids would use the proceeds for college if something happens. But don't assume anything. That niece may decide that with her sudden windfall she'd rather party in Ibiza than get a college education. So instead of leaving it to her directly, it may make more sense to use some trust structure.

SPECIAL CONSIDERATIONS FOR SPECIAL-NEEDS CHILDREN

If you have a child with special needs, you know that a portion of his or her support is provided by public assistance. If someone with special needs has money in her own name, the eligibility for these dollars can be put at risk. Thus, for most people with special needs, it does not make the most sense to directly leave them assets. Instead, you should leave whatever resources you deem appropriate to a special-needs trust (SNT). SNTs are "special" and are subject to some very stringent rules and regulations. It is vital that any family contemplating using an SNT consult an experienced attorney, not just one who does general estate planning, but one who is very knowledgeable about SNTs and current government benefit programs. One wrong word or phrase can make the difference between an inheritance that really benefits the person with a disability and one that causes the person to lose access to a wide range of needed services and assistance.

SPECIAL CONSIDERATIONS FOR PETS

Some of you may be rolling your eyes right now, but for some pet lovers, making sure that their pets are properly cared for once they pass is of great importance. Take, for example, Leona Helmsley and her dog Trouble. If you recall, when she died she left $12 million dollars in trust for the care of her favorite companion.

If you have concerns about what will happen to your pet in case of your incapacitation or passing, you may want to set up a "pet trust" that allows you to designate a specific amount of money for your pet's care and name a trustee to carry out your wishes. These trusts can come under your will or you can create one during your lifetime. Some people prefer a separate trust document because it can be immediately available for the care of an animal if a pet owner, for example, has to go into a nursing home or becomes incapacitated. States have different rules, so check out your state statutes. You may want to look at www.estateplanningforpets.org for more information.

You worked so hard to earn your wealth. It's important to put some effort into preserving and sharing it as well. I am sure I don't have to tell you that getting this right requires focus and frank discussion with family members and others. Communication is key. It also requires you to work with professionals who are experts in these matters. A poorly drafted will or trust can be worse than no will or trust at all. So, if possible, search out an estate-planning attorney instead of using the attorney you used to buy your home.

Furthermore, just like with your investment plan, your estate plan needs to be monitored and adjusted over time. So don't throw those documents into the bottom drawer or into a safe-deposit box and think you are done until you die. Your plan should be reviewed at least every five years or so, or when there are life changes.

I believe that the last thing most of us want to happen is that our estate plan destroys the memory we leave our loved ones. As a very wise estate-planning attorney once said to me, "The best surprise in an estate plan is no surprise at all."

AT THE VERY LEAST

Check your beneficiary designation of your investment and retirement accounts and life insurance policies to make sure they are up-to-date, and if you haven't already, make sure to execute your health-care directives.

CHAPTER SUMMARY

. . . .

1. Estate planning is first and foremost about making sure your property (and minor children) are distributed according to your wishes upon your demise.
2. Once you establish the who, what, when, and how of your estate plan, then look to do it in the most tax-efficient manner.
3. Beneficiary designations and property titling have precedence over a will or trust
4. If your situation is somewhat complex or is not typical, make sure to work with an attorney who specializes in trust and estate planning.
5. Make sure to be an active partner in the estate-planning process. Ask questions and more questions until you have clarity and comfort.
6. What you've learned:

SOME CLOSING THOUGHTS

· · · · · · · · · · · · · · ·

Give yourself a big hug. You have just given yourself a fabulous present by reading this book—knowledge. Without that key ingredient it is difficult to muster the confidence and the drive to be an active participant in your own finances.

Always keep in mind that being an active participant doesn't mean that you are as knowledgeable and as deft with the markets as a portfolio manager involved in the day-to-day management of your portfolio. What it does mean is that you have defined goals, an understanding of your personal risk capacity, and have realistic expectations. Without those three things, it is too easy to allow our emotions to take over and to lose the discipline to stay the course. We end up being our own worst enemy.

As you know, nothing is guaranteed in life. No investment plan can guarantee exact results. But knowledge and discipline can put the odds in your favor. And that is what this book was all about: increasing your probability for your success.

Note the words "your success." It is not your neighbors, your friends, or your colleagues. It's all about you. What you want and what you need may be very different from what all those other people want and need. They may need or want to shoot for the stars and you may not. So whenever you hear someone talking about how they "beat the market," remember this: A rate of return is not a life goal. What you want is an investment plan that's tailored to your specific needs and objectives.

Believe me, I understand how hard it is to find the time to focus on your long-term needs when too often we are overwhelmed by short-term priorities. But this is not a luxury, it is a must-have. It takes a little work up front, and then, if there are no extenuating circumstances, will take just a few hours per year. You owe it to yourself as well as to your family. Ignorance is just not bliss. Don't be afraid to ask question after question after question. In the words of a Chinese proverb, "One who asks a question is a fool for five minutes; one who does not ask a question remains a fool forever."

So please don't be one of those women who end up saying, "If I only knew," or "I can't believe this happened to me," or "I should have, could have, would have." Instead, be one of those women who is aware, knowledgeable, and says, "I did the best I could to maximize the likelihood of achieving the life goals that I desired."

Now that you have completed this book, you have taken the first step to being that woman. Congratulations on your journey to being fabulous with your finances and now having the tools and the awareness to make your assets look abundantly fat.

APPENDIX

. . . .

1. THE CHOICE IS YOURS

Credit Score

The credit score, also well known as a FICO score, is a statistical or numerical interpretation of the information portrayed through your credit file. Your file is a compilation of the history of your credit cards, auto loans, student loans, mortgage, and so on. Think of it as the litmus test for financial responsibility. The overall purpose is to help lenders determine if you basically would pay a loan back on time—the higher your credit score, the higher your credibility in the loan market. It can affect your interest rates, insurance rates, and other rates as well.

To find out what your score is, you can use a FICO calculator to get a rough idea. It's free; go to www.annualcreditreport.com. Or you can purchase your credit score from any of the credit-reporting agencies like Equifax, TransUnion, Experian, or FICO. If your credit score is:

- Above 760, you are charged the lowest prevalent market rates.
- More than 700, you are usually charged a relatively lower rate of returns.
- Below 660, normally you have to pay relatively high loan rates.
- Most creditors find the credit score of 620 acts as a break-even point.

2. NAKED IN FRONT OF THE MIRROR

Additional Calculations to Determine Your Financial Health

The inflow over outflow formula is total cash inflow divided by total cash outflow multiplied by −1.

What we would like to see here is a number of 1 or greater. Below 0.8 may indicate frivolous spending habits and/or too aggressive saving goals.

The debt-to-income ratio formula is total debt payments divided by total monthly income.

Most lenders will tell you that:

- Less than 30% is excellent
- Less than 36% is good
- More than 40% is concerning.

If yours is above forty, it may indicate a sign that your credit situation requires attention.

3. THE FOUR BASIC FOOD GROUPS

Price-Earnings Ratio

When people talk about growth and value, they often use the term "P/E ratio" or talk about a stock trading at a "high multiple" or "low multiple." At the root of their comments is something known as the price-earnings ratio, which is the number derived by dividing a company's stock price by the company's annual per-share earnings. A high P/E ratio tells us that when compared to other stocks of similar companies the stock in question is perceived as more valuable by investors who are willing to pay more for that stock because they believe it has a higher potential for growth (and vice versa for value).

The Secondary Market—Discounts and Premiums

You do not always buy a bond when it is first issued by an organization. A secondary market exists in which investors buy and sell previously issued bonds. The prices of the bonds in the secondary markets depend on their stated interest rates compared to current rates, the amount of time remaining before the bond matures, and the creditworthiness of the bond. Bonds can sell at a discount to the face value or at a premium to their face value. In other words, just because an existing bond has a face value of $5,000 does not mean it will sell for $5,000 in the secondary market. Look at the chart on the top of the next page.

	FACE VALUE	COUPON RATE	CURRENT INTEREST RATE	COUPON VERSUS CURRENT RATE	IN SECONDARY MARKET, THE BOND WILL SELL AT A
Bond A	$5,000	8%	5%	Higher	Premium to the face value; that is, greater than $5,000
Bond B	$5,000	5%	8%	Lower	Discount to the face value; that is, less than $5,000

Thus, if the bond has an interest rate greater than today's prevailing rates, then someone will be willing to pay you more than $5,000 to get that higher interest. The bond then will be said to be selling at a premium. If the coupon rate is lower than the prevailing rate, a buyer will want to pay you less than $5,000 because she could get a higher interest rate somewhere else. In other words, the bond is selling at a discount.

Buying and selling bonds in the secondary market is far from simple. There is no central place or exchange (like there is for stocks) where bonds are bought or sold. Rather, there are a vast number of independent dealers who buy and sell to one another. Commissions—the fees for using a broker's services as a buyer or seller—also vary. That is why you won't find the price of bonds listed in your newspaper alongside the stock price tables.

The Yield Curve

In its simplest terms a yield curve is a graph on which you plot today's yields for various maturities of U.S. Treasury bills and bonds, going from the shortest to the longest maturities. U.S. Treasuries are used because no matter the maturity they have the same credit risk, essentially zero. That way we see the differences between short-term and long-term interest rates without having to bother about credit risk and how that affects those rates.

To understand the importance of the yield curve, we have to return to the concept of risk and reward. Long-term bonds tend to have a greater risk that inflation will overtake the interest rate they pay, so they tend to pay higher interest rates. Under normal economic conditions if you plot the interest rates paid by various maturities of Treasury bonds, you would see them slope gently upward as maturities lengthen and yields rise.

A normal yield curve usually means that bond investors expect the economy to continue to grow normally—not too fast and not too slow. As we know, the economy sometimes grows too fast (inflation) and sometimes grows too slowly (recession). That's why the yield curve won't always look "normal." Sometimes instead of a gentle slope upward, it has a sharp, steep slope. With a "steep yield curve" the yields on the short terms are relatively low when compared to the long terms. Usually we see this as we leave some bad times (a recessionary period) and enter into better times (an expansion period). Thus, investors want to be in the longer-term bonds. Other times the curve can be "flat." The difference between short- and long-term rates is relatively small. Thus, investors will want to be in the short-term bonds. Why tie your money up for longer than necessary? A flat curve usually happens during transition periods, either upward or downward. A curve with a downward slope is said to be "inverted." That means short-term yields are higher than those on longer-term bonds. This happens when investors think rates and the economy will go lower in the future—in other words, when the economy seems to be heading into a recession. During periods of an inverted yield curve an investor would obviously want to stay short.

SHAPE	ECONOMY	INTEREST RATES
NORMAL	Normal conditions	Short-term rates are lower than long-term rates
STEEP	Entering an expansion period	Short-term rates are relatively low as compared to long-term rates
FLAT	Transition period, either way	There's no great difference between the two
INVERTED	Heading into a recession	Short-term rates are higher than long-term rates

4. PORTION CONTROL

Concentrated Positions

A concentrated position is typically defined as an investment that is 10 percent or greater of your overall portfolio. (If you are a corporate executive, you may not even realize you have a concentrated position. Add up the value of your corporate stock in your 401(k) plan, deferred compensation plans, stock plans, bonus plans, and so on—it may amount to much more than 10 percent of your portfolio.)

There are two fundamental challenges with concentrated positions. They can be very bad, but they can also be very good for your bank account. Here's what I mean. The bad is that your success becomes very dependent on one thing and if there is some kind of unexpected (bad) event, a heavily concentrated position can bring dire results. The good is that concentrated positions have created great wealth for some people. And this is the great paradox of concentrated positions: They can be a great way to create wealth, but they can also be a great way to destroy wealth.

When you look at the Forbes 400 list as of 2007, most of the people on that list—Donald Trump and Bill Gates are two examples—created their wealth through a concentrated investment in one specific sector or in one specific company. But what you don't see when you look at the list is all the people over the last twenty-five years who have been taken off the list because their wealth was concentrated in real estate, oil, or one specific company. For example, over the last several years Howard Schultz of Starbucks and Steve Case of AOL and Time Warner fame were dropped from the list due to large declines in the stock prices of their respective companies.

Now, I am sure your heart is not bleeding for these people because they have great sums of wealth. For example, if Howard Schultz owns 17.7 million shares of Starbucks stock and the shares are off 32 percent over the past year, he has lost about $229 million! But if the stock is at $18 a share, he still has $339 million of it. It's probably safe to say he can achieve his "must-have" goals on that. But the question is, if your portfolio suddenly dropped by 32 percent, would you have the financial capacity to absorb this loss and be able to reach your goals?

After meeting with people who have suffered the woes of a concentrated position I have found that they suffer from several misconceptions. One of their biggest misconceptions is that they optimistically assumed that they would be able to sell out in time. But human nature being what it is, we do not let go easily. This phenomenon is called the disposition effect. In its simplest terms the disposition effect can be thought of as people holding on to losses too long. Studies have shown that when the loss becomes almost certain, people actually tend to increase risk taking, hoping to beat the odds and avoid the loss. This is often exactly the wrong behavior.

Another misconception is the fact that investment analysts have a "buy" recommendation on a stock. What people don't realize is that analysts make their recommendations in the context of a diversified portfolio, often in relation to whether the position should have a slight over- or underweight compared to its percentage weight in an index. Their published recommendations are never intended for positions that have a weight of 10 percent or more of a particular portfolio.

A third challenge I see is when people inherit concentrated positions. Often for the person that is leaving you the stock, that stock is a symbol of a life's hard work or success. They have a lot of loyalty and/or sentimentality attached to the stock and frequently advise you that upon your inheritance, "No matter what you do, don't let anyone ever let you sell the stock." Unfortunately, they are saying this out of ignorance. The stock may have performed well over their lifetime, but did it truly deliver to them the best reward for the given level of risk that they took on and, most important, will it do so in the future? Keep in mind that just because you own stock in a good solid company doesn't mean it's a good investment.

Another mistaken belief I often hear is from corporate executives with concentrated holdings in their own company's stock. They reason that because they work there they know what is going on with the stock. They have "inside" information. That's just a simple matter of "overconfidence." In essence, they are confusing familiarity with knowledge. That familiarity or comfort with the company's stock often gives an illusion of control, but unfortunately it really is only an illusion. Even the chairman of the board doesn't really know what will happen to the stock since it's largely in the hands of other investors.

Lastly, one of the most common reasons people wind up with a concentrated position and refuse to diversify it is that they are worried about the tax liability (capital gains taxes) on any appreciation. First, capital gains taxes apply if your holdings are not in a tax-deferred type of account like a 401(k) plan or an IRA. Many of us have such an aversion to paying taxes that we immediately shun voluntarily doing something that will create additional taxes. But the truth is that sooner or later you will have to pay the tax. To delay and refuse to diversify out of a concentrated position is to trade the certainty of taxes for the uncertainty of a potentially much more costly loss if your concentrated investment plunges. Don't let the tax dog wag the investment tail. Your first goal should be risk management and only then turn to tax management.

5. GOING SHOPPING

Five Unique Features of Mutual Funds

1. *Open Ended:* Open ended is usually omitted when talking about mutual funds; it's nevertheless important to understand what that means. In essence, an open-ended mutual fund will create new shares to sell to whoever wants to invest in the fund. In other words, there are an open-ended amount of shares available to investors so that I don't have to find someone willing to sell his shares to me (like I do with a stock, for example). As a result, the performance of a specific mutual fund is driven only by

movements of the underlying investments the fund holds and not by the supply and demand of that specific fund.

The underlying investments affect the value of a mutual fund in three ways: dividends (or interest), realized capital gains (and losses), and increases (decreases) in market value.

- *Dividend payments*: A fund may earn income in the form of dividends (interest and short-term capital gains) on the underlying securities in its portfolio.
- *Long-term capital gains distributions*: When a fund sells a security that it has held for at least a year and which has increased in price, the fund has a long-term capital gain.
- *Increases in market value*: The market value of a fund's underlying portfolio may increase, which is shown as a higher NAV (see value). For you, the investor, a higher NAV is only a paper gain. You have to sell your shares in the fund to realize that gain (or, if the NAV is lower, a loss).

2. *How they are purchased*: Because of the open-ended nature of a mutual fund, you purchase them somewhat differently than the way you buy individual stocks, exchange-traded funds, and closed-end funds. These are bought and sold from an exchange (such as the New York Stock Exchange or the American Stock Exchange), whereas open-ended funds are bought directly from the sponsoring fund company. Therefore, they have unique pricing and value characteristics.

3. *Pricing*: The price of a mutual fund share is stated in the form of *net asset value*, which is simply the total value of the stocks (or bonds) the fund holds divided by the number of shares the fund has issued. For example, say a mutual fund has a portfolio of stocks worth $10 million and there are 1 million shares outstanding, the NAV is calculated as so:

$$\frac{\$10 \text{ million}}{1 \text{ million shares}} = \$10 \text{ NAV per share}$$

That means to buy 100 shares of that fund, it would cost you $1,000 (100 shares = $10 per share = $1,000 along with any commissions or fees charged if applicable by your broker or the fund). That $10 NAV is also what you would get if you sold shares in the fund.

4. *Value*: A fund's NAV is calculated once a day, usually after the U.S. stock market closes and the fund can get closing prices for each of the stocks it holds. No matter

what the stock market does over the course of a day, the only value that counts for you is the end-of-the-day NAV calculation. Therefore, from day to day, the NAV will fluctuate in value in line with the underlying investments as compared to an ETF, closed-end fund, individual stocks, and so on, whose prices fluctuate all day long.

5. *Distributions*: Keep in mind that when an underlying stock pays a dividend, or an underlying bond pays interest, or if either is sold at a gain, you do not automatically get cash in your hand. Think about it; administratively it would be a nightmare. Because each fund can own hundreds of different investments, the fund's managers would spend all their time and resources paying out the income instead of finding the best investment opportunities for you. Instead, they accumulate it and pay it out at certain points during the year.

Important dates for mutual funds:

- *Record date*: This is the official date when the fund determines which shareholders will receive the distribution.
- *X-date*: This date indicates the day the fund recognizes the drop in net asset value according to the amount it intends on distributing.
- *Distribution date*: This date reflects the day the fund actually pays out the distribution due.

Mutual Fund Expenses

Mutual funds have two kinds of costs:

- The cost of buying and selling
- The cost of owning

Not all funds have a cost of buying and selling, but they all have a cost of owning.

Costs of buying and selling: Certain funds charge a sales commission when you buy them and others don't. Some funds charge a redemption fee when you sell them and others don't. Generally speaking, the funds that charge either a sales commission or a redemption fee rely on advisers to sell their funds. These costs—referred to in mutual fund lingo as "loads"—come in different shapes and formats. It's important to understand how and when they apply, because sometimes they do and sometimes they don't.

Costs of owning: Fees for owning a fund apply to every fund and are set by the fund company itself. Generally speaking, these fees cover a fund's operating expenses, such as management and distribution fees. Knowing what fees a fund charges allows you to calculate a fund's "expense ratio," which is the fund's total operating expenses expressed as a percentage of the fund's average net assets. These fees eat into the overall performance of a fund. Therefore, if you were looking at two similar funds, with similar investment philosophies, processes, and objectives, the one with the lower cost may have a better overall performance. Looking at expense ratios can help you make comparisons among similar types of funds.

Style Drift

It's not only individual investors who chase performance, sometimes it's portfolio managers as well. This is especially important if you are a believer in asset allocation and are buying a fund to fill a specific asset class. If you bought a fund because you want your portfolio to include, say, small-cap stocks, then you want its manager to stay committed to that discipline and you don't want them drifting (or jumping) into large-growth issues just to enhance the performance of that fund. A down-and-dirty way to determine if there may be style or asset class drift is by comparing the performance of a fund to its benchmark and to funds with similar objectives (that is, its peers). If the performance is much greater or much less compared to the benchmark or to peers, you need to ask why. I know this sounds counterintuitive, but if a fund is doing so much better than its peers, the reason may be that it is including stocks from the outperforming styles or asset classes that are not really supposed to be part of the fund's holdings. You may be saying, "Who cares as long as they make money?" But when it doesn't work in your favor you're going to be very unhappy and, more important, most likely taking on additional risk that you did not want.

Shorting

Think of a shorting strategy this way: You borrow a designer bag from a friend and sell it on eBay for $500. You do this because you believe that a week from now you can buy the same bag for $200. You also are fairly certain that you can take the $500 and buy a different bag that you can sell on eBay later for $600. If you can execute that strategy perfectly, you wind up making $400 on your friend's investment—$300 from the difference between selling her old bag for $500 and then replacing it for $200 and another $100 from using the $500 from the first sale to buy another bag that you then sold for $600. But it only works as long as you can replace your friend's bag for less than you sold it. If you can't find a bag for less, it's going to cost you to replace it for her. The same can be done with stocks. A portfolio manager selects stocks that he believes will decrease in value, borrows them, and sells them at the current price. Then he later buys those same stocks at a lower price and returns them to the original owner, pocketing the difference as a profit. So remember that short sellers are betting that stock prices will fall. Obviously you want a portfolio manager making the choices who has demonstrated some skill in shorting stocks.

7. KEEPING UP

Common Investment Benchmarks

Benchmarks measure the market performance of a specific asset class. They are often compared to the performance of a personal portfolio—so it is crucial that you compare apples to apples. In other words, make sure you choose the best representative benchmark for the right portfolio.

- IBC's Money Fund Report Averages
- Barclays Capital Aggregate Bond Index
- Ten-Year U.S. Treasury Bond
- Standard & Poor's 500 Index
- Dow Jones Industrial Average
- NASDAQ Composite Index
- Morgan Stanley Capital International Europe, Australasia, Far East Index

10. PASSING IT ON

Married Couples with Larger Estates

The best way to demonstrate the benefit of each spouse taking advantage of his or her respective exemption amount is by looking at the estate of Lucy and Ricky. In our first example, Lucy and Ricky do not take advantage of the respective exemptions and in the second one they do.

Lucy and Ricky are married, have two grown children, and their respective estates are $5 million each (the house is in her name, the investment accounts are in his, and they have no debts).

	RICKY	LUCY	TOTAL
GROSS ESTATE	$5,000,000	$5,000,000	$10,000,000

Ricky dies first and leaves all his assets to Lucy. The assets fall under the "un-limited marital deduction" estate tax free. Lucy's estate is now worth $10 million.

	LUCY	TOTAL
GROSS ESTATE	$10,000,000	$10,000,000

Lucy dies (the next day, so she didn't spend anything nor did her assets grow), and passes her assets on to her children.

Net Estate	$10 million
Estate Tax Exemption (a)	$3.5 million
Net Taxable Estate (b)	$6.5 million
Tax Rate (c)	45%
Net after tax $(b \times (1-c)) = (d)$	$3,575,000
Total inheritance $(a + d)$	$7,075,000

The total amount that Lucy and Ricky's children will receive is $7.075 million. Let's look at example 2, where they will take advantage of their respective exemption amounts to see if the result is different.

As in example 1, both Ricky and Lucy each have $5 million dollars in their name. Ricky passes on and leaves assets up to his exemption amount ($3.5 million) to their children and his remaining assets ($1.5 million) to Lucy. These transfers are not taxable since they fall under the estate tax exemption and the unlimited marital deduction rules. After Ricky's passing, the asset ownership will be as follows:

	LUCY	KIDS	TOTAL
GROSS ESTATE	$6,500,000	$3,500,000	$10,000,000

Lucy dies (the next day, so she didn't spend anything nor did her assets grow), and passes her estate on to her children.

Net Estate	$6.5 million
Estate Tax Exemption (a)	$3.5 million
Net Taxable Estate (b)	$3.0 million
Tax Rate (c)	45%
Net after tax $(b \times (1-c)) + (d)$	$1,650,000
Total inheritance from Lucy $(a+d)$	$5,150,000

Do you see the difference between example 1 and example 2, where both Ricky and Lucy take advantage of their estate exemption amounts? The difference lies in the overall total inheritance to the kids.

	INHERITANCE TO TO KIDS FROM RICKY	INHERITANCE TO KIDS FROM LUCY	TOTAL INHERITANCE TO KIDS
DOES NOT TAKE ADVANTAGE	$0	$7,075,000	$7,075,000
DOES TAKE ADVANTAGE	$3,500,000	$5,150,000	$8,650,000

When Lucy and Ricky utilized both spouses' exemption amounts, the kids inherited $1.575 million more than when they did not, because in example 2 they are getting $3.5 million estate tax free when Ricky passes, whereas in example 1, $3.5 million gets passed to Lucy and then to the kids where it will be subject to an estate tax of $1.575 million ($3.5 million at a rate of 45 percent).

Gifting

Laverne and Shirley each give a gift of $13,000 to their respective sisters. Laverne gives cash and Shirley gives stock.

	ASSETS OWNED	ASSETS GIFTED TO SISTERS
LAVERNE	$13,000 cash $13,000 stock	$13,000 cash
SHIRLEY	$13,000 cash $13,000 stock	$13,000 stock

When Laverne and Shirley happen to both die ten years later, the value of the stock has grown to $10 million (I want that one!), and the value of the cash is $20,000.

	ASSETS OWNED	ASSETS OWNED BY SISTERS
LAVERNE	$10,000,000 stock	$20,000 cash
SHIRLEY	$20,000 cash	$10,000,000 stock

Now, let's look at the net result to Laverne's and Shirley's estates and their respective sisters.

	LAVERNE'S ESTATE	SHIRLEY'S ESTATE
Gross Assets	$10,000,000	$20,000
Estate tax exemption	$3,500,000	$20,000
Net taxable estate	$6,500,000	0
Tax rate	45%	0
Net after tax	$3,575,000	0
Net assets passed on from estate	$7,075,000	$20,000
Value today of the gifted assets in hands of the sisters	$20,000	$10,000,000
Total assets to sisters	**$7,095,000**	**$10,020,000**

So at the end of the day the beneficiary of Laverne has $7.095 million and the beneficiary of Shirley has $10.2 million because Shirley was able to transfer all of the growth on the stock free of estate tax.

Forms of Ownership

- *Joint tenancy*: Joint tenancy has rights of survivorship, meaning that if one of the joint tenants dies, the remaining rights automatically go to the surviving person(s). And a will is not required to transfer this remaining title to the surviving person(s). The advantage to joint tenancy is that it avoids having an owner's interest probated upon his death, but it is not the best for protection against creditors and estate taxes.
- *Tenancy in common*: Tenancy in common allows for multiple people to hold title in unequal shares, with each having the right to sell their share, or will their share, as they want. Allows the individual owners the greatest flexibility, which can cause issues with consensus decisions.
- *Tenancy by the entirety*: Tenancy by the entirety is not available in all states and not available to all people. It mainly applies to married

couples. This type of title is similar to joint ownership, where the property automatically reverts to the survivor when one spouse dies, bypassing probate, but it offers better protection if one spouse is in debt or files for bankruptcy.

- *Community property* (or co-ownership): There are nine states that allow married people to purchase property, either together or individually, as community property. This basically means that each person owns 50 percent and each needs to write in their will how their share is to be divided when they die. It is also allowed to take title in these states as community property with rights of survivorship. The nine states that allow community property are Arizona, California, Idaho, Louisiana, Nevada, New Mexico, Texas, Washington, and Wisconsin.

GLOSSARY

·················

A

Actively managed fund. A fund that uses a manager or team to analyze securities and to try to beat the market index returns

Adjusted basis. Cost. It is used to calculate short-term and long-term gains or losses for tax purposes.

Adjusted gross income (AGI). A line on your tax return that represents taxable income less certain adjustments.

Alpha. The value that a portfolio manager adds to or subtracts from a fund's return.

American depositary receipt (ADR). Certificates traded on U.S. stock exchanges that represent ownership of a specific number of shares of a foreign/international stock.

Appreciation. An increase in the market value of an investment.

Asset. Something you own.

Asset allocation. The process of dividing investment funds among the different categories of asset classes.

Asset Allocation Fund. An "all in one" mutual fund that includes stocks, bonds, and cash-equivalent assets in its portfolio.

B

Balance sheet. A statement of the actual value of your financial situation on a specific date.

Balanced fund. A mutual fund that combines investments in a combination of stocks and bonds. Its goal is to provide income plus some capital appreciation.

Basis point. Is one-hundredth of a percentage point, or 0.01 percent. It is used to discuss fees, interest rates, yields, and so on.

Bearish. A bear thinks the market is going to go down. Bearish is the opposite of bullish.

Benchmark. An index or other performance indicator against which an investment's performance is measured.

Beneficiary. An individual(s) identified to inherit specific property.

Blue-chip stock. There is no set definition of a blue-chip stock; typically it refers to the stock of well-known, respected companies that have a good track record of earnings and dividend payments. The name "blue chip" came about because in the game of poker the blue chips have the highest value.

Bond premium. The amount above the face value of a bond that you pay to buy a bond paying higher-than-market rates.

Bond rating. A judgment about the ability of the bond issuer to pay the interest and repay the principal when due. The best-known bond-rating companies are Standard & Poor's and Moody's.

Bullish. A bull is someone who thinks the market is going to go up. Bullish is the opposite of bearish.

C

Capital gain. The net profit from the sale of property. "Short-term" capital gains are from the sale of assets owned for one year or less; "long-term" gains are from those held for greater than a year.

Capital gain distribution. A mutual fund's distribution to shareholders of the profits derived from the sale of stocks and bonds within the fund.

Capital loss. The loss from the sale of investment assets.

Cash flow. The difference between cash in and cash out.

Closed-end fund. A pooled investment fund that issues a set number of shares versus an open-ended fund (mutual fund) which continually issues new shares. Closed-end funds trade on an exchange.

Common stock. A share of ownership in a corporation.

Compounding. Earnings on earnings.

Consumer Price Index (CPI). A measure of inflation used by the U.S. Bureau of Labor Statistics. Changes in the price of more than three hundred goods and services are tracked and recorded.

Correlation. The relationship between two assets. A correlation coefficient of 1.0 indicates that both asset classes tend to move in a similar fashion. The lower the correlation, the better the expected diversification; −1.0 means perfect negative correlation.

Coupon rate. The rate of interest payable annually on a bond.

D

Default risk. The risk that a company will be unable to pay the interest or principal on its debt (bond) obligations.

Designated beneficiary. The recipient of a specific asset as instructed by a form aligned with that specific account.

Disability insurance. Type of insurance that replaces lost earnings when someone is unable to work due to an accident or illness.

Discount bond. A bond that is valued at less than its face amount.

Discretionary account. An account in which the investor has given the financial adviser the authority to buy and sell securities at his or her discretion.

Dividend. A share of company earnings paid out to stockholders.

Dollar-cost averaging. Investing a set amount on a regular schedule regardless of the price of the shares at the time.

Dow Jones Industrial Average. A price-weighted average of thirty actively traded blue-chip stocks that are primarily those of industrial and service-oriented firms, prepared by Dow Jones & Company.

Due diligence. The act of examining an investment for consistency and reliability.

Duration. A measure of the sensitivity of the price (the value of principal) of a fixed-income investment to a change in interest rates.

E

Earnings per share. A company's earnings, divided by the number of shares of common stock outstanding.

EBITDA. Earnings before interest, taxes, depreciation, and amortization.

Equity. Another word for stock.

Estate planning. A plan that utilizes various strategies for the transfer of your assets to the next generation(s).

Estate tax. A tax levied on the value of an estate after it exceeds an exclusion limit set by law.

ETF. Short for "exchange-traded fund," a fund that tracks an index but trades like a stock.

Expected return. The average of a probability distribution of possible returns.

Expense ratio. A percentage of a fund's assets that represents management and 12b-1 fees but not sales loads.

F

Face value. The stated principal amount of a bond.

Family of funds. A group of mutual funds under the same management company.

Fannie Mae. The nickname derived from the acronym for the Federal National Mortgage Association, which buys mortgages on the secondary market, repackages them, and sells off pieces to investors.

Federal Deposit Insurance Corporation (FDIC). Federal agency that insures bank deposits up to a set amount.

Federal funds rate. The interest charged by banks to other banks.

529 plan. A tax-deferred college-savings plans named after the section of the tax code that deals with them.

Fixed expenses. Expenses that don't vary over time.

Fixed-income investment. A catchall description for debt-based instruments that pay a fixed amount of interest.

401(k) plan. An employer-sponsored defined-contribution retirement plan that employees contribute to. The earnings grow on a tax-deferred basis. The 401(k) is named for the section of the federal tax code that authorizes it.

403(b) plan. Similar to 401(k) plans, but set up for public employees and employees of nonprofit organizations.

Freddie Mac. The nickname derived from the acronym for the Federal Home Loan Mortgage Corporation; it operates very much as does Fannie Mae.

Fund category. A description of how a mutual fund's manager intends to invest the fund's assets. The fund category should reflect your investment objectives, time horizon, and risk tolerance

Fundamental analysis. Study of the balance sheet, earnings history, management, product lines, and other elements of a company in an attempt to discern reasonable expectations for the price of its stock.

G

General obligation bond (GOB). A municipal bond backed by the full faith, credit, and taxing power of the issuing unit rather than the revenue from a given project.

Gift tax. Tax on lifetime transfers to heirs in excess of exemption and exclusion amounts.

Ginnie Mae. The nickname derived from the acronym for the Government National Mortgage Association, which buys up mortgages in the secondary market.

Government bond. A debt obligation issued by the U.S. government. Also known as a Treasury.

Grantor. Creator of a trust, also known as the settler or trustor.

Growth-and-income funds. Mutual funds that strive for both dividend income and capital appreciation.

Growth fund. A mutual fund that invests in stock with an objective of capital appreciation.

Growth stock. The shares of a company whose earnings are expected to grow at an above-average rate.

H

Health-care proxy. A legal document that grants authority to make medical decisions for another person if that person is incapacitated.

High-yield bonds. Non-investment-grade bonds. They must pay a higher interest rate to attract and to compensate investors for the increased risk of default. Often referred to as "junk bonds."

Home equity. The difference between the fair market value of the home and the balance of the mortgage.

I

Income fund. A mutual fund that invests in stocks or bonds with a high potential for current income, either dividends (e.g., utility stocks) or interest (e.g., bonds).

Index. A set collection of securities whose overall performance is used as an indication of stock or bond market trends, for example, Dow Jones Industrial Average or Standard & Poor's 500.

Index fund. A mutual fund that is passively managed and designed to track a particular market index.

Individual Retirement Account (IRA). A tax-deferred retirement savings vehicle.

Inflation. The erosion of purchasing power over time through an increase in the cost of goods and services.

Inflation risk. Uncertainty over the future real (after-inflation) value of your investment.

Interest rate risk. The risk that the value of fixed-income securities (e.g., bonds) will decline when interest rates rise.

Intestate. Dying without a will.

Investment style. A description of the "personality" of a fund as determined by the securities in which it invests.

Irrevocable trust. A trust that can't be materially altered.

J

Junk bond. See High-yield bonds.

L

Lagging indicator. Economic indicator that changes direction after business conditions have turned around.

Large-cap stocks. Stocks with more than $10 billion market capitalization.

Leading indicator. Economic indicator that changes direction in advance of general business conditions.

Leveraging. Investing with borrowed money in the hope of multiplying gains.

Liability. An obligation owed.

Lipper. An investment analysis company that provides peer-based mutual fund comparisons in the form of relative rankings.

Liquidity. The ability to quickly convert an investment portfolio to cash without suffering a noticeable loss in value.

Load. A sales commission to buyers that a mutual fund may charge. They can be front, back, or deferred loads.

M

Marital deduction. The estate and gift tax deduction that allows any amount of property to go from one U.S. citizen spouse to the other U.S. citizen spouse—via lifetime gifts or bequests—tax free.

Market capitalization. The relative size of a company. Generally speaking, those companies with less than $1 billion in capitalization are small cap and those with more than $10 billion are large cap. Companies with market caps between $1 billion and $10 billion are known as mid-cap stocks.

Market timing. Attempting to sell shares before a market downturn begins or to buy shares before a market rally begins.

Maturity. The length of time until the principal amount of a bond must be repaid.

Maturity date. The date when the principal amount of a security becomes due and payable.

Mid-cap stocks. Stocks with a market capitalization between $1 billion and $10 billion.

Minimum investment. The dollar amount it takes to open an account.

Modern Portfolio Theory (MPT). Overall investment strategy that seeks to construct an optimal portfolio that maximizes expected return for a given level of risk.

Money market mutual fund. A mutual fund that invests in very short-term financial securities, usually of less than thirty days' maturity.

Morningstar. An investment research company known for its ratings of the performance of mutual funds.

Municipal bond. Debt obligations of a state or local government entity that support general government needs or special projects. See General obligation bond and Revenue bond.

N

NASDAQ. The acronym for the National Association of Securities Dealers Automated Quotations System, a computerized security price-reporting system.

Net asset value (NAV). The price at which mutual fund shares are bought and sold by investors. Most funds calculate the net asset value after each trading day.

Net worth. A "snapshot" of your financial situation calculated by subtracting liabilities from assets.

New York Stock Exchange (NYSE). The largest and oldest stock exchange in the United States, which trades the stock of established companies that meet its stringent listing requirements.

O

Objective. Investment goal.

Open-ended fund. A mutual fund. It issues new shares to accommodate new purchases.

Option. The right to buy or sell a security at a given price within a given time.

P

Par. The face value of a stock or bond.

Passively managed. A fund that emulates a market index.

Portfolio rebalancing. Periodically adjusting the holdings in an investment portfolio to maintain a certain asset allocation.

Preferred stock. A class of stock that pays a specified dividend set when it's issued.

Premium. The price of an insurance policy, typically charged annually or semiannually.

Premium bond. A bond that is valued at more than its face amount.

Present value. The value today of a future payment, or stream of payments, discounted at some appropriate interest rate.

Prime rate. The interest rate a bank charges its best customers.

Principal. The amount owed; the face value of a debt; the amount invested.

Probate. The procedure by which state courts validate a will's authenticity, thereby clearing the way for the executor to carry out necessary tasks involved with settling an estate.

Prospectus. The document that describes a securities offering or the operations of a mutual fund, a limited partnership, or other investment.

Q

Qualified plan. An employee benefit plan—such as a pension or profit-sharing plan—that meets IRS requirements designed to protect employees' interests.

R

Real estate investment trust (REIT). A fund that invests in real-estate enterprises, primarily the ownership, renting, and managing of properties.

Real rate of return. The annual percentage return realized on an investment, adjusted for changes in inflation or deflation.

Required rate of return. The rate of return needed to meet your goals.

Return. The capital appreciation and income earned on an investment.

Revenue bond. A municipal bond supported by the revenue from a specific project, such as a toll road, bridge, or municipal coliseum.

Revocable trust. A trust that can be changed or revoked.

Risk. Variability of returns.

Rollover. A tax-free transfer of funds from one tax-deferred retirement savings plan to another.

R-squared. A measurement of how closely a portfolio's performance tracks an index. It tells you what portion of the portfolio's performance can be explained by the performance of the overall market or index.

The Rule of 72. Formula used to determine at what interest rate or during what time period a sum of money will double. The answer is found by dividing the known variable into 72.

S

Sallie Mae. The nickname derived from the acronym for the Student Loan Marketing Association, which buys student loans from colleges, universities, and other lenders and packages them into units to be sold to investors.

S&P 500. An index of stocks often considered a fair representation of the stock market in general.

Secondary market. The general name given to stock exchanges, the over-the-counter market, and other marketplaces in which stocks, bonds, mortgages, and other investments are sold after they have been issued and sold initially.

Sector. The broad general industry classification for stocks.

Share classes (class A, class B, etc.). Ownership of shares in the same mutual fund but with different fee structures.

Short selling. A technique whereby the investor borrows stock from a broker and immediately sells it, hoping that the price of the stock declines, so that the investor can replace the borrowed shares by buying them at a reduced price, thus netting a profit (the difference between the sales price and the later purchase price).

Small-cap stock. Shares issued by companies with capitalizations between $20 million and $3 billion.

Standard deviation. A measure of the degree to which returns of an asset vary around the mean.

Stepped-up basis. The basis of inherited property is adjusted to the appreciated value on the date of death of the original owner.

Stock. Shares that represent ownership in a corporation. The shares or stock are claims on a corporation's earnings and assets.

Stock dividend. A dividend paid in additional shares of stock rather than in cash.

T

Tax-deferred. Investments in which earnings are not taxed in the current year but will be later, usually at the time of withdrawal. Examples of tax-deferred investments are Individual Retirement Accounts (IRAs), employer 401(k) and 403(b) plans, and annuities.

Tax-exempt interest (Tax-free). Interest paid on bonds issued by states or municipalities that are tax-free for federal income tax purposes.

Taxable-equivalent yield. The pretax rate that a taxable bond must yield to generate the same income as a tax-free municipal bond.

Technical analysis. An approach to market analysis that attempts to forecast price movements by examining and charting patterns.

Term insurance. Insures you for a certain amount of money for a fixed period of time and charges you an annual premium based on your age and the amount of coverage you're buying.

Trading range. The spread of prices within which a stock normally sells.

Transaction costs. Costs incurred buying or selling securities.

Treasury bill. Short-term securities with maturities of one year or less. They are issued at a discount from face value.

Treasury bond. Long-term debt instruments with maturities of ten years or longer issued in minimum denominations of $1,000.

Treasury note. Intermediate securities with maturities of one to ten years. Denominations range from $1,000 to $1 million or more.

Trust. An arrangement whereby you give assets to a legal entity (the trust) to be administered by a fiduciary for a beneficiary, who may be yourself or some other person.

Trustee. A person or financial institution that manages the property of others.

Turnover. Indicates how frequently the fund's manager trades stock. The higher the amount of trading, the higher the turnover.

U

Umbrella liability coverage. Excess liability insurance that supplements the liability limits of a homeowner's or renter's policy and automobile insurance policy.

Universal life insurance. Insurance that allows you to raise or lower the face amount by the amount of premium used for insurance versus cash value buildup.

Unlimited marital deduction. The provision of federal estate tax laws that allows individuals to leave their entire estate to a surviving spouse tax-free if the surviving spouse is a U.S. citizen.

V

Value stock. Stock of companies whose price looks cheap relative to earnings, assets, dividends, or cash flow.

Variability. The possible different outcomes of an event.

Variable life insurance. A form of whole-life insurance that allows the cash value portion to be invested in stock, bond, or money market portfolios.

Volatility. The degree of price fluctuation associated with a specific investment or market index. The more price fluctuation that is experienced, the greater the volatility.

W

Whole-life insurance. Insurance that charges you the same premium for as long as you keep the policy.

Will. A legal document that states what people want done with their property after they die and who they want to manage their financial affairs, settle their estate, and serve as guardian for minor children.

Y

Yield. A measure of the income generated by a bond.

Yield curve. A curve that shows interest rates at a specific point for all securities having equal risk but different maturity dates.

Yield to maturity. The yield on a security assuming that interest payments will be made and reinvested until the final maturity date, at which point the principal will be repaid by the issuer.

Z

Zero-coupon bond. A deep-discount bond that pays all its interest at maturity.